The
Sea
We
Swim
In

ALSO BY FRANK ROSE

The Art of Immersion

The Agency

West of Eden

Into the Heart of the Mind

Real Men

The
Sea
We
Swim
In

How Stories Work in a Data-Driven World

Frank Rose

W. W. NORTON & COMPANY
Independent Publishers Since 1923

For information about permission to reproduce selections from this book, write to
Permissions, W. W. Norton & Company, Inc., 500 Fifth Avenue, New York, NY 10110

For information about special discounts for bulk purchases, please contact
W. W. Norton Special Sales at specialsales@wwnorton.com or 800-233-4830

Manufacturing by LSC Communications, Harrisonburg
Book design by Chris Welch
Production manager: Anna Oler

ISBN 978-1-324-00313-7

W. W. Norton & Company, Inc., 500 Fifth Avenue, New York, N.Y. 10110
www.wwnorton.com

W. W. Norton & Company Ltd., 15 Carlisle Street, London W1D 3BS

1 2 3 4 5 6 7 8 9 0

In memory of Susan Kamil,
who loved great stories and
the people who tell them

There are these two young fish swimming along and they happen to meet an older fish swimming the other way, who nods at them and says "Morning, boys. How's the water?" And the two young fish swim on for a bit, and then eventually one of them looks over at the other and goes, "What the hell is water?"

—David Foster Wallace, *This Is Water*

We live in a sea of stories, and like the fish who (according to the proverb) will be the last to discover water, we have our own difficulties grasping what it is like to swim in stories.

—Jerome Bruner, *The Culture of Education*

Contents

Preface

I GREW UP IN A DIFFERENT TIME. It was the mid-1960s when I was in high school, on the outskirts of a small city in Virginia. Our house was out in the country, on a hill above the valley where the Blue Ridge Mountains meet the Alleghenies. I was an only child. Sometimes at night I would go outside and gaze over the woods and pastures at the city down below. It was a railroad town, home base of the Norfolk & Western, the line that brought coal down from the Appalachian mining camps and hauled it on to the sea. You could see a lot of lights down there, streetlights, store lights, house lights, electric evidence of human activity. And though I couldn't see them or feel them, I was also acutely aware of the signals that were flying through the air— radio waves from the city's two television stations, carrying information from other cities far beyond my view.

I knew then that I wanted to be where the signals come from, not where the signals go to. So I did the only thing I could think of to get started: I volunteered for the school paper. I was painfully shy back then, and I figured if nothing else it would give me an excuse to talk to people.

Today, of course, the signals come from everywhere. They are as ubiquitous as the lights outside my lower Manhattan apartment.

Social media are there even for people who never wrote for the school paper. But more than that, the idea that you would sit back and passively "consume" an article or a television show now seems quaint. Digital technology changes the way we tell stories and the way we respond to them. It allows for an interplay between author and audience that didn't exist in mass media. It blurs the line that made most of us passive receptors for more than a century.

That was the subject of my last book, *The Art of Immersion*, published just as these changes were coming into focus. As a journalist for *Wired* reporting on media in the early 2000s, I could sense something happening. The first real tip-off came when I was interviewing James Cameron for a story on 3-D. We were on a soundstage at Mel's Cité du Cinéma in Montreal, where Cameron was on hand for the shoot of Eric Brevig's *Journey to the Center of the Earth*, the first feature film to be made with Cameron's newly invented stereoscopic camera system. When I asked about *Avatar*, which had been in development for years but had yet to be green-lit, he described it as an Edgar Rice Burroughs–type "manly adventure film" that would exist not only on the big screen but in other forms—forms that would let you delve deeper and deeper into the story and its world. *Avatar*, he said, would be "the kind of fantasy that as a geek fan you can hurl yourself into. I think the role of this type of film should be to create a kind of fractal-like complexity. The casual viewer can enjoy it without having to drill down to the secondary and tertiary levels of detail. But for a real fan, you go in an order of magnitude and, boom! There's a whole set of new patterns."

This brief quote, this notion of going ever deeper, changed the way I thought about everything I was writing about. But just as I couldn't have written *The Art of Immersion* without my experience at *Wired*, I couldn't have written this book without the past few years at Columbia University. In 2014, when I came to Columbia at the invitation of David K. Park, dean of strategic initiatives at the time, and Ira Deutchman, the independent film producer and then-chair of the School of the Arts' film program, I was able to continue my study of digital media in an academic environment rather than a journalistic one.

A couple of fortuitous things soon happened. First, I partnered with Paul Woolmington, one of the most forward-thinking people in advertising, to create an executive education program in storytelling for people who need to know how stories work but aren't professional storytellers themselves—marketing executives, for instance. And I joined Lance Weiler's Digital Storytelling Lab, where with Lance's support I launched an awards program that would scrap the whole idea of categories—film, television, advertising, books, what have you—and honor the most innovative efforts in storytelling in any medium. Digital technology erases distinctions, so why try to hang on to them? That's the idea behind Columbia's Digital Dozen: Breakthroughs in Storytelling awards, our annual list of the 12 most inventive digitally enabled stories from the previous year. It's also the idea behind this book. It's why, as you read, you'll find yourself moving from movies to television to marketing to live performance to journalism and books and back again.

Meanwhile, the executive education program has evolved from the one-day seminar I led with Paul to a more ambitious effort I've run on my own since Paul returned to advertising in 2016. We call it Strategic Storytelling because it's about how to tell stories that are strategic—that are designed to achieve a goal that is long-term and fundamental, as opposed to short-term, immediate, and tactical.

Tactical stories are important, sometimes critical. They are what you need when one of your oil-drilling platforms in the Gulf of Mexico explodes, killing nearly a dozen workers and injuring even more, and the subsequent oil spill fouls 1,300 miles of coastline. But that's also when you want to have a strategic story or two to fall back on. Maybe your organization has a wonderful heritage that speaks of trust built up over decades. Or better yet, maybe you have a sterling safety record and employees who have spoken volubly and unprompted about your efforts to keep this sort of accident from happening. No? Quite the opposite? And then your CEO gets tired and flustered and blurts out "I'd like my life back" in a television interview?*

That's unfortunate—for your company, for the firm's management, for investors. It's why you need to have a storytelling strategy long before the oil well blows.

I READ AN ARTICLE in *The New Yorker* a while back in which the writer started to wax on about the Greek philosophers. "Appetites we share with animals," he wrote, summarizing Socrates; "reason is what makes us human." Well, sure. Reason, to the extent that we employ it, does appear to be uniquely human. But so are stories.

"Man—let me offer you a definition—is the story-telling animal," Graham Swift wrote in *Waterland*, his meta-novel about a history teacher whose students are bored with history. "Wherever he goes he wants to leave behind not a chaotic wake, not an

---

* This is what happened with BP when its *Deepwater Horizon* exploded off the coast of Louisiana and sank in April 2010. What followed wasn't pretty. That October, after the well was finally capped, the CEO was replaced. Eight years later, after extensive legal battles, the company had racked up some $65 billion in cleanup and legal costs. The stock price fell from around $60 shortly before the disaster to less than half that a few weeks later and has yet to recover.

empty space, but the comforting marker-buoys and trail-signs of stories. . . . As long as there's a story, it's all right."

Two things are going on here. One is the assertion that stories give us patterns—they comfort us by helping us make order out of chaos. The other has to do with that word "animal." Storytelling may be unique to humans—it's difficult, though hardly impossible, to tell stories without language—but stories are a product of our animal instincts. They have little to do with reason and everything to do with emotion. Reason has always been an aspirational goal. When humans lived more like other animals—architecture and language and religion, yes, but no electricity, no air conditioning, no jet travel, no germ theory, no anesthesia, no indoor plumbing, no flush toilets, horses to take us places, shit everywhere—those who could afford to took great pains to raise themselves above the barnyard. Reason did the trick; so did exquisite clothing in satin and lace, which cost more in pecuniary terms but far less in mental effort. Now we exist by the billions in 24-hour high-tech cocoons wearing—young or old, rich or poor—some combination of worn jeans, T-shirts, and designer sneakers. We don't have to worry about what separates us from the animals because the iPhone makes it obvious. We can finally relax—maybe not completely, but at least enough to think about what's going on with stories.

Part I

~

THE NARRATIVE TURN

SOMETIMES THE ODDEST THINGS arouse controversy. "There are two modes of cognitive functioning, two modes of thought," the psychologist Jerome Bruner wrote in 1986, "each providing distinctive ways of ordering experience, of constructing reality." Parallel to logical reasoning, Bruner was saying, there exists another mode of thought that's far less well understood—what I call "narrative thinking."

William James had said as much in 1878: "To say that all human thinking is essentially of two kinds—reasoning on the one hand, and narrative, descriptive, contemplative thinking on the other—is to say only what every reader's experience will corroborate." James was the most eminent American psychologist of his day, just as his brother Henry was America's preeminent novelist. Yet when Bruner made essentially the same assertion a century later, the novelist and philosopher Rebecca Goldstein, writing in the *New York Times Book Review,* called it a "truly radical claim." It seemed that way then because, in the intervening years, science had largely blinded itself to stories. They were frivolous. Unworthy of serious study. If we live "in a sea of stories," as Bruner put it, most psychologists would have been the last to know.

Eminent in his field yet relatively little known to the wider public, Bruner was one of those people whose ideas shape culture in ways most of us are barely aware of. He had already backed one revolution in his field, in the 1950s, when as a professor at

Harvard he helped lead a rebellion against radical behaviorism, then the dominant school in American psychology. Behaviorism, championed by his Harvard colleague B. F. Skinner, sought to limit psychology to that which can be scientifically and empirically observed—which is to say, behavior. It rejected anything so vague and fuzzy as the mind, along with such related concepts as intentions, beliefs, and desires. In Skinner's view, the mind is a black box; humans, like any other organism, can be properly understood only through objectively observable behaviors which various stimuli produce. To consider anything else would be "unscientific." Human behavior becomes entirely predictable in such a scheme, free will an illusion. We are input-output machines, nothing more.

Skinner was a towering yet polarizing figure in Harvard's psychology department—holder of a prestigious professorship, awarded the National Medal of Science by President Lyndon Johnson, author of the influential utopian novel *Walden Two* as well as the 1971 bestseller *Beyond Freedom and Dignity*. Or, as some of his less admiring students called it, *Toward Slavery and Humiliation*.

By this time, however, behaviorism was on the way out. The "cognitive revolution" was well underway in 1960, when Bruner launched the Center for Cognitive Studies with another Harvard colleague, George Miller. Where behaviorists assumed the mind was a black box, cognitive psychologists like Bruner and Miller, along with such people as Noam Chomsky and Marvin Minsky at the Massachusetts Institute of Technology, presumed to look inside, exploring the processes of cognition (memory, language, perception) to see how we work. Bruner's approach was further rooted in the notion that we make sense of the world by constructing our own reality. "Nothing that is out there in the world is there in and of itself," he once told an interviewer. "You're always constructing it."

During the sixties and seventies, Bruner applied this idea to child development and education reform. In 1972, alienated from Harvard by its treatment of student activists during the Vietnam War era, he and his wife, Blanche, sailed their yacht across the Atlantic with a small crew and he took up a professorship at Oxford. By the start of the eighties, when he returned to the US to accept a chair at the New School for Social Research in New York City, he was starting to believe that our concept of reality is shaped if not defined by stories—that reality is a construct, and narrative the chief means of construction.

The "narrative turn," as this growing interest in stories came to be known in psychology and other fields, was also a turning point for Bruner. He was approaching 70 at the time, with a long history of advancing radical claims, and he would have another 30 years to promote this one before he died in 2016. Behaviorism had long been eclipsed; now he was taking issue with his fellow cognitive psychologists, who tended to reject anything that appeared "unscientific"—stories included. "Why are we so intellectually dismissive towards narrative?" Bruner demanded years later. "Why are we inclined to treat it as rather a trashy, if entertaining, way of thinking about and talking about what we do with our minds?"

Yet others were already starting to echo Bruner's claim. Oliver Sacks, the maverick neurologist, had asserted in his 1980s bestseller *The Man Who Mistook His Wife for a Hat* that "each of us constructs and lives" a narrative that forms our identity. In 1989, the Harvard psychiatrist Robert Coles published *The Call of Stories*, which begins with his own account of how he learned the importance of stories. As a young resident at Massachusetts General Hospital in Boston in the 1950s, Coles recounts, he had two supervisors—a Dr. Binger, "vigorously analytic," and a Dr. Ludwig, whose focus on patients' stories made him slyly, subversively indifferent to standard procedure:

"Let's try to formulate this case," Dr. Binger would exhort, and if I hesitated, he was ready to weigh in, much to my pleasure and edification. He was known as a brilliant theorist, and he saw me as the lucky resident who, early in his career, was learning to follow suit. Dr. Ludwig was known as a nice guy; he was also regarded as a bit slow on the draw, perhaps over the hill. . . . Yet "that other supervisor," as I began to call him in my mind (the "other" signifying for me a certain gradual divergence on his part from prevailing practice), kept nudging me in a different direction.

Different and, as Coles makes clear, far more productive—for it was Ludwig's insistence on listening to a problem patient's story that enabled Coles to make a breakthrough that had eluded other doctors for years.

By the late nineties, neuroscientists too were investigating narrative and how it works. Within a few years, the view that storytelling was central to human experience had become so entrenched that a lonely dissenter felt compelled to cry out against this "new narrative orthodoxy." Today we have not only narrative psychology but narrative medicine, narrative criminology, even narrative economics—as in *Narrative Economics*, the most recent book by the Nobel Prize–winning economist Robert Shiller.

Shiller maintains that narratives are critical to understanding economic events—the Roaring Twenties and the Great Depression, to cite two particularly noteworthy examples. And it's not just the stories people tell that matter, it's how viral they are, how contagious the ideas they express. He's felt this way since he encountered *Only Yesterday*, Frederick Lewis Allen's 1931 bestseller about the decade leading up to the stock market crash, as an undergraduate:

After I read Allen's book, it seemed to me that the trajectory of the stock market and the economy, as well as the onset of the Great Depression, must have been tied to the stories, misperceptions, and broader narratives of the period. But economists never took Allen's book seriously, and the idea of narrative contagion never entered their mathematical models of the economy.

Like psychologists, most economists thought stories unworthy of their attention.

Today, with academic papers explaining how stories can sway a jury or encourage Dutch college students to have safer sex or sell conflict-ridden cities as travel destinations, we are approaching what Bruner called "a 'psychology' of literature"—a field of study that aims to discover, as he put it, "what happens when a reader enters the Dublin of Stephen Daedalus" through the portal that is James Joyce's *A Portrait of the Artist as a Young Man*. What researchers are finding is that we seem to understand stories by projecting ourselves into them; that the more fully we project ourselves, the more immersed in the story we become; and that the more immersed we become, the more likely the story is to affect our attitudes on what the story is about.

Murder at the Mall

One of the earliest and most intriguing contributions to the study of narrative came in the late nineties from Melanie Green, a graduate student in social psychology at Ohio State. Green, now a professor at New York State's University at Buffalo, wanted to know how stories affect the way people feel about the world around them. To find out, she asked fellow students to read a grisly account of a nine-year-old girl named Katie who was chosen at random and stabbed to death by a psychiatric patient in a suburban Ohio shopping mall. The story, called "Murder at the Mall," was adapted from a true account in Sherwin Nuland's *How We Die*, a bestseller and National Book Award winner about—well, how we die. Nuland used the story to explain exsanguination—bleeding out. It was vivid and engrossing, all the more so because the gruesome events were recounted in a dispassionate manner.

Not all the students participating in Green's experiment saw the same version of the story. Some were given what looked like a newspaper clipping from the *Akron Beacon Journal* and were told the stabbing had actually happened. Others were handed the identical story, formatted to look like a reprint from a literary magazine called *Akron Best Fiction*, and were told it was a short story. Some were questioned beforehand about the issues it raised—whether psychiatric patients should be allowed out unsupervised, how likely violence is to occur in public places, whether we live in a fundamentally just world. All were asked about these issues after they'd read the story. Would readers who were told it was true react differently from readers who were told it was fiction? Would those who were deeply immersed in the story react differently from those who were less so?

In order to figure that out, Green and her faculty adviser, Timothy Brock, had to determine which readers were immersed—or "transported," to use the term preferred by psychologists. Immersion had been observed in a literary context for decades, if not centuries. J. R. R. Tolkien referred to it as "the enchanted state." But psychologists were influenced by Richard Gerrig, a cognitive scientist at Stony Brook University on Long Island, who introduced the idea of "narrative transportation" in his 1993 book *Experiencing Narrative Worlds*. Readers who become lost in a book, moviegoers who are surprised to see the lights come up, television viewers who care what happens to their favorite soap-opera characters: "In each case," writes Gerrig, "a narrative serves to transport an experiencer away from the here and now."

Now Green and Brock were proposing to measure how far to quantify enchantment. They began by developing a "transportation scale" that has since become a standard measure of immersion. Participants were given 15 statements on the order of "I wanted to learn how the narrative ended" and "While reading the narrative I had a vivid image" of a particular scene or character. For each statement, they were asked to rank their responses on a seven-point scale, from "not at all" to "very much."

The findings were unequivocal. For people reading about the little girl being stabbed, the immersion scores ranged from 31 to 99, out of a potential high of 105. The higher their score—that is, the more transported they were by the story—the more likely they were to say that people were being stabbed to death in Ohio shopping malls on a regular basis and that mental patients should not be let out unsupervised. Asked to circle passages in the text that rang false, readers who were transported found far fewer than those who were not. Whether they'd been told the story was fact or fiction made no difference.

Black Early, or Black Late?

Other researchers have reported similar results. People who are transported by a story tend to be less critical of the attitudes and beliefs the story carries with it and more likely to express those same attitudes and beliefs. "Advocacy messages" such as ads and editorials can have the opposite effect. When their beliefs are challenged, people often harden their positions no matter how strong the evidence—unless the person challenging them resembles themselves, in which case, research shows, people find the argument less threatening and may even agree with it.

With stories, it turns out, we tend to respond to the main character in a similar way. It's fairly widely accepted among psychologists today that as we read or watch a story we essentially rehearse what happens in our heads, a process that's been compared to a computer simulation. It follows that we would tend to spontaneously assume the identity of a main character, adopting the character's mindset and perspective and subsuming our own. But how the story is told can make a crucial difference.

This was demonstrated by Geoff Kaufman, a researcher at Carnegie Mellon who at the time was a PhD candidate at Ohio State. A few days before the 2008 primary election, Kaufman and his faculty adviser, Lisa Libby, asked a group of undergrads to read a story about a student trying to vote. The student runs into all sorts of obstacles, from rain to car trouble to long lines at the polls, but he manages to cast his ballot nonetheless. The test subjects were randomly assigned one of four versions of the story— told either in the first person or in the third, and about a student either at Ohio State, a 60,000-student public university in the state capital, or at Denison, a small, private, liberal arts college in a picture-postcard village a half-hour away.

When the results were tallied, it was clear that those who'd read the first-person story about the Ohio State student were most likely to assume the identity of the main character. But the real test came a week later, when the students were asked in a follow-up whether they had voted on Election Day. As it happened, nearly two-thirds of those who'd read the first-person Ohio State story voted, compared to 43 percent of those who'd read the first-person Denison story and only a quarter of those who'd read one of the third-person stories. Intriguingly, the best predictor of who would vote turned out to be how closely the readers identified with the main character—which corresponded in turn with whether they had read the first-person Ohio State story or one of the others.

Kaufman designed two more studies to test this identification factor. For these he borrowed a narrative technique from the 1975 Broadway musical *A Chorus Line*. The show, which depicted what happens behind the scenes at such productions, featured several characters who said they were gay—but this being the seventies, when homosexuality was still more widely considered a perversion than a preference, not before they'd been onstage long enough to connect with the audience.

Kaufman gave a group of straight, male students one of three versions of a story to read—one about a day in the life of a student who gets a call from his boyfriend in the first paragraph, one in which he gets a call from his boyfriend about two-thirds of the way through, and one in which he gets a call from his girlfriend. Another group of undergrads, all of them white, were given one of three versions of an entirely different story—this one involving a student who refers to himself by a stereotypically Black name in the first paragraph, or by the same name later on, or by a name more often used by whites. Toward the end of the story, he engages in behavior that might be considered hostile—demanding his money back from a store clerk for no good reason, for example. How would the test subjects react?

Exactly as Kaufman expected they would. The straights who read the "gay-early" story, as it was called, were significantly more likely to describe the character as effeminate. Those who read the "gay-late" story were as likely to identify with him as those who read the version in which he was straight. "Gay-late" readers also came away with a more favorable attitude toward gays in general.

White students who read the Black-late story were significantly more likely to identify with the protagonist than those who read the Black-early story. They were less inclined to rate him as hostile than the Black-early readers and less inclined to express attitudes that are subtly racist—Blacks getting too demanding in their push for equal rights, Blacks getting more economic rewards than they deserve. By the time they learned he was Black, they had already accepted him—and the hostility he then displays came too late to change that acceptance.

Kaufman's studies suggest that prejudice may hinder immersion—but immersion, once achieved, may overcome prejudice. They also suggest how easy it is to manipulate people through storytelling. As Tom van Laer, a narratologist at the University of Sydney, put it, "nothing is less innocent than a story."

Neural Coupling

Meanwhile, Uri Hasson, a neuroscientist at Princeton, has conducted a series of experiments involving movies and television shows that appear to show how the mental link between storyteller and audience—the "neural coupling," he calls it—actually works.

Hasson started out as something of a renegade. He felt that there was no way to understand the brain without understanding how it interacts with other brains in the real world. But if psychologists in the eighties were loath to accept Jerome Bruner's view that stories were worth studying, that was mild compared to the backlash Hasson got two decades later when he decided to find out how brains respond to *The Good, the Bad and the Ugly*, Sergio Leone's 1966 spaghetti Western. The accepted way to study brain processes—the proper way, in the view of most scientists—was to isolate them in a laboratory setting.

"The philosophy was, the more controlled the experiment, the more it was science," explains Chris Baldassano, who did a postdoc with Hasson at the Princeton Neuroscience Institute before joining the psychology department at Columbia. "The idea of using a movie was kind of heresy."

In fact, Hasson argues, the more controlled the experiment, the more limited the results. Using functional magnetic resonance imaging (fMRI), he and his colleagues found that when a story is successful, it activates the same parts of the brain in different listeners, putting them in sync with one another.

In the spaghetti Western study, conducted when he was at the Weizmann Institute of Science in Israel, they found that brains of different individuals tended to respond to the movie in unison. In a later study at Princeton, he compared the brain activity of people watching *The Good, the Bad and the Ugly* with that of a second group watching an episode of the Larry David comedy series *Curb Your Enthusiasm* and a third group viewing a 1961 episode of *Alfred Hitchcock Presents*.

The Hitchcock show—"Bang! You're Dead," the last in the series that Hitchcock himself directed—is a highly suspenseful drama about a six-year-old boy who's playing with a loaded pistol he thinks is a toy. It evoked similar responses among viewers in more than 65 percent of the neocortex—a bigger slice of the brain than *The Good, the Bad and the Ugly*, and way more than *Curb Your Enthusiasm*. This, Hasson and his collaborators conclude, suggests that a master storyteller—and who better than Hitch?—is able to orchestrate the responses of many different brain regions in many different viewers, "turning them on and off at the same time"— which in the case of Hitchcock "may provide neuroscientific evidence for his notoriously famous ability to master and manipulate viewers' minds."

By the simple act of telling a story, Hasson told me, "I'm making your brain similar to mine." This has serious implications. "Is it a good thing or a bad thing about Hitchcock? Is it a good thing that Hitchcock can control your brain? Because he doesn't leave anything to ambiguity."

Narrative Thinking

If we live in a sea of stories, then narrative thinking means being aware of the sea we swim in. It means realizing that stories constitute a distinct mode of thought, one that plays such a central role in human experience that anyone who wants to sell something, communicate ideas, motivate people, or change their minds should understand how they work. And while narrative thinking relies in large part on Bruner and his progeny, it also benefits from the example of "design thinking," a concept that has come to guide decision-making in organizations large and small.

The essence of design thinking is creative problem-solving. Designers face problems all the time: how to build a smartphone that's intuitive and easy to use, how to structure a shopping site so people won't abandon it in frustration, where to put the "on" switch or the "buy" button so people can actually find them. Design thinking applies techniques designers use to problems outside the traditional realm of design: how to get people to stick to a drug regimen, or what to do about the rise of obesity in children.

The idea has been around since at least the sixties. But it wasn't until the nineties, when engineering professors Rolf Faste and David Kelley joined forces at Stanford, that it started to gain traction outside the field of design. Kelley headed a small firm in Palo Alto, Stanford's hometown, that grew through a set of mergers to become the global design and consulting firm

IDEO. Throughout the nineties, Kelley and his colleagues sys-
tematized their methodology into a five-step process—*empathize*
with the user, *define* the problem, *ideate* around it, *prototype* a
solution, *test* it, and then start over if necessary. The process is
broad and robust enough to be applied to almost any problem.

Design thinking was ideal for the Silicon Valley business
environment, which valued creativity in a fast-changing, com-
petitive landscape. An analysis by the Design Management
Institute found that 16 design-centric firms—Apple, Nike, Starbucks, and Target among them—collectively outperformed the
S&P 500 by 211 percent between 2005 and 2015. As IDEO chief
executive Tim Brown put it, "Design is now too important to be
left to designers."

Just as storytelling is too important to be left to storytellers.
We're all storytellers in the digital world, as we were in the pre-
industrial age, before mechanical reproduction relegated most of
us to the role of passive consumers. But narrative thinking is not
design thinking cloned. There is no five-step process, and stories
are not about problem-solving—quite the opposite. Story, Bruner
pointed out, "is an instrument not so much for solving problems
as for finding them. . . . Something goes awry, otherwise there's
nothing to tell about."

The relationship of narrative thinking to design thinking is by
analogy. Just as design thinking adapts the tools of professional
design for nondesigners, narrative thinking adapts the tools of
professional storytellers—novelists, journalists, filmmakers—
for use by nonprofessionals. Just as design thinking means
applying design principles at a strategic level rather than a
purely tactical one, narrative thinking is a long-range process
that requires buy-in at the top. It's the difference between sending out a press release and viewing everything your organization

does as part of an ongoing narrative—one you conceivably might be able to control.

The Emotional Appeal of Reason

One more thing about design thinking: it assumes that by applying brainpower in the right way we can arrive at an optimum solution—in other words, that there's some basic rationality at work. Narrative thinking makes no such assumption.

As a species, humans have an enormous investment in the idea that we are rational creatures, far too cerebral to be persuaded by something so personal and emotional as a story. It's not hard to see why. The laws of reason form a bulwark. Our ability to follow them is what separates *our* group from all those other groups— the ones that don't think right. Unfortunately, our attachment to this idea is much more emotional than it is rational.

Economists long assumed that we are "rational actors," wild stock market swings and tulipomania notwithstanding. Then, about 20 years before narrative economics, came the rise of behavioral economics—a marriage of economics and cognitive psychology that began when Daniel Kahneman and Amos Tversky, both psychologists, broke into the field and pointed out that humans aren't so rational after all. Robert Shiller—the future author of *Narrative Economics* and no mean storyteller himself—further eviscerated the rational-actor conceit in his 2000 book *Irrational Exuberance*, which predicted the dotcom crash that came, in fact, the very month it was published. A few years later, despite pointed warnings from Shiller and others, the housing bubble produced a global recession so deep it took countries years to dig themselves out. "We are finally beginning to understand that irrationality is the real invisible hand," wrote Dan Ariely, author of the bestselling book *Predictably Irrational*, in an article called "The End of

Rational Economics." "If humans were comic book characters," he added parenthetically, "we'd be more closely related to Homer Simpson than to Superman."

People in advertising and marketing are coming to the same realization. In the fifties, ad execs used to talk about the "unique selling proposition," the singular benefit that, properly touted, would give their product an edge over all competitors. Even after the theory behind it fell out of favor during the "creative revolution" that rocked Madison Avenue in the sixties, marketers continued to obsess about their product's USP. If the ad didn't hawk the product's benefits, they insisted, it was wasted money. Yet psychologists and neuroscientists point out that buyers are no more rational in their product choices than they are in their investment decisions.

Our understanding of emotion got a boost with the 1995 best-seller *Emotional Intelligence* by the psychologist and science writer Daniel Goleman. Much as Bruner had argued for the study of "the narrative mode of thought" a decade earlier, Goleman maintained that we need to understand our emotions if we are to understand ourselves. "A view of human nature that ignores the power of emotions is sadly shortsighted," he wrote. "We have gone too far in emphasizing the value and import of the purely rational—of what IQ measures—in human life. For better or worse, intelligence can come to nothing when the emotions hold sway."

And it can indeed be for better or worse. The coronavirus that started to devastate the world in 2020 had many precedents: AIDS in the eighties, the influenza pandemic of 1918–19, tuberculosis in the nineteenth century, the Black Death of the fourteenth. The 1918 pandemic was the first in which humans faced such threats with any real knowledge of what caused them or how lives could be saved. Yet the scientists who had advanced such knowledge—people like Ignaz Semmelweis, the Hungarian physician who in the 1840s famously demonstrated that simply by washing their hands, doctors could keep their patients from dying—had been ridiculed or ignored by the medical establishment for years before their ideas were accepted. So maybe I shouldn't be surprised that the response to the coronavirus was led in many countries, including my own, by people who routinely denigrate science and deny its findings.

To them and to many others, disease is not a fact but a story. In *The Black Swan*, a book that's often cited to explain the suddenly-out-of-nowhere nature of the coronavirus, Nassim Nicholas Taleb writes about the "narrative fallacy," our "limited ability to look at sequences of facts without weaving an explanation into them"— without fitting them into some sort of story. Thus we've had tuberculosis as a signifier of the victim's romantic psyche, AIDS as a punishment from God, and perhaps most bizarrely of all, the coronavirus as a conspiracy against Donald Trump. The brain is a pattern-seeking organ, but there are times when almost any pattern will do, and what stories lack in logic they often make up for in emotional appeal. The struggle between reason and emotion is rarely an even contest. The problem is that reason—science— can offer us solution and salvation, while emotion only leads to more stories.

Which is what happened with the coronavirus. Like others before it, this pandemic was accompanied by an "infodemic"—a glut of stories, many of them false and some that themselves resulted in illness or death. An international team of researchers counted more than 2,300 instances of misinformation on social media in the first three months of 2020 alone. Nearly 90 percent of these were unfounded rumors about COVID-19 and supposed treatments for it, such as camel urine mixed with lime in Saudi Arabia or, in Western countries, a so-called "Miracle Mineral Solution" that was actually chlorine bleach. Hundreds of people died, thousands were hospitalized, and many went blind from drinking methanol. Then there were the conspiracy theories: that the virus had been engineered in China as a bioweapon, or that it was created as part of a population-control scheme, or that it was created by the Bill and Melinda Gates Foundation to promote vaccine sales. Rumors and conspiracy theories were found to be more prevalent in the US and India than anywhere else in the world.

Often the most effective stories don't even register as stories. They're just the way things are. Growing up in Virginia, which my mother's family has called home since the seventeenth century, I never thought to wonder about the Confederate soldier on the courthouse lawn or the larger-than-life statues of Confederate leaders on Richmond's Monument Avenue. They were just . . . there. Not until African-American activists started targeting such statues a few years ago did I see them for what they are: part of a large-scale effort to rewrite the story of the Civil War.

Usually the victors write history, but in this case Southern whites staged a remarkably successful campaign to rebrand the Confederacy. Instead of an insurrection led by slaveholders bent on preventing Abraham Lincoln from "annihilating in effect property worth thousands of millions of dollars," as Confederate president Jefferson Davis put it in 1861, the war was transmuted after the surrender at Appomattox into the "Lost Cause," a doomed yet noble campaign to preserve a way of life marked by chivalry and crinolines. Instead of a pecuniary defense of property rights, it became a principled defense of states' rights. The "Waw Between the States," as my mother used to call it, became "the Waw of Northern Aggression," a fight to preserve an agrarian way of life against the rapacious, industrialized North. Slavery in this telling was a strangely benevolent institution, and not the real cause of the war in any case.

The tale was told across many media, as tales so often are. It reached its apogee in the 1930s with the release of *Gone with the Wind* and the publication of Douglas Southall Freeman's worshipful, four-volume biography of Robert E. Lee. Freeman, who lived in a white-columned, plantation-revival mansion in Richmond's West End, is said to have saluted every time he drove past the Lee statue on Monument Avenue. But long before that, the United Daughters of the Confederacy (UDC) sprang forth to memorialize Confederate valor in stone.

The Ku Klux Klan had been stamped out by 1871, but in 1915 D. W. Griffith's *The Birth of a Nation*—the first historical epic on film, the first American blockbuster, the first movie to be screened in the White House, a film that lampooned freed slaves for eating fried chicken on the state house floor and demonized them for daring to sully white womanhood— sparked the KKK's rebirth in North and South alike. The regeneration took place on Georgia's Stone Mountain, which the UDC, with the support of Klan leaders, set out to transform into a Confederate memorial.

For Blacks, lynch law prevailed—Black bodies dangling from trees, hanging from bridges, strung up in the town square. The practice was championed by such upstanding citizens as Atlanta newspaper editor John Temple Graves, a Stone Mountain enthusiast who in a public lecture in Chautauqua, New York, hailed lynching as "the sternest, the strongest, and the most effective restraint that the age holds for the control of rape." Blacks, Graves declared, are creatures "of the senses, and with this race and with all similar races the desire of the senses must be restrained by the terror of the senses." But for whites—or at least, white Protestants—the bitter enmities of the Civil War were fading away in a haze of reconciliation. On the fiftieth anniversary of the Battle of Gettysburg, which had left some 46,000 dead or wounded in three days, veterans from both sides converged on the small Pennsylvania town for a reenactment marked not by animosity but by handshakes. As a title card in *The Birth of a Nation* put it, "The former enemies of North and South are united again in defense of their Aryan birthright."

Stories have been weaponized throughout history. Only by understanding how they work, how they can prey on the emotions, can we create better stories to counter them.

Part II

~

THE ELEMENTS
OF STORY

Author

Journey

Audience

Character   World   Detail   Voice   Platform   Immersion

I N MY COLUMBIA PROGRAM I've identified nine key elements
of story, each of which will be addressed in this section of
the book. The first three are fundamental. Author: Who is
telling the story. Audience: Who the story is for. Journey: The
events of the story itself, which—having a beginning, a middle,
and an end—will start at one point in time and space and conclude in another, with some sort of conflict a given along the way.

Any story, stripped to its essentials, is an experience in which
an author takes her audience on a journey. The author is a guide
to parts unknown, and like any guide she needs a sure footing.
That's why the first thing you need to know as a storyteller is:
Who are you, and why are you telling this story? What is your
purpose, and how will the story you're telling help further it? And

the next thing you need to know is, who are you telling this story to, and why would they want to hear it? Only then are you ready to start the journey.

But the six other attributes are no less essential, and in some cases they perform quite differently in a digital world than in the pre-digital era of mass media. Character: The humans (or humanoids) who inhabit the story. World: What used to be called the setting, before our sense of setting expanded to make room for the audience as well as the characters. Detail: The specifics of the story. Stories are nothing if not specific, but the need for detail can vary dramatically depending on what kind of story you are telling, and to whom. Voice: The way the author speaks. Platform: What used to be called the medium, before our sense of the medium expanded to embrace all possible media. Immersion: The story's propensity to seize the imagination, to cause us to lose ourselves within it. Or, alternatively, to engage with it on a level bordering on obsession.

All nine play an important role, and each is intertwined with the others in ways that can make them hard to tease apart. What makes them so powerful is the way they work together. In isolation they are inert; put them together and, like Walt Whitman, they can contain multitudes.

1. Author

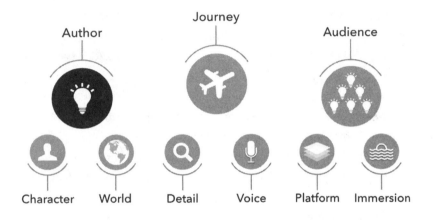

Author

Journey

Audience

Character World Detail Voice Platform Immersion

I f we want to create better stories, how do we go about it?

Arijan Kurbasic had an idea. Kurbasic—also known as Zero One, after the code name his father used during the 1992–95 war in Bosnia and Herzegovina—was the proprietor of War Hostel Sarajevo for several years, an establishment in the Bosnian capital. His War Hostel violated every known rule of hospitality. It did not promise comfort, relaxation, or a good night's sleep. Quite the opposite: it offered a form of time travel, a narrative conduit straight to the civil war that erupted during the breakup of Yugoslavia, turning neighbor against neighbor and leaving more than 100,000 of Bosnia's four million people dead.

The hostel comprised two floors of the house Kurbasic grew up in. Walking in, you saw a room lined with sandbags, the walls hung with automatic weapons. Instead of beds, you'd find sponge mats on the floor; instead of sheets and pillows, heavy woolen blankets that seemed designed to make you itch. The experience, it was said, was like sleeping with a dead horse. The electricity went off at night, but you could read by candles made from cooking oil—not that it was easy to concentrate with all the gunfire and explosions coming in over the sound system. If they really wanted to, visitors could stay in the windowless bunker his family escaped to whenever the shelling started, its floor packed with mud, air thick with smoke, lit only by a flashlight whose batteries were about to run out.

Kurbasic was a toddler when the war started. Sarajevo was besieged for nearly four years, and though he and his family survived, more than one city resident in eight ended up dead or wounded—some blown up by mortar and artillery shells from Yugoslav army and Serbian militia positions in the hills above, others (many of them children) picked off by snipers. Water and electricity were cut off; thousands of buildings were destroyed; the suicide rate soared. The three-way fighting among Orthodox Serbs, Catholic Croats, and Muslim Bosniaks was marked by atrocities on all sides, though the overwhelming majority of victims were Bosniaks. Kurbasic refused to say what his own ethnicity is. "My family and I experienced a war we didn't ask for, and we survived it out of pure luck," he told a reporter. "I offer immersive experiences and war tours to show what happens when people get divided into 'us and them.'"

Today, Sarajevo has its share of hip bars and clubs, a couple of cool hotels, and even an elegant restaurant or two. Yet it's also a destination for "dark tourism"—travel to sites marked by death and destruction. Kurbasic, having started out as a tour guide, knew there would be a market for his hostel. Even so, he seemed to have mixed feelings about it. "Millennials come and say, 'This is so cool,'" he said. "But it is not cool. It is not a game. If you grow up thinking war is a game, you will make some very bad decisions." Visitors, he added, need to know that "what happened here can happen wherever there are people."

"The Netflix of Eyewear"

Because of his background, Kurbasic has a very special story to tell. Most of us, fortunately, don't have anything so dramatic. At most we might have a story that's more like, say, Warby Parker's, the outfit that sells eyeglasses online.

In February 2010, when Warby Parker was launched, selling eyeglasses on the web was a dubious idea. Who would buy glasses without being able to try them on? The four founders, all MBA candidates at Wharton, had gotten the idea a year and a half earlier, after one of them—a hiking enthusiast named Dave Gilboa—got off an airplane in Chiang Mai, Thailand, and realized too late that he'd left his Prada glasses behind. He couldn't afford to replace them, and he also couldn't believe he'd blown $700 on them. When he mentioned this to a classmate—Neil Blumenthal, who'd spent five years running a nonprofit called VisionSpring that helps people in poor countries get glasses—an idea was born.

Blumenthal shared the idea with a couple of friends, Jeff Raider—who was wearing a $500 pair of designer glasses held together by duct tape—and Andrew Hunt. The four guys spent months researching the field, trying to establish a clear idea of what they wanted to do. But before they'd even put together a website, they got word that *GQ* was planning to feature them in its March 2010 issue. It was a small mention—just a single paragraph in the middle of a long photo feature about eyeglasses that featured such notables as Andy Warhol, Yves St. Laurent, David Hockney, and James Dean. But it did say that Warby Parker would ship you five pair of glasses to try on at no charge, let you mail them all back for free, and then send you the pair you'd picked out with prescription lenses included for $95. Best of all was the heading: "The Netflix of Eyewear."

The Warby Parker website went live on February 15, the same day the magazine hit the newsstands; within 24 hours the four were so swamped with orders they had to temporarily suspend the home try-on offer. Some would-be customers asked if they could come by the office to try on glasses, not realizing that there was no office. So they came to Blumenthal's apartment, or sometimes Raider's, and looked at options laid out on the dining table. Since the guys hadn't thought to put a SOLD-OUT button on the website, they soon had a backlog of 20,000 orders. As they worked their way through that, they realized they'd sold as many glasses in three weeks as they had expected to sell in their first year.

What Warby Parker did, on its website and in media coverage that followed its hasty debut, was tell a story about itself. A key part of that story involved the competition. When the four partners were planning their business, they found out why eyeglasses are so expensive: a single company controls almost the entire industry. That company is Luxottica, an Italian outfit that owns Ray-Ban and Oakley, licenses designer brands ranging from Armani to Burberry to Prada to Versace, owns major retail chains like LensCrafters and Sunglass Hut, and even controls EyeMed, the second largest insurer in the United States.

As a vertically integrated company with a dominant position in the market, Luxottica can charge whatever it wants—which, in some cases, means a markup of 1,000 percent or so, according to the *Los Angeles Times*. By selling its eyeglasses online, Warby Parker was able to bypass Luxottica-controlled retail networks, sell glasses for a fraction of Luxottica's inflated prices, and establish a direct relationship with its own customers in the process. So

Warby Parker became the saga of four guys who took on a retail octopus and sold fashionable if slightly nerdy-looking glasses at the certifiably crazy price of 95 bucks.

But it wasn't just their story that had Warby Parker's glasses flying off the shelves before the shelves were even built. It was why they were doing this. In a TED talk he gave in 2009—one of the most-watched TED talks ever, as it happens—Simon Sinek, the author of *Start with Why*, observed that "people don't buy what you do; people buy why you do it." Selling what you do makes you one among many. Selling why you do it (assuming you know) makes you unique. It's how Steve Jobs rebuilt Apple from the wreckage left by the professional managers who'd all but destroyed it in the nineties: he wanted people to "think different." And it's how, operating on a slightly less cosmic level, Gilboa, Blumenthal, Hunt, and Raider built Warby Parker. They wanted to make glasses affordable, the way glasses ought to be.

That was the start of it. What further established Warby Parker, both as a brand and as a story, was the Warby Parker Class Trip. When they were getting started, Raider told me, the plan if PR and word of mouth weren't enough was "to drive across the country ourselves, bring the glasses with us, and host trunk shows across the country." They even thought about buying an old school bus they'd found for sale for $10,000. As it turned out, that wasn't necessary—but in 2012 they did it anyway on a somewhat grander scale, transforming an old yellow school bus into a rolling eyewear boutique and sending it across America. What Ken Kesey did for acid in the sixties, the scruffy little band of Warbyites on the Class Trip would do for eyeglasses.

So a guy from their customer experience team got a bus-driving permit and set off with four other people who were handling social media and sales. For months they rambled from city to city, meeting fans and blogging about anything they encountered that seemed artisanal and hipsterish: a quirky little clothing shop in Nashville, the best barbecue joint in Atlanta, a pie shop in Dallas, a gastrotruck in San Diego, a coffee roaster in downtown LA, a San Francisco bookbinder who makes iPad cases, a leather crafter in Portland, the indie music pioneer Sub Pop Records in Seattle, a bicycle shop in Denver, a woodworking shop in Minneapolis . . . By September 2013, when they finally called it quits at Camp Wandawega, Wisconsin, they'd been on the road for nearly a year.

The Class Trip was brilliant in several ways. Compared with advertising, its cost was trivial. On a purely practical level, it enabled the folks back at headquarters in downtown Manhattan to supplement the customer data they'd been collecting online with detailed impressions of actual individuals who liked their products—to put faces to the numbers. It also forged a bond with those people, cementing the cult-brand status that had been developing since launch. Nearly every photo they posted showed the Warbyites to be the mirror image of their customers. Facial hair? Check. Denim? Check. Food-obsessed? Check. All-natural everything? Check. They were cool, their fans were cool, and because the two were such a close match they had every reason to tell a story that was, as a research psychologist might put it, cool-early.

One final factor: Though the fan interactions were heavily documented on the company blog and on Instagram, and therefore infinitely shareable, they happened in the real world. This put Warby on point with an emerging appreciation among Millennials—easily the most digitally savvy generation of adults at that time—for physical objects such as books and vinyl records. I'd just designed a survey on attitudes about digital vs. physical with JWT Intelligence, the trend research unit of the J. Walter Thompson ad agency, which showed that American Millennials were more likely than older generations to express nostalgia for things like record players and film cameras, to say they'd miss printed business cards and mail-order catalogs if they disappeared, even to say they liked the smell and feel of books and magazines. The Class Trip resonated with that: it was about the smell and feel of life.

Two Thousand Names to Choose From

One of the most effective stories to tell is the origin story. When the marketing agency Merkle teamed up to do a study with Levo, an online community for Millennial women, they found that nearly half of the women surveyed knew their favorite brand's origin story and two out of five could name the founders.

The guys who started Warby Parker gave a remarkable amount of thought to who they were and what they wanted their start-up to become—starting with its name. They came up with some 2,000 alternatives which they mulled over for more than six months. The name they settled on was quirky—half strange, half familiar, and memorable for that reason. The story behind it is that Gilboa had seen a Jack Kerouac exhibit at the New York Public Library one day and started reading some of Kerouac's journals on display. He came across a couple of characters with curious-sounding names, Warby Pepper and Zagg Parker. A decade later, new employees were being given a copy of Kerouac's *Dharma Bums* to maintain the connection.

Warby Parker defined itself early on as "a lifestyle brand offering value and service with a social mission"—a three-part identity statement that establishes a clear purpose as well as a straightforward hierarchy of goals. The social mission is its buy-a-pair/give-a-pair program: for every pair of glasses bought, Warby gives a pair to someone in need. Value and service are what the company promises its customers. And by identifying itself above all as a lifestyle brand, Warby is signaling that it wants to do more than sell a product—that it aspires to be part of people's lives, even to help define their identity.

Books, and reading, are an important piece of this. Old books were lined up on wooden shelves on the school bus for the Class Trip. When Warby started opening retail stores in 2013, books from independent publishers like Brooklyn's powerHouse Books and McSweeney's were for sale there. Books are a good fit with Warby's fashionably geeky style and with eyeglasses in general, plus they reinforce the real-world connection that the Class Trip made so pointedly.

The retail stores take that connection further. The first, in SoHo in lower Manhattan, has been joined by dozens of others, many of them in hip neighborhoods like Venice, California, and downtown Detroit. They proved phenomenally successful: by 2015, five years after the company's launch, in-store sales were averaging $3,000 per square foot per year—a figure roughly equal to Tiffany's and far above the retail average of $325. (Apple leads everyone with pre-pandemic sales of roughly $5,500 per square foot.) Two things made the retail stores work: intensive data analysis to identify locations that would flourish, and a focus on creating a pleasing and shareable physical experience, with ample space for people to move around and full-length mirrors so they could try on glasses and post the results on Instagram. As bricks-and-mortar retail seemed to be cratering, with department stores closing willy-nilly and shopping centers being repurposed as Amazon "fulfillment centers," Warby's shops were overtaking online to become the company's leading source of sales.

Other aspects of Warby Parker's identity are less obvious. Take the color blue, which can be found on its website, in its stores, in its packaging, and lining the inside of its glasses cases. This is not just any blue: it's blue-footed booby blue. The blue-footed booby is a marine bird that's found in the Galapagos Islands and elsewhere in the Eastern Pacific. The boobies have bright blue feet, and they're known for a strange mating ritual in which the males lift their feet one by one and show them off to discerning females. The bluer the feet, the healthier the bird, and the more likely to find a mating partner.

Blumenthal encountered the boobies on a trip to the Galapagos. He loved their look, which is as goofy as it is earnest. "It's sophisticated, because it's found in these far reaches of the globe, and part of the Warby Parker brand is being worldly and informed," he told *Fast Company*. Boobies also tend to view the world with a quizzical expression, which fits because the brand is also about learning and being curious. But the most amazing thing, he went on, is those bright blue webbed feet, "which have a little bit of flair, a little bit of quirkiness. One of our core values here is to inject fun and quirkiness into everything that we do."

Pink Sweater at the Biker Bar

The blue-footed booby is a reminder that, subliminally or otherwise, every choice we make feeds into the story we're trying to tell. It doesn't matter if we're a direct-to-consumer company like Warby Parker or a nonprofit or a political organization. Our story isn't just what we say it is, and it isn't told only in words. It's the sum of everything we do.

This realization was key to the success of an earlier start-up that in some ways served as a model for Warby Parker. Kate Spade Handbags was launched in 1993 by a former *Mademoiselle* editor named Kate Brosnahan and her soon-to-be-husband, Andy Spade. The two had met in the mid-eighties when they were students at Arizona State University who were working in the same clothing store. A few years later, he was a budding entrepreneur who created restaurant ads in exchange for food; she was the Kansas City preppy who wore pink crewneck sweaters while waitressing at a Scottsdale motorcycle bar. Eventually they settled in New York, where Andy worked at an ad agency while Kate moved up the editorial ladder at *Mademoiselle*—until it hit her that this was a ladder she didn't want to be on. So she quit and, at his suggestion, started making handbags—functional bags with simple, architectural lines, because everything that was out there at the time struck her as gaudy and overcomplicated. Her name was on the outside of the bag—but in lower-case, Andy explained, "because we're lower-case."

Like a lot of young entrepreneurs, Brosnahan and Spade didn't have money to spend on advertising. They were putting everything they had into the business, emptying out Andy's retirement account and using their apartment as a warehouse. It was all they could do to keep up with their orders, once orders started coming in. But they did have a story.

The story of Kate Spade Handbags wasn't about handbags. It was about Kate and her personal style. It was about a way of life the handbags represented—upscale, yet unfussy and unpretentious. An attainable luxury that was playful and casual and quintessentially American. "It was about this world we were creating, which was about graciousness," Andy told *Inc.* magazine. "We built it around Kate's personality."

Because they knew how to evoke that feeling of graciousness, the Spades were able to expand their product line over time to include stationery, shoes, beauty products, eyewear, china, and wallpaper. In 1997 they invented Jack Spade, a fictional ad-agency-type guy whose name they used to expand into men's clothing and accessories. Every decision they made along the way—where to open their first shop (in lower Manhattan, in the gallery-district-turned-shopping-mecca of SoHo), what color soap to put in the bathrooms, whether to sell flowers in the shop too or just handbags—became part of the story. As Andy put it, "What does it say if we're in SoHo? What does it say if we're on the Upper East Side," in the silk-stocking district? "All of these things communicate something about the brand."

Sadly, there were aspects of Kate's personality that conflicted with the story. Like other fashion figures—Alexander McQueen, Isabella Blow—she suffered for years from depression, a condition that, as the novelist and critic Daphne Merkin wrote in the *New York Times* after Kate's death, "can be covered up with a smile and denied even by the one enduring it." Increasingly her world took on a darker cast. On June 5, 2018, at the age of 55, to the shock of her family and friends, she went to her bedroom in their sprawling Park Avenue apartment—the apartment success had bought—and hanged herself with a red scarf.

By this time, she and Andy had long since sold the company and moved on to other ventures. For Andy, that meant joining forces with Anthony Sperduti, a former art director at their company, in a branding studio called Partners & Spade. Among their clients was Warby Parker, for whom they helped brainstorm both the initial store in SoHo, with its highly Instagrammable interiors, and the Class Trip.

Though the Kate Spade story was about an imaginary world and Warby Parker's was about eyeglasses, there's still a direct line between the kind of storytelling that went into Kate Spade and the storytelling that built Warby nearly 20 years later. In both cases, the focus was on the sensibility of the founders and the motivations behind what they did. "It seems straightforward now, but back then no one thought like that," Sperduti said. When Kate Spade was started, companies advertised on TV and sold their products in stores. But ads and products grow dated. "There is the idea of having a narrative and concept and a level of wit,"

Sperduti went on. "That doesn't have a shelf life. The aesthetics and style do have a shelf life. But the bigger notion of having an experience built on a narrative does not."

An experience built on a narrative: beyond the simple matter of good, cheap eyeglasses, that was the essence of what Warby Parker offered its customers.

The Company That's Fixing Shaving

If Warby Parker's was version 1 of the origin story for the Internet age and Kate Spade was the prelude, then version 2 would be Harry's, the shaving company. Warby's story is compelling; Harry's is immersive.

Harry's was launched in March 2013, three years after Warby Parker, by a Stanford MBA named Andy Katz-Mayfield and one of Warby's four cofounders, Jeff Raider. Like Warby, it had its genesis in sticker shock. It happened when Katz-Mayfield was shopping for razor blades at a drugstore in Santa Monica, where he was working at a start-up. First he had to find a store clerk to unlock the case ("I wasn't in some high-end jewelry store shopping for diamonds," he said later), but the real surprise came when he got to the cash register and the bill for a four-pack of razor blades and a can of shaving cream came to $25. "I was like, 'How did I just spend that kind of money?' I can remember the emotion," he told *Inc.* "You know as a consumer when you are getting taken advantage of."

The experience made him think of Warby Parker. Before he went to Stanford, he and Raider—both natives of the Boston area—had worked together, first at Bain & Company, a Boston-based management consultancy, and then at Charlesbank Capital Partners, a Boston-based private equity firm. Katz-Mayfield rang up his old friend, and eventually they agreed they should do a Warby on

Gillette—itself a Boston company, founded in 1901 and now owned by Procter & Gamble. Gillette had 70 percent of the US men's shaving market and almost as much of the world market, and it enjoyed the profit margins that kind of dominance makes possible. Harry's, they decided, would be "the company that's fixing shaving."

What distinguishes the Harry's story from the Warby Parker story is that Harry's is much more personal. Neil Blumenthal and Dave Gilboa have been fixtures in the business press for years, but Warby itself, while often alluding to its founders, rarely shows them in a photograph or even mentions them by name. Harry's put Katz-Mayfield and Raider front and center from the start, and for good reason.

"One of the insights we had early on," Raider told me, "was that for people to believe in our brand, they had to believe in us. Razor blades are like a knife that you take to your face. People want to understand how and why two founders could credibly make those products and offer them at a fair price. And the answer is that we had this journey where we spent years trying to learn about how the best razor blades in the world were made."

Dollar Shave Club, their bargain-priced online competitor, was selling razors from a South Korean company. But if people were to believe in Harry's, Raider felt, that wouldn't work. Raider grew increasingly obsessed with razor-blade technology until finally, while reading a shaving blog late one night, he came across a mention of Feintechnik, a German company that was said to make some of the world's best. "And so I called them," he said. "I literally picked up the phone and said, Hey, my name is Jeff, I started this company Warby Parker in the US, it's had some success, the model is pretty straightforward, we deliver great products that people are really proud to wear and love. And I think there's an opportunity to do something similar with razors and razor blades and shaving gel." It worked:

Feintechnik agreed to make blades for them, and less than a year after launching, Harry's raised $100 million to buy the company. Which is how Feintechnik—now known as Harry's Deutschland—became part of the story too, lending, as one report put it, "an important air of credibility and authenticity" to the startup.

When Harry's ran its first television ad, in January 2017, it was a mini-documentary that told the company's origin story in a deft and witty fashion. It started with the founders' baby pictures, highlighted the German factory, featured Katz-Mayfield's proud parents on a Skype call ("Did we conceive Andy to take on Big Razor in an epic battle of David vs. Goliath? Oh, hell yes"), and even showed the two founders in their boxer shorts after Gillette "threatened to sue their pants off." (Gillette had filed suit for patent infringement shortly after Harry's launched but dropped the suit a week later.) "Jeff and Andy are two guys who put their pants on one leg at a time, just like you," the spot concluded. "Who need to shave, just like you. Who don't want to pay too much and like good design—like you."

By this time, Harry's was causing real pain. Procter & Gamble, the company behind Tide and Pampers and Crest and Tampax and who knows how many other big-name consumer brands, had paid $57 billion to buy Gillette in 2005. Business was good for a while. But between 2010 and 2016, as first Dollar Shave Club and then Harry's began to grow, Gillette's share of the men's-razor market fell from 70 percent to 54 percent—and it was still falling.

Belatedly, P&G decided to fight back. Shortly before the Harry's television ad ran, Gillette launched a "Welcome Back" campaign aimed at Harry's customers. It was a hapless effort. The 30-second spot at the center of it used the theme song from *Wel-*

come Back, Kotter, a sitcom that had been a big hit on TV—for two seasons, 40 years before. Even more inept was Gillette's claim that most guys leave Harry's after trying it. "We said, 'Hey Gillette, like you make these assertions in your ad—here's the actual data,'" Raider recalled. "The actual data said that customers love Harry's and come back over and over and over again. 'So we'd love you to run the ad—just change the claim from, you know, "leave Harry's" to "stay with Harry's" and we're great.' And then we took the letter and we put it online and our customers, like, flocked to our defense. It was awesome to see."

Meanwhile, Nelson Peltz, the billionaire hedge fund manager, had announced that he'd spent more than $3 billion to amass a huge stake in P&G. It was not because he liked what he saw there. That summer, as he launched a proxy fight to win a seat on the P&G board, he singled out the company's failure to stop its online shaving competitors as evidence of its incompetence. "I spoke to a lot of the ex-Gillette guys," Peltz told CNBC, "and you know what they said? If Dollar Shave Club, and whoever the other guy is, were around when they were running Gillette, they would have put a group of them together—five or 10 guys in a room—and say 'how do we put these guys out of business now?'"

The proxy fight—the most expensive ever fought in the US up to that time—ended when the company called a truce and added Peltz to its board. But if he was expecting to effect a dramatic turnaround, he didn't succeed. Gillette kept on losing market share, and Harry's continued to grow, even as sales at Dollar Shave Club flatlined after it was acquired by P&G's archcompetitor, Unilever. Several months later, P&G admitted defeat, taking an $8 billion write-down on the $57 billion it had paid for Gillette 14 years earlier. Headline writers responded with a lot of bleeding references.

"Drowning in Pitches to Buy"

Like Warby Parker and Kate Spade, Harry's is a lifestyle brand. The word "lifestyle" has been used in its current sense, as a mode of living, since the early sixties, and we've had lifestyle brands for almost as long. Harley-Davidson, a quintessential lifestyle brand, set up the Harley Owners Group—HOG for short—in 1983; its million-plus dues-paying members get discounts on insurance and access to members-only rides and other events, not to mention special merch that boosts the company's bottom line. Red Bull energy drink seems to have extreme sports woven into its DNA, thanks to decades of sponsorships that back up the slogan "Red Bull gives you wings." So in 2012, when the brand sponsored Felix Baumgartner in a daredevil leap to earth from 24 miles up, no one viewed it cynically. "In the apex of the age of consumerism, we're just drowning in pitches to buy," wrote a *Forbes* editor on the day of the jump. "Then comes today, with Red Bull."

As conventional advertising has become less and less effective, the appeal of such stunts has become ever more obvious. A couple of decades ago, people objected mainly to advertising that interrupted their television viewing. Now it's not only interruptive but "transactional" advertising that people find objectionable. In a 2017 survey, Deloitte found that more than 30 percent of American adults and fully 50 percent of those aged 25 to 34 use an ad blocker on their personal computers, while roughly half the adults in the US and Canada fast-forward through ads on TV. It's gotten to the point that we almost don't want to be sold to, period. And when we can go online and get information on any subject we choose in a matter of milliseconds, why should we?

We'd rather be entertained by stories—stories we weave from our own experience, as in the case of HOG. Stories we can watch as they happen, as in the case of Red Bull Stratos, which was the name given to Baumgartner's leap from the edge of space. Or stories about a couple of guys who seem a lot like ourselves, except they raised hundreds of millions of dollars to start their own shaving company because one of them felt ripped off when he had to shell out 25 bucks for four razor blades and a can of shaving cream. Harry's stories work because they feel earned, and because they feel earned they make a deep connection with the company's fans.

That Harry's customers can even be called fans is telling. Like Warby Parker, the company cultivates relationships that go well beyond transactional. When people place their first order, they get an email saying, essentially, we're here to answer any questions about Harry's or about life in general. Often, Raider said, "People start reaching out to us, saying hey, this is going on in my life or that's going on in my life and I don't really have anyone to talk to." Looking into these replies, Harry's customer experience team realized that frequently what was going on was a feeling that person writing had to live up to being something he wasn't. "So we started to build this perspective within Harry's that guys can be confident *and* vulnerable, strong *and* open-minded—that you don't have to be one or the other," Raider said. "If you think about being a brand that's really about men's care and cares about guys, we should help you."

This has found expression in a variety of ways: support for anti-suicide hotlines for military veterans and gay youth, for an organization that promotes "healthy manhood" and another group that treats PTSD among veterans. In 2018, Harry's took the connection a notch further with "A Man Like You," a three-minute video in which a space alien asks a young boy what it means to be a man. After reciting some answers by rote—a man needs to know about cars and sports, a man needs to not be afraid—the kid 'fesses up: "I mean there really aren't any rules, honestly."

The ad drew complaints from grumpy old men. But it fit well with attitudes among younger people, who increasingly expect brands to take a stand on social issues. (One recent survey found that 75 percent of US Millennials support such stands, versus less than a third of Boomers.) It also seemed to make sense for this stage in the development of Harry's. "We're five years old, and I think we've done a pretty good job of introducing ourselves," Lorna Peters, Harry's head of marketing, said when the video was released. "Now we want guys to understand what we care about and recognize their voice in Harry's values."

The key words here are "recognize their voice." Even when Harry's tells a story about Harry's—about its founders and why they started the company, say—the story looks outward, not in. If you're going to talk about yourself, you need to do it in a way that reflects the people you want to connect with: your audience.

2. Audience

Author · Journey · Audience

Character · World · Detail · Voice · Platform · Immersion

Connecting with an audience is the point of any story. The question is, how? And how do you know when you've done it?

Matt Locke, a veteran of the BBC and the UK's Channel 4 who now heads an innovative consultancy called Storythings, recounts an anecdote from a BBC documentary on the making of *Blackadder*, a cult comedy series from the eighties. The documentary included an interview with Richard Curtis, one of *Blackadder*'s writers, who would go on to script such hit movies as *Four Weddings and a Funeral* and *Love Actually*. "I still don't know how many people watched any episode of *Blackadder*," Curtis recalled. "I used to wander 'round Shepherd's Bush"—the West

London neighborhood where the BBC had its television studios—"looking in people's windows, particularly people with basement flats, to see whether or not anyone was watching."

Curtis, in other words, was entirely cut off from his audience—and he was hardly alone. Even the broadcasting executives who had access to the ratings found themselves looking at shadow figures. "By the time I started working for the BBC in 2001," Locke himself said on a subsequent BBC show, "multiple generations of TV executives and creatives had only ever understood audiences as numbers."

In the years since, digital platforms have connected author and audience—or at least distributor and audience—with a vengeance. Amazon knows exactly how long it took you to finish the last book on your Kindle and where you stopped if you didn't finish it. Newspaper editors can see what stories people are reading, how long they spend on each one, and what they're sharing online. Netflix knows how many people are watching its shows, who they are, how avidly they're bingeing on them, whether they binge on a whole season or stop partway through, where they pause or rewind or fast-forward, what (if anything) they watch next, and how they rated what they saw.

But it's still entirely too easy to lose sight of those people watching TV in their living rooms or on their smartphones or wherever they may happen to be. The goal is not simply to harvest the most data. The goal is to experience the feedback loop that data can approximate. To re-create the bond between author and audience that existed in earlier days, before the advent of prerecorded mass media a century and a quarter ago. To get back to what Locke calls "the call and response" of Victorian-era music halls, the noisy back-and-forth that used to connect the performer with the crowd, back when the performer was a few feet away and the crowd was usually drunk.

Digital, Physical, Ethereal

At least you don't need to peer in people's basement windows any longer. Sometimes all you have to do is look out onto the street. In late 2013, thousands of people stood in line for hours outside a lower Manhattan art gallery, often in a cold rain, in order to spend 45 seconds in a work of art—not looking at it, but standing inside it. The work in question was Yayoi Kusama's *Infinity Mirrored Room—The Souls of Millions of Light Years Away*, a selfie-friendly and highly Instagrammable piece that took the form of a small, mirror-lined room hung with flickering LED bulbs in a multitude of colors. Meanwhile, the 27 new Kusama paintings in an adjacent room went largely ignored. It was hardly the 84-year-old artist's first exhibition in the city— the year before, she had had a major retrospective at the Whitney Museum of American Art—but her infinity room's ethereal, otherworldly presence seemed strangely of the moment. "It felt like eternity," a 25-year-old computer technician told a *New York Times* reporter, referring not to the wait but to his 45 seconds in the room. "Very surreal, seeing how small you are but how beautifully everything works together."

Kusama is not the only artist to gain a following with work that slips the customary bounds of art. A year later and 4,000 miles away, I found myself in one of James Turrell's *ganzfeld* ("total field") pieces, *Sight Unseen*, an immersive and wildly disorienting work that tends to produce confusion and astonishment in equal measure.

I was in Varese, a small city in the foothills of the Italian Alps, at an eighteenth-century hilltop villa that was owned for decades by Giuseppe Panza di Biumo, a Milanese businessman whose adventurous tastes and frequent purchases made him one of the most important art collectors of the twentieth century. "It's not bad," admitted his daughter, Maria Giuseppina Panza di Biumo, a smile escaping her lips as our eyes swept across eight acres of topiary and fountains.

Now an art museum, the villa had a small exhibition of works by Turrell and Robert Irwin, pioneers of Southern California's Light and Space movement—artists whose concern with the limits of perception appealed to "Count Panza," as he was known in the art world. ("He was never a count," his daughter said with a laugh, "but people liked to call him that.") Light is Turrell's medium—he has worked in it for more than 50 years, starting in the sixties—and perception is his subject. Trading the physicality of art objects for the immateriality of light, he makes light look solid, even as it seems to float in space and dissolve into air.

After signing a release (lawsuits have been filed over injuries sustained in other ganzfelds) and donning little plastic booties, I joined about a dozen other people as we were ushered up a set of steps to what looked like an extremely large artwork on the wall. Then the guide stepped through it and invited us to do the same. Entering a large and seemingly boundless space suffused in white, I felt as if I had floated into a cloud—or I would have felt that way if the floor weren't sloping downward, reminding me that gravity had not gone on holiday.

"Stop!" the guide said when I was 25 or 30 feet in. "No further."

There seemed to be an edge ahead, barely visible but suggesting a sharp drop. Then the light began to shift, from an all-encompassing white to intense reds and blues. I felt as if I were deep within a Mark Rothko painting, bathed in nonspecific spirituality. I also felt the need for a wall to lean against, but I couldn't make one out. It's important to remain upright, I told myself. I still had five or six minutes to go.

Follow the Actors, or Rifle the Set?

The kind of all-encompassing experiences created by Yayoi Kusama and James Turrell are hardly limited to art. A few blocks from the gallery that had staged the Kusama show, a theatrical performance called *Sleep No More* played for nine years before being put on hiatus by the pandemic. *Sleep No More* has no stage, no auditorium, no seats, and most importantly, no proscenium arch. It plays out in a rambling series of rooms in a five-story loft building that has been styled the McKittrick Hotel—rooms the audience is invited to explore at will. Actors come and go. You can follow them or not. You might rather rummage through drawers in an old desk or explore a room that looks like a taxidermy studio. At some point you're liable to encounter a man and a woman having a terrible fight, slamming each other against the walls; later he slips naked into a bathtub, smeared with blood. There's a story involved, a sort of Hitchcock/*Macbeth* mashup, but it's mostly wordless and entirely nonlinear: no matter how many times you come back, you won't experience it the same way twice.

Sleep No More and Punchdrunk, the London-based theater company behind it, are the brainchild of Felix Barrett, a man who has been devising ways to break down the conventional expectations of theatergoers since he was a university student in the nineties. Thin and wiry, with shoulder-length hair in a dirty shade of blond, Barrett has been described, not inaccurately, as "elfin." Conventional theater "shuts off most of your brain and all of your body," he said one evening when we met at a wine bar on the south bank of the Thames, just across the river from the houseboat he and his wife were living in. "You're switching everything off. So what I want to do is physically wake people up. I'm always searching out sensations that take your mind to a different place."

There's precedent for this sort of thing: medieval drama depended on "communal participation," the historian Stephen Greenblatt notes, and often "there was no sharp distinction between theatrical spaces and the spaces of ordinary life. . . . All the world was a stage." The spot where Barrett and I were sitting was less than a mile downriver from the original site of Shakespeare's Globe Theatre, which was one of the first purpose-built public playhouses to go up in England since Roman times.

When I asked Barrett what prompted him to dispense with the four centuries of theatrical tradition that followed, he flashed a sly grin. "I know what my mum would say—that I've always been obsessed with the visceral and with things you can feel. I'm fascinated by people entering a space—the adventure of a transition, the idea of the reveal." The reactions we have in such circumstances, he added, are primitive, instinctual, beyond our control. "If you're truly present in a place, your body is making a decision before your mind is. That's what's immersive. And the fact that it's visceral, that it's sensation-based, helps you get there."

Punchdrunk has put on more than two dozen productions since Barrett founded the company in 2000, but his personal favorite may have been his first: *The Moon Slave*, created for an audience of one when he was still a student at the University of Exeter. He invited four theater critics, each of whom arrived on a separate night to discover an empty theater with programs laid out on the seats. Onstage a phone would ring, and after an initial hesitation the audience—that evening's critic—would answer it and be told a car was waiting outside. A masked chauffeur would usher the critic into the car and speed off into the night, Stravinsky playing at high volume on the stereo.

The car would eventually stop on the grounds of Poltimore House, the burned-out shell of an eighteenth-century stately home, and let you out at a spot where a torchlit path led into a dense forest. Wearing headphones to hear the story, you would venture forth into the woods and into Barrett's production. You were in a fairytale, following an unseen princess deeper and deeper into the forest as she dances alone in the night, wildly and with increasing abandon. Night after night the princess comes back, and as she grows ever more obsessed with her dancing, the call of her day-to-day life slips away. One evening she misses her engagement party, but she keeps coming back. Then, on what was supposed to have been her wedding night, the night of a lunar eclipse, a night when the music seems louder and more fervent than ever, she suddenly realizes she is no longer dancing alone. At that point the music explodes and so does the sky, in a blinding, blood-red flash that reveals 200 grinning scarecrows surrounding you in a clearing.

On the drive back to the theater, the soundtrack explains that the prince found bloody footprints in the clearing the next morning, and next to them another set of footprints, made by a pair of cloven hoofs. As for the audience—"you always know it's working," Barrett said quietly, "if people can't speak afterwards."

The Age of Immersion

What Yayoi Kusama's *Infinity Mirrored Room*, James Turrell's ganzfelds, and Punchdrunk's *Sleep No More* have in common—beyond the fact that they're all physical experiences—is the seductive power of immersiveness. You don't just look at them. You inhabit them, and in doing so, even very briefly in the case of the Kusama, you undergo a transformation that is rarely achieved by viewing a painting or watching a stage production. You're not on the outside looking in, you are inside. The experience is visceral, emotional, and not, as Barrett pointed out, entirely within your control.

Immersion is the experience of losing yourself in another reality. It's what happens when you are so in thrall to a story—or an art work, in the case of Kusama and Turrell—as to slip into a world of someone else's creation. The whole idea defies logic. Not only is it inherently subjective, but the term "immersion" is a metaphor derived from an entirely different state, the physical experience of being underwater. "Transportation," the term preferred by psychologists, is similarly metaphorical. To be immersed, as Janet Murray wrote in her landmark book *Hamlet on the Holodeck*, is to have "the sensation of being surrounded by a completely other reality, as different as water is from air."

People have been immersing themselves in stories for centuries—it's a natural human impulse, the inevitable result of our understanding stories by projecting ourselves into them. But twenty-first-century audiences show a heightened desire for stories that encompass them. A 2013 survey of US and UK adults by JWT Intelligence found "a growing desire and appreciation" for immersive experiences of all sorts—especially among Millennials, much more than among older generations. A 2016 report noted a vogue for "unreality," with Millennials in particular eager to immerse themselves in make-believe settings.

Want to sleep in Van Gogh's bedroom? The Art Institute of Chicago partnered with Leo Burnett, the Chicago-based ad agency, and Airbnb to realize the little bedroom in Arles he painted in 1888 and 1889 as an actual, three-dimensional room in a downtown apartment building. For a mere $10 you could spend the night in it and have the opportunity, *Vice* suggested, "to inhabit the painter's mind and gain a tacit feel for the man without hours of scholarship and observation of his works." Online ticket sales for the institute shot up 250 percent.

We are living in an age of immersion. Technology is of course a factor. The trend is always toward gadgets that do more work and leave less to the imagination. The late nineteenth century saw a vogue for cycloramas, which displayed large-scale reproductions of Civil War battles, volcanic eruptions, even the Crucifixion. When moving pictures were invented, they seemed so realistic by comparison as to make these static illusions look superficial and tawdry. Orson Welles inadvertently demonstrated the immersive power of radio a few decades later when his adaptation of H. G. Wells's *The War of the Worlds* led some listeners to think that New Jersey was being invaded by Martians. A half-century after that, the proliferation of video games created a generation accustomed to actively participating in a story rather than passively consuming it. (Not for nothing have *Sleep No More* and its ilk been called "theater for the video game generation.") Now we have virtual reality, which can produce a startlingly realistic-looking computer-simulated environment within a totally enclosed stereoscopic headset.

But as Punchdrunk has demonstrated, you don't need digital technology to create an immersive experience. VR provides a shortcut, but you can get there without it. What you need is the illusion VR provides—the sense that there are no limits, no boundaries, no frame around the picture, no proscenium arch to signal a fourth wall, not even a screen to come between you and the experience, because audiences that once viewed the screen as a window are now coming to see it as a barrier. The word "media," after all, comes from the Latin for "middle": a medium is the middle-thing that comes between us and the information it conveys. What we want is an unmediated experience—art without a frame, theater without an arch, movies without a screen.

Steven Spielberg made this point in a 2013 discussion with George Lucas at the University of Southern California. The two old pros were on hand for a discussion with a Microsoft executive and the dean of USC's School of Cinematic Arts to mark the opening of a $50 million interactive media building. The headline news was their prediction of the imminent collapse of several mega-budget movie franchises, and with it the end of Hollywood as it exists today. So far, that hasn't happened. But they also indulged in some intriguing speculation about what will come next.

Lucas predicted that blockbusters will eventually become big-ticket events, priced like ball games and Broadway plays, and that the rest of the movie business will migrate to online video. Spielberg offered a more radical vision. At a time when screens of every size, shape, and level of connectivity are proliferating, he foresaw an end to screens and a new role for the audience. "We're never going to be totally immersive as long as we're looking at a square," he declared. "We've got to get rid of that and put the player inside the experience, where no matter where you look, you're surrounded by a three-dimensional experience. That's the future."

I Was Arthur Hudson

No one has yet invented a technology that dispenses with screens entirely. But Gene Roddenberry, the creator of *Star Trek*, offered a blueprint for one in *Star Trek: The Next Generation*, the 1987 follow-up to his original series. In the pilot episode, the first officer of the Starship *Enterprise* goes to the ship's "holodeck," a chamber specially outfitted to project a holographic simulation of reality, and enters a verdant woodland. For the moment, the closest we've come to this is immersive theater.

Sleep No More is probably the best-known example, at least in New York. But even there it's easy to spot the audience: they're the people wearing masks. The mask is the sole remaining barrier between the audience and the experience—a vestigial relic of theater's fourth wall. Fabien Riggall's approach is more radical.

Riggall is the founder of another London-based production company, Secret Cinema, which thrusts you into the world of a movie and then screens the movie for you at the end. The "secret" is that you don't know what movie you're in until the screening begins. "When people discover something, they become emotionally connected to it," Riggall told me. "What we're doing is allowing the audience to discover everything."

Riggall launched Secret Cinema in 2007, when he was 32. Over the years he has produced spectacular live-action realizations of dozens of movies—*Blade Runner*, *The Empire Strikes Back*, the 1949 film noir *The Third Man*. "By us creating a real experience," he said, "it produces a blur between fact and fiction." I saw what he meant when I joined a production that began in a dilapidated, Victorian-era library in the still-gritty East End neighborhood of Bethnal Green and ended hours later in some place I'd never heard of. By then I'd been treated to a screening of *The Shawshank Redemption*, the 1994 movie starring Tim Robbins as an innocent man sent to prison for murder. For an extra £30 (about $50 at the time), I could have spent the night in a cell with four or five fellow "prisoners." Instead I stumbled out into the night and tried to figure out how to get back to my hotel.

The experience had started the day before, when I'd gotten an email informing me that I would be assuming the identity of a man named Arthur Hudson and that I should wear a suit, a tie, and long underwear. (It was late November, and cold.) I showed up to find several hundred people, many of them young couples, waiting in what was clearly supposed to be a courthouse. ("Secret Cinema is the biggest dating destination in London," said Riggall.) Eventually my name was called and I got in line in the courtroom, only to be pronounced guilty the moment I stood before the judge. My group was led out to an asphalt courtyard, lined up against a brick wall, yelled at by guards, and marched around the neighborhood and onto a rickety-looking prison bus. When a fellow prisoner pulled out his smartphone to snap a photo, a guard went berserk and grabbed it away from him. "You just wait til tonight!" he snarled as the guy cringed in his seat and his date looked on in dismay. "My balls are gonna be on your chin."

The prison was dark and forbidding—a disused Victorian parochial school, I learned later. It certainly seemed better suited to its current, fictional role than to anything involving children. We were led into a gym, lined up in rows, and ordered to strip down to our underwear and pick up our prison garb. We were marched through the shower room, where a guard loomed menacingly over a prisoner cowering naked in a corner. The guard said something I couldn't quite catch and the prisoner went hysterical, falling to his knees and screaming, "No, no, *not that, please!*" (The production employed 45 actors and 60-odd crew.) Eventually we found ourselves shoved together on a narrow, U-shaped balcony that was lined floor-to-ceiling with chicken wire. When we were packed shoulder-to-shoulder, face-to-face, breathing one another's air, the guards started banging their billy clubs against the iron railings. Maximum compression; no release. As the throng started keening wildly, I got for the first time a glimmer of what prison must be like: total control, always verging on utter chaos.

Even if you've paid to be there, standing amid a crowd that's trapped in a cage and being threatened by armed guards is a searing experience. The *Telegraph* called the production "frighteningly immersive," and I can see why. It felt personal and intimate and direct in a way that conventional plays and movies cannot and that digital simulations don't manage either. It combined the first-person involvement of the holodeck with the animal engagement of flesh-and-blood interactions. In that sense, at least, the future Spielberg imagined is already here—but in a way that makes it available only to the small number of people who can attend something like this. Live theater doesn't scale, no matter how immersive it gets.

The Experience Economy: Business Is Theater

Dramatically immersive experiences like Secret Cinema have become increasingly common in entertainment. What's remarkable is how common they're becoming in other industries as well. Joseph Pine and James Gilmore predicted as much in 1999 when they published *The Experience Economy: Work Is Theatre and Every Business a Stage*, a book that radically shifted our understanding of business.

Since the late sixties, people in the West had grown accustomed to living in a "service economy," where products are undifferentiated and economic value lies in the intangible activities people do for us—banking, medical care, driving a taxi. As manufactured goods became increasingly standardized, with price the main distinguishing factor, manufacturing moved to countries where it could be done more cheaply. In places like North America and Western Europe, services began to employ more and more people and make up an ever-bigger share of the economy. But by the late nineties, Pine and Gilmore pointed out, services too were becoming commoditized. To stand out, businesses had to offer something more.

Services are useful but ordinary. Experiences are memorable, even magical—and worth paying extra for. You can buy ground coffee pretty cheaply, and for a little more you can get a cup of coffee already made for you. But if you pay a good deal more than that, you can get a more exotic cup of coffee prepared on the spot by a friendly barista and enjoy it at a window seat at Starbucks.

Long before the advent of free Wi-Fi, people went to Starbucks to hang out, just as they hang out at bars, bookstores, and other places that are neither home nor work. "People want to be with people," the architect Robert A. M. Stern once told me. "Why do we think Starbucks is such a success? Don't we think you can make coffee at home?"

As with coffee, so with other businesses. "Experiences have always been around," Pine and Gilmore wrote, "but consumers, businesses, and economists lumped them in with the service sector along with such uneventful activities as dry cleaning, auto repair, wholesale distribution, and telephone access. When a person buys a service, he purchases a set of intangible activities carried out on his behalf. But when he buys an experience, he pays to spend time enjoying a series of memorable events that a company stages—as in a theatrical play—to engage him in an inherently personal way."

As work becomes theater, workers become performers. "Two guys tossing pizza dough back in the kitchen . . . a floor full of claims adjusters shuffling papers for an insurance company . . . workers on an assembly line": they may not realize it, but they are putting on a show—a show for which, as Pine and Gilmore noted, "audience = customers." They might have added, customers = fans.

Why is this happening—and why now? For two reasons, Pine said when I rang him up. "On the supply side, companies are always in search of differentiation. As goods and services are being commoditized, the natural thing is to move into experiences. And on the demand side, experiences make us more happy. We *want* goods and services to be commoditized—to get the lowest possible price and the greatest possible value. Experiences are really about time—and time has become so much more precious to us."

The Audience Moves onto the Stage

The emergence of the experience economy dovetailed neatly with the development chronicled by the urbanologist Richard Florida in *The Rise of the Creative Class*. Florida's newly identified demographic, comprising by his account more than 40 million Americans (about a third of the workforce) by the early twenty-first century, was made up of an eclectic mix of scientists and engineers, architects and designers, artists and performers, as well as "creative professionals" in fields like business, finance, and law, plus an amorphous group we might call hipsters. "The Creative Class is experience driven," Florida writes, with a strong preference for "active, participatory recreation over passive spectator sports" as well as for "a teeming blend of cafés, sidewalk musicians, and small galleries and bistros, where it's hard to draw the line between participant and observer." In other words, Brooklyn.

C. K. Prahalad and Venkat Ramaswamy, professors at the University of Michigan business school, had their own take on this. To them, it wasn't just theater that explained what was happening: it was a particular kind of theater—the precursor of the immersive productions we have today. Business competition, they wrote, "seems more like the experimental theater of the sixties and seventies; everyone and anyone can be part of the action." Consumers, they added, "have moved out of the audience and onto the stage."

To Prahalad and Ramaswamy, the big news was that, because customers were now informed and connected online, they were no longer passive consumers—that is, no longer just an audience. This led the two to the concept of "co-creation"—the idea that informed consumers influence the development of a product and thereby add value to it. Eventually, buttressed by developments in cognitive science, co-creation would turn out to be a more powerful and expansive concept than they knew.

Co-creating the Experience

One of the curious things about Secret Cinema's production of *The Shawshank Redemption*, once I'd calmed down enough to register anything curious, was that the audience, while clearly having a role in what was happening, did not have any say about where it was going. We were like extras, except we didn't know what movie we were in. Acting on instinct, we "co-created" the experience in partnership with the actors. But audiences don't have to be as actively involved as we were.

Gerald Zaltman of Harvard Business School has applied the idea of co-creation to ads. "Advertising does not work by injecting consumers with meaning," he asserted in a 2007 ad-industry task force report on the effectiveness of television spots. Instead, "consumers and advertisers engage in a process I call the co-creation of meaning." Even when we're vegging out in front of the TV screen, we don't just "consume" whatever flickers before our eyes; we co-create it, interpreting it and imbuing it with meaning according to our own background and experiences.

This runs counter to conventional thinking in the advertising world, where the audience is given little credit for anything. People in the ad business have long tried to gauge the effectiveness of what they do with memory measures like "spontaneous recall" (what brand names you can think of in a given category) and "ad awareness" (what brands in a given category you recall being advertised on TV). These lend a pseudoscientific air to the endeavor, as if it were being run by PhDs in white lab coats. But to Zaltman, such standard-issue ad-measurement techniques aren't worth much—not least because they rely on a fundamental misunderstanding of memory.

Memories aren't thoughts we store intact in the brain like so many old photographs. All evidence suggests that we construct our memories on the fly, recalling some things and forgetting others, unconsciously altering them in response to subtle suggestions, even making up stuff that never happened. Asking us what we remember about an ad is about as scientific as asking us to identify a suspect in a police lineup—which research and DNA evidence have shown to be not scientific at all.

Much the same can be said for focus groups, another frequently used tool that's somewhere between misleading and worthless. "Focus group folly," Zaltman calls it in his book *How Customers Think*: "Contrary to conventional wisdom, they are not effective when developing and evaluating new product ideas, testing ads, or evaluating brand images. Nor do they get at deeper thoughts and feelings among consumers."

To get any realistic measure of how the audience responds to anything, you need long, in-depth interviews with at most two or three people. Focus-group researchers "take people out of the context of their regular lives and pepper them with questions about discrete ideas, products, or policy ideas," writes Christian Madsbjerg of ReD Associates, a consultancy that takes an anthropological approach to brand research. "By decontextualizing experiences . . . they miss almost everything that can shed light on human behavior. This is why their conclusions are wrong most of the time."

Neuromarketing: Emotion Meets Memory Meets Story

The current ad-industry frontier is neuromarketing, pioneered by Zaltman in the late nineties in a series of brain-imaging experiments that measured consumer responses to marketing efforts. Now, more than 20 years later, neuromarketing is a growing industry propelled by such people as Mihkel Jäätma, a London-based entrepreneur who heads a firm called Realeyes. A native of Estonia, Jäätma was working toward his MBA at Oxford when he started Realeyes with two fellow students from Eastern Europe, both of them PhD candidates in computer science. Companies like Coca-Cola, Condé Nast, Nestlé, and the advertising conglomerate Publicis Groupe come to Realeyes to learn how people feel about their marketing campaigns, as opposed to how they say they feel. To find out, Realeyes records people's faces on its webcams as they watch a video and then analyzes their reaction, microsecond by microsecond, with a vision system that has been trained through machine learning to recognize human facial expressions and the emotional states they signify.

Like its competitors, chief among them the MIT Media Lab spin-off Affectiva, Realeyes builds on the work of Paul Ekman, the University of California psychologist who in the seventies identified what he considered six universal emotions—happiness, sadness, fear, anger, disgust, and surprise—that are registered the same way by human faces regardless of culture, gender, and other differences. Since ads rarely provoke anger, Jäätma and his team replaced it with confusion, which is a much more common reaction to marketing efforts. Their system analyzes ads and ranks them on a 10-point scale according to the emotions they engender, the level of attention they get, and the overall brand impact they're likely to have.

This kind of work has its critics, as does Ekman's classification system—many of them psychologists who argue that facial expressions are not a reliable gauge of people's emotions. Still, Realeyes did a study of 130 automobile ads early on and found that the commercials that scored highest on its ranking system were also the ones that were most frequently viewed online and shared on social media. At the low end of the spectrum was a dreary Ford Fiesta spot promoting fuel economy; it scored a 4 and got 54,000 views online and five tweets. At the opposite end was Volkswagen's "The Force," a 2011 Super Bowl ad in which a little boy in a Darth Vader costume apparently manages to start his father's new Passat by invoking the *Star Wars* energy field—while his dad looks on from the kitchen window, car keys in hand, slyly working the remote. Realeyes gave this 60-second mini-movie a 9; in the two years after it aired, it was viewed 59 million times and generated more than 101,000 tweets, making it one of the most-shared spots in advertising history.

By the time I met Jäätma at Realeyes' Soho offices in 2019, the company had analyzed more than 20,000 video campaigns. The Volkswagen spot, which fails to mention anything about how great the Passat is, performed considerably better than most, but it fit the overall pattern. "We consistently show that you want to use people to tell a story," Jäätma said. "Authentic people—celebrities have basically zero effect." Compared to ads that focus on product benefits, he added, "story ads have about double the effectiveness."

This should not come as a surprise. "Human memory is story-based," explains the cognitive scientist Roger Schank, former director of artificial intelligence at Yale, in his book *Tell Me a Story*. To make his point, he tells a story about having a discussion with a friend

> about Jewish attitudes toward intermarriage. He said that two Jewish friends of his mother had gone out when they were young women, and when they'd returned home, their mother had asked them what they had done that day. They'd responded that they had played tennis. Their mother had

asked whom they had played with, and they had said, "Two guys." The mother had then asked what kind of guys, and they had responded, "Italian," to which the mother had said: "Another day wasted."

But what if instead of reciting this anecdote, Schank continues, his friend had simply said, "I know someone who thought that playing tennis with Italians was a waste of time" or "Some mothers don't want their daughters to spend time with non-Jews"? Obviously it wouldn't have been as memorable. Stories are effective, Schank concludes, because "if the story is good enough, you usually don't have to state your point at all; the hearer thinks about what you have said and figures out the point independently. The more work the hearer does, the more he or she will get out of your story."

Schank's assessment lends further heft to the idea of cocreation. But the concept is natural to anyone adept at telling stories or making art of any sort. "Description begins in the writer's imagination, but should finish in the reader's," Stephen King declared in *On Writing*, his helpful and entertaining memoir/howto. "The creative act is not performed by the artist alone," Marcel Duchamp once declared; the spectator "adds his contribution."* The author fashions the story, and we imbue it with meaning. We respond, as Anthony Sperduti of Partners & Spade pointed

---

* Admittedly, the spectator's contribution can go too far. I was at the 1989 Andy Warhol retrospective at the Museum of Modern Art in New York when somebody got sick and threw up in front of a painting. I don't know what happened to the person, but the offending upchuck was immediately surrounded by a velvet rope—had the staff been training for just such a moment?—and almost as quickly swept away. Meanwhile, a friend took in the scene and quipped, "Well—every man a critic!"

out when discussing Warby Parker, to an experience that's built on a narrative. We project ourselves into that narrative and react according to our own background and experience. And the storytelling that creates these narratives is not a static affair but an elaborate dance between author and audience. An act of seduction.

The Power of #Pepsi?

Like any attempt at seduction, storytelling can go painfully awry. We've seen that the more closely the story reflects its audience, the more likely we are to become immersed, and the more immersed we become, the more persuasive we find the story. But what happens when people who are supposed to look like us turn out to be a mindless caricature instead? That's when you get something like the uproar that greeted Pepsi's "Jump In" ad in April 2017.

Here was a 2-minute-40-second commercial that featured supermodel Kendall Jenner, costar of the famously fatuous reality TV hit *Keeping Up with the Kardashians*, getting swept up in the artificial fervor of a pretend street demonstration that had people carrying signs with milquetoast slogans like "Join the conversation." Cans of Pepsi appear frequently, always with the logo turned in our direction. At the video's climax, Jenner walks up to a line of cops and hands one of them a Pepsi. Warily the cop takes the can, and then—pop! fizz! End of conflict.

Whatever else you say about this spot, it got Pepsi a lot of attention. Twitter mentions were up 21,675 percent over a two-day period, with sentiment about the brand swinging from overwhelmingly positive before the video was posted to well over half negative. Instead of recognizing themselves in the crowd, people saw a weirdly distorted mirror. "Tone-deaf" was by far the dominant reaction.

"If only Daddy would have known about the power of #Pepsi,"

tweeted Bernice King, Martin Luther King's daughter. *Slate* published a list of 30 questions for the brand, among them "What type of role does Pepsi believe cola can play in the resistance?" and "Were the police expecting trouble from the notorious Nothing in Particular movement?" Pepsi pulled the ad from YouTube and apologized the next day, but the damage was done. As a consumer psychologist told *Ad Age*, "There really isn't anything they can say to explain why the ad that was supposed to show how connected and central they are to our culture said exactly the opposite."

Pepsi has targeted young people for decades with slogans like "For Those Who Think Young" (1961) and "the Pepsi Generation" (1963). A crucial difference is that those campaigns didn't try to co-opt a protest movement or suggest that soda pop could bridge racial and ethnic divides. Similarly, the idea of casting a celebrity like Kendall Jenner may not have seemed off-base, given the success Pepsi had putting Michael Jackson in its ads in the eighties. It's only when you mix the vapidity of a Kardashian with a bland mimicry of Black Lives Matter that you get such a toxic result.

The irony is that PepsiCo, Pepsi's corporate parent, was a socially aware enterprise that for years had been governed by the aphorism "Performance with Purpose"—and like just about everything else that happened at PepsiCo, "Jump In" would have been developed with that dictum in mind. PwP, as it was called, was the brainchild of Indra Nooyi, PepsiCo's CEO from 2006 to 2018. Nooyi had advocated social responsibility and healthier products at Pepsi for years before she became CEO, engineering the spin-off of its fast-food chains—Pizza Hut, Taco Bell, and Kentucky Fried Chicken—and the purchase of Tropicana and Quaker Oats at a time when most executives at Pepsi and its snack-food sibling, Frito-Lay, saw no reason to move beyond fat, sugar, and salt. She instituted Performance with Purpose shortly after being named CEO, ultimately tying it to the United Nations' sustainable development goals. And she delivered on performance: revenues nearly doubled under her watch to $65 billion, while the stock price went from $62 to $110. Little wonder she became a star of the business press.

The flip side of her stardom, according to a former marketing executive who asked not to be identified, was a corporate culture in which Nooyi reigned supreme and top executives were loath to cross her. This person and others realized the ad was going to be a disaster, but their warnings were ignored. Other people may have been too intimidated to speak up. Nooyi herself didn't see the problem: "I looked at the ad again and again and again trying to figure out what went wrong—because it was a peace march not a protest march," she later told *Fortune*. "It was people in happiness coming together." This despite the fact that Black Lives Matter protests had been roiling cities across America for the past three years in response to an unremitting spate of police killings. Happiness was not on the national agenda.

Pepsi's misstep may seem particularly egregious given the wealth of data the company possesses. But for all the facts and figures at their command, Pepsi's marketing people did not have a clear understanding of the people who would be seeing their ad. If anything, the Pepsi debacle suggests the limitations of data in a world where the resource that's limited is not information but attention. Pepsi got people's attention, but not in a good way.

The Attention Economy: Living in a Rabbit-Rich World

A half-century ago, in a lecture sponsored by Johns Hopkins University and the Brookings Institution, the economist and future Nobel laureate Herbert A. Simon told a story about bunny rabbits. It seems his neighbors had purchased a pair of bunnies for their daughter as an Easter present, and since the rabbits were of different genders the neighbors soon found themselves living in, as Simon put it, "a rabbit-rich world." This would have consequences for the neighbors and for the local food supply as well. "A rabbit-rich world is a lettuce-poor world," Simon pointed out, "and vice versa."

Alas for leporidologists, Simon was not there to talk about bunny rabbits. His actual topic was information, which even then appeared to be exploding, and he offered an observation that has been cited many times since:

> In an information-rich world, the wealth of information means a dearth of something else: a scarcity of whatever it is that information consumes. What information consumes is rather obvious: it consumes the attention of its recipients. Hence, a wealth of information creates a poverty of attention and a need to allocate that attention efficiently.

And so, at the dawn of the information age, was born the notion that we live in an "attention economy" in which a glut of information leaves us with a deficit of attention. It was a radical idea. For most of human history, information was in short supply while attention was overabundant. But Simon was prescient. In a few quick sentences, he predicted a reversal of the economic relationship between media producers and media consumers— between authors and publishers on one side and audiences on the other. In the future, the value of information (the stuff being published) would trend toward zero, while the value of attention, which is owned by audiences but can be leveraged by companies that help them allocate it, would only rise. Google, its founders as yet unborn, would triumph; most newspapers would collapse.

The information glut has had another, less obvious effect: it has fueled the triumph of design. As Richard Lanham, a professor emeritus of rhetoric and English at the University of California at Los Angeles, points out in a fascinating book called *The Economics of Attention*, when attention becomes the scarce resource,

> some fundamental changes occur. The devices that regulate attention are stylistic devices. Attracting attention is what style is all about. If attention is now at the center of the economy instead of stuff, then so is style. It moves from the periphery to the center. Style and substance trade places.

No reason to be surprised, then, that design thinking should come to the fore just as we began to be deluged by information. "'Design' is our name for the interface where stuff meets fluff," Lanham observes—where physical objects, which used to be what mattered, meet our willingness to give them our attention, which is what matters now. Apple's performance began to sky-rocket after Steve Jobs returned from exile, put a little-known but highly talented Londoner named Jony Ive in charge of design, and made style a key concern. The ascendancy of style applies as well to websites, video games, travel experiences, ad campaigns, art works, just about anything.

And anything with style can become what Lanham calls an "attention structure"—a shiny object that exists not for its own sake or to serve some greater purpose but to engage our atten-tion. Dairy farming in Switzerland, Lanham reports, is subsidized at a rate of $1,000 per cow per year so the Swiss and their visi-tors can enjoy a pastoral landscape. (Well worth it, in my view.) Warby Parker puts a few hipsters in a converted school bus and sends them across America. Yayoi Kusama puts twinkly lights in a mirrored room and people wait for hours to experience a few seconds of "eternity." Andy Warhol—almost Kusama's exact contemporary, though he had the misfortune to die at 58—achieved celebrity in the early sixties by painting Campbell's soup cans and Brillo boxes and putting them in art galleries, where they became an instant media sensation. Art critics who had championed the abstract expressionists—Jackson Pollock and Willem de Kooning and all their self-consciously heroic friends—were aghast at the lack of depth and personal feeling in pop art. Andy feigned indifference. Lanham again: "The surface, he said, was all there was. . . . He sung not of the soup but of the can it came in."

Where Experience and Attention Meet

It is hardly an accident that we have moved into the attention economy and the experience economy at the same time. They are flip sides of the same development. Time, attention, and money, Pine and Gilmore note, are "the currencies of the experience economy." In their view, every company needs to "create an experience that first gains potential customers' attention, then gets them to spend time experiencing [its] offerings and finally causes them to spend their money by buying those offerings." In many cases— Starbucks, for example—the experience serves as marketing to generate demand for whatever the company is selling. Other times, the experience itself is what people pay for: a museum visit, say, or a farm that hosts wedding parties or kids' birthday celebrations.

Both the experience economy and the attention economy celebrate, as Lanham would say, fluff over stuff. In the US, Capital One Bank introduced Capital One Cafés, where anyone—no need to be a bank customer—could drop in and have a Peet's coffee while enjoying "fun, inspiring, free events and experiences," from learning how to check your credit score to tasting samples from a local ice cream shop. In Manchester, England, as in Manchester,

New Hampshire, abandoned woolen mills and machine shops are transformed into stylish apartment complexes (exposed brick! central air!) so people can experience luxury loft living in the one-time sweatshop where their great-grandparents might have made trousers or widgets.

For years, trend-spotters have noted a growing preference, particularly among young people, for experiences over possessions. A 2018 Expedia survey found that 74 percent of Americans prioritize experiences over products or things. A 2019 Deloitte survey found that significantly more Millennials and Gen Zs worldwide would rather travel the world than own a home or start a family. And why not, since so few of them can afford to buy a home or to raise a family as comfortably as they themselves were raised? Not to mention that they'd better see the world while they can—whether because much of it will soon be lost to impending climate disaster or simply because so much of what makes it special is being lost anyway. As Lanham writes,

> Tourism seems an oddly self-destructive business. When that South Seas island is discovered by "the tourists" we say it has been "ruined." It has lost its reality, its genuine substance. It has become an attention structure, a cruise ship stop, the nonstuff of which Disneylands are made. The more cruise ships we launch, the fewer real ports there will be for them to visit. Mountain climbers have to make a reservation for Everest. . . . Every city worth its salt has parked up its "old town" or, if unlucky enough to be new, has invented one. In such a world, all the world does indeed become a stage.

Little wonder, then, that Pine and Gilmore would call their next book *Authenticity*.

Freaky Times and Human Ant-eaters

It's a short leap from attention structures to attention traps. Clickbait and linkbait—web posts that use sensational headlines as come-ons to maximize page views—are classic attention traps:

> "32 Freaky Times the World Was Creepy in the Worst Ways Imaginable"
>
> "She Was Hit by a Car, Struck With a Hammer, Buried . . . and She STILL Wags Her Tail"
>
> "He Thought He Could Be a Human Ant-eater, But What Happened Was . . . OMG"

These examples are from ViralNova, a site *Bloomberg Businessweek* once declared "one of the defining media companies of this convulsive era." That was in 2014. Sites like ViralNova are designed to suck viewers in and serve them up to advertisers. People often feel used when they fall into the trap, but no matter: because of the way web traffic is measured, such sites need the audience's attention for only a moment to succeed. What does matter is that Google and Facebook revise their algorithms from time to time to punish the most egregious offenders. These changes cut ViralNova's traffic so dramatically that in 2017, two years after it was bought by a "digital-first media company" called Zealot Networks for $100 million, it was sold along with several other sites for just $25 million. But the fight against clickbait continues.

The temptation to build online attention traps is intensified by metrics that value fleeting impressions at the expense of actual engagement. Herb Simon thought attention should be measured by the amount of time an average business executive—a man (this was in the sixties) he identified as having a bachelor's degree and an IQ of 120—spends focused on something. These "attention units," as he called them (a catchier name might have been "simons"), would capture the cost, in addition to any monetary outlay, of receiving information. But Simon was years ahead of everyone else. By the time the rest of the world caught up with his ideas, cruder metrics had come into use—monthly average users for social media sites like Twitter; unique visitors per month and the number of pages they view for media sites, whether Viral-Nova or the *New York Times*, no matter if these visitors stay for 10 minutes or half a second.

This fixation on uniques and pageviews assumes that value online is where it has always been in the media business—in space that can carry advertising. But because the Internet is essentially unbounded by physical constraints, web pages are free to multiply like bunnies. What's needed to generate value is scarcity—and that can come from just one place. "Time is the only unit of scarcity on the Web," said Tony Haile, founder of the web analytics firm Chartbeat and currently CEO of the online news network Scroll. "You've only got 24 hours a day per person."

Herb Simon would have approved.

The problem is that time belongs not to the publisher but to the audience. Online distribution is largely determined by the audience too, whether through search engine queries or by links posted to social media. This means that the scarcity of attention inverts not only the economic relationship between publisher and audience; it inverts the power dynamic as well, since the audience—through its proxies, such as Google and Facebook and Twitter—now has the power to drive traffic.

Meanwhile, the proliferation of ever-cheaper and easier-to-use digital production tools has turned the flood of information

Herb Simon saw coming into a torrent and the torrent into a deluge. Almost anyone can shoot a video, record a music track, write an article, or publish a book. This helps explain Hollywood's fixation on blockbusters: "Very few entities in this world can afford to spend $200 million on a movie," Disney Studios chief Alan Horn told the Harvard Business School professor Anita Elberse. "That is our competitive advantage." And what an advantage it can be, if handled properly: Disney had seven of the top 10 highest-grossing movies of 2019, each of them based on a preexisting property, for a combined worldwide box office take that year of $9.9 billion. Other studios didn't fare as well, thanks to mega-budget fiascos like Universal's *Cats*, Paramount's *Terminator: Dark Fate*, and Fox's X-Men spin-off *Dark Phoenix*.

But even as the major Hollywood studios have been releasing fewer, more expensive films, others have been making more. At this point you could watch two new films a day every day of the year and still not see them all—not that anyone would try. As the director of the South by Southwest Film Festival lamented, "The impulse to make a film has far outrun the impulse to go out and watch in a theater." The head of the British Film Institute's funding office put it even more succinctly: "There's just too much stuff out there."

The explosion of stuff has led to the rise of a new gatekeeper: the curator. Curators are humans, not algorithms, and their emergence signals yet another inversion in the media business. Just as the crisis of attention has inverted the economic relationship and the power dynamic between media producers and media consumers—that is, between author and audience—so it has inverted the gatekeeper role. For well over a century, publishers—book publishers, studio executives, network programmers, music-label executives, every one a suit—decided what we should read, what we should watch, and what we should listen to. When production and distribution were expensive, this made sense. But now that they aren't, the audience has started to generate its own gatekeepers.

Media executives still determine what gets published, though the proliferation of self-publishing tools makes it easy to get around them. Curators determine what gets noticed. Both act as filtering mechanisms, but curators aren't there to select some people for a shot at success and deny it to others. Their function is to fine-tune the attention machine. Like the gatekeepers of old, they are valued for their taste. But their taste is not broad and bland like a broadcast television programmer's: it is specific and niche. Some, like Taylor Swift and Mindy Kaling, are celebrities in their own right. Others, like the folks who recommend books on the Warby Parker blog, represent a brand. But most are ordinary people—millions upon millions of people whose playlists and endorsements are followed by friends and strangers who would rather respond to a human presence than to mindless, algorithmically generated tips like "Customers who bought this item also bought . . . ."

What Data Won't Tell You

As their taste-making role is being usurped by curators, media executives are turning to a new source of authority: audience data. For decades the Nielsen Family, carefully selected to be representative of society, their every channel change recorded in the attempt to divine the people's taste, was the arbiter of broadcast television. But as networks increasingly seek a direct relationship with their viewers, ratings are becoming obsolete. The new order was signaled in 2011, when Netflix did what no television network had even contemplated: order up two entire seasons of a new series without even asking for a pilot.

The series was *House of Cards*, starring Kevin Spacey as a scheming congressman, and for Netflix it was a $100 million gamble. Having driven Blockbuster to bankruptcy with its no-late-fee DVD-by-mail service, the Silicon Valley company was switching to a streaming model, and it needed original programming to build excitement and membership. What made *House of Cards* a sane bet was the direct relationship Netflix had with its subscribers, who constantly fed it information about their likes, their dislikes, and their viewing habits.

With access to billions of data points, Netflix could build statistical models to produce a risk profile of any show it might want to license or produce, based on such variables as genre, subject matter, stars, and Emmy and Oscar wins. So when the film director David Fincher was pitching Ted Sarandos, Netflix's chief content officer, on *House of Cards*, Sarandos knew how many subscribers had watched the original British series, how many had watched *The West Wing*, how many liked David Fincher movies, and how many were Kevin Spacey fans. Broadcast and cable networks didn't have that direct relationship with subscribers, so the best they could do was consult Nielsen.

What's important is not just what Sarandos did with all the information at his command; it's what he didn't do. Any television network would have conducted extensive "likability" research, corralling focus groups and test audiences to get their feedback and using it to tell the creators what to do. Some assumed that Netflix would use data to the same end. As one critic wrote on *Salon*, "What will the Big Data approach mean for the creative process? . . . Can the auteur survive in an age when computer algorithms are the ultimate focus group?"

A Few Words about Eyeballs

If you work in any aspect of the media industry, you will be tempted to refer to the audience as so many "eyeballs." Don't. Yes, it's a convenient shorthand. Maybe it really does make you sound professional and sophisticated. But it's also a tell. It says you are dehumanizing your audience.

Let's think about what an eyeball really is: an organ at the surface of the body that is sensitive to light. Light comes in through the pupil, the black opening at the center of the iris, and is focused on the retina at the back of the eyeball. The information the retina receives is transmitted via the optic nerve to the visual cortex at the back of the brain, which interprets it as sight. The real action happens deep within the brain, in other words, and it's far more complicated than anything the eyeball can handle. But if you treat your audience like so many eyeballs, that surface interaction is all you'll get.

But having concluded that the combination of elements in *House of Cards* would work, Netflix gave Fincher total creative freedom. Otherwise the series premiere would never have opened with Frank Underwood, the Kevin Spacey character, kneeling in front of a dog that's just been hit by a car. "There are two kinds of pain," Underwood says to the camera, breaking the fourth wall as he wrings the dog's neck. "The sort of pain that makes you strong, or useless pain. This sort of pain is only suffering. And I have no patience for useless things." It was a defining moment for the show—and never mind that a huge portion of the audience, predictably, stopped watching on the spot. *House of Cards* wasn't made for them anyway.

When Metrics Meet Magic

Netflix is not the only media company to put audience data to good use. Marriott International, the world's largest hotel corporation, publishes online travel magazines, produces podcasts, commissions short films, and even set up a glass-enclosed "nerve center" in the lobby of its Washington-area headquarters to monitor and respond to social-media mentions. The company seems bent on proving that any organization in the digital age can be a media company, and it's using data to find its way.

Marriott's data-collection efforts go well beyond the who-are-they-and-what-kind-of-pillow-do-they-like norm. Karin Timpone, the company's global marketing officer from 2013 to 2020, calls it "metrics meets magic": data-driven insights into your audience—what they care about, how to get their attention—coupled with the emotional impact of storytelling. "People just didn't imagine there was a story sitting in the numbers," she told me. In fact, there are many stories.

To ferret them out, Timpone brought in Matthew Glick, an Emmy Award–winning television producer with extensive experience at NBC and at CBS News. Glick's operation includes a social media feed to monitor trending topics and mentions of Marriott's many brands, an emerging trends desk to identify "zeitgeist moments," and a social media unit to tap into them. But its most innovative component may be the "surprise and delight" team, which aims to turn hotel guests' social mentions of having fun at Marriott properties into cause for celebration.

"We're looking to identify consumers who are posting on social media that they're having a great time," Glick explained. People who do so might find a bottle of champagne in their room or a round of drinks delivered to them at the bar or poolside, courtesy of Marriott. Almost inevitably, he added, "you'll be so wowed that you'll take a picture of the drinks and post that too. So you're creating a story for us, and you're distributing it as well."

The surprise and delight initiative relies on geofencing, an electronic technology that monitors activity within a certain pre-defined area—the grounds of a hotel, for instance. Though commentators sometimes raise privacy concerns, it's hard to cry privacy when people have already posted what they're doing online. In any case, Glick said, "what we've found is that consumers love being recognized by a brand."

With outposts in south Florida, London, Dubai, and Hong Kong in addition to its Washington-area home base, the team also works directly with hotels to surface guest stories and to promote upcoming events that might generate more of them. When a total eclipse of the sun was predicted to cut a swath across the US in August 2017, for example, Marriott set out to create an "awe-inspiring guest experience," as the press release had it, at hotels in its path— viewing parties augmented by local art in Bend, Oregon, for example, or by a Pink Floyd cover band in Jackson Hole, Wyoming. In cases like this, "data is terrific to help inform your decision making," said Glick. "But you always need that human element to tell and shape a great story. Technology will only get you so far."

That's because technology gives you abstractions, not audiences. For overstressed media executives, abstractions are comfort food. Silent. Predictable. But to fully connect with the audience, to reestablish the feedback loop, to issue the call and get the response, authors and publishers alike need to look away from the numbers and engage with actual humans. This is not easily done, as Matt Locke noted in an essay about his time at the BBC, when he joined a retreat at which top executives were shown video footage of fellow Brits discussing their media habits:

Then the Audience Insight team announced a surprise—the people they interviewed were *here, in the same room,* and we were going to get one of them assigned to each group so we could find out more about their media consumption.

You could almost feel the air being sucked out of the room as a couple of hundred BBC top brass gasped. The audience was actually *here?* The people who listened, viewed and clicked on our stories? In the *same room as us?*

We were given a "gamer" for our group—a nice enough guy in his early 20s who very politely answered the questions of the dozen or so media execs on my table. Yes, he did play games for a couple of hours a day. No, they weren't all about killing things. No, he didn't play alone—his friends would come round for the night. Yes, he did find time to watch a bit of television as well. Yes, he did prefer gaming to television. No, he didn't think that was weird.

The reaction in my group was almost as if an alien had landed. I realised that behind the ratings, media execs had all sorts of assumptions about who their audience was, but none of them were anything like these real people, in the room, with *us.*

Data and people are not the same—and while data can tell you a lot, it's people you need to connect with, and not in a superficial, focus-group kind of way. Making that connection is what Warby Parker did with the Class Trip. It's what Punchdrunk did with *Sleep No More* and Secret Cinema with *The Shawshank Redemption.* It's what Pepsi so disastrously failed to do with "Jump In." It's the bond you need to make if you want to take the audience on the journey you've prepared for them.

3. Journey

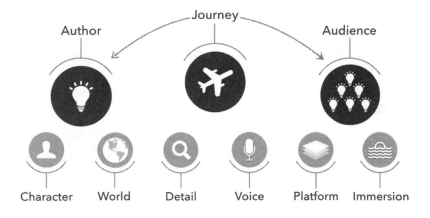

A couple of years ago I was in Paris, reporting for the *New York Times* on a monumental exhibition on the Beats. The show was at the Centre Pompidou, the 1970s architectural incursion in the heart of the city. The Pompidou, with its famously inside-out design, is quite literally an attention structure, and as usual it was mobbed. As I glided toward its upper floors on escalators that seemed glued to its outside walls, the plaza with its crowd of pedestrians fell away and half of Paris rose up before me, its soft gray presence punctuated by the grand exclamation point of the Eiffel Tower. Arriving at the show, I was greeted by a glass-topped vitrine stretched out for 120 linear feet. Unspooled inside it was the original 1951 typescript of Jack Kerouac's *On the Road*, unedited and uncensored, page after page of tracing paper taped together by Kerouac himself to form a single continuous sheet, the ultimate American road novel laid out like so much two-lane blacktop.

"That river of words," mused Jean-Jacques Lebel, an artist who'd befriended William S. Burroughs and Gregory Corso at a Left Bank poetry reading in 1957, who'd translated Allen Ginsberg's "Howl" into French and helped find a publisher for Burroughs's *Naked Lunch*, and who had now helped organize this show. "That Mississippi of words."

"The last part of it got chewed off by a dog," he added.

A good story is like a road. It takes you on a journey. Things happen along the way—conflicts rear, defeat looms, the battle is won or lost, a transformation occurs. And not only to the protagonist: the audience will be taken on a journey as well, starting in one state, emotionally or intellectually or imaginatively speaking, and ending in another.

Like any journey, a story unfolds over time. "Time is the context that gives meaning to everything in this world," wrote Iain McGilchrist in *The Master and His Emissary*, his extraordinary account of the workings of the brain, "and conversely everything that has meaning for us in this world, everything that has a place in our lives, exists in time. This is not true of abstractions . . . but all that *is* is subject to time." Here we have a clue to the appeal of stories over logic: logic is an abstraction, timeless and time-free; but stories unfold in a way that mimics our experience of life.

Because they play out over time, stories almost invariably have a beginning, a middle, and an end (though as the New Wave filmmaker Jean-Luc Godard once quipped, "not necessarily in that order"). The most effective stories—movies and novels, but also much shorter tales, 60-second television spots among them—generally follow a narrative arc. This arc is both literal and metaphorical. It is literal in the sense that action and suspense rise and then fall when you lay them out on a graph, and metaphorical in the sense that "rising and falling" stand in for the changing levels of tension that accompany conflict and resolution.

The three-act structure allows for setup, confrontation, and conclusion, the triad that defines conventional Hollywood story structure. In the first act, you introduce the characters and set the scene—hopefully with as little exposition as possible. You don't want to tell people about your characters; you want to show them in action. At some point early on, often in the opening scene, an "inciting incident" occurs—a dramatic development that "sets the story in motion," in the words of the late screenwriting guru Syd Field, grabbing the audience's attention and catapulting the characters into action.

Once that's been done, the screenwriter must move the story forward. There are various schemes to accomplish this, but

The Narrative Arc

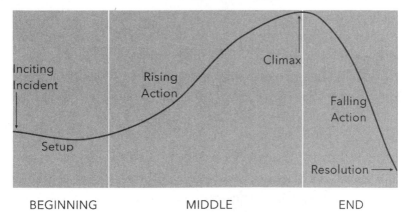

Field's approach has become canonical. It identifies two critical plot points, one at the end of act one and another at the end of act two, each designed to advance the action. There will be other plot points along the way, but these two are pivotal. The first

The Inverted Pyramid

The Lede
Who, What, When, Where, Why, How

Context

Details

Minor
Details

Cut from the - - - - - - -
bottom as needed

pushes us into the second act, where the conflict that defines the story plays out. This is a period of "rising action"—of growing tension as the protagonist encounters one obstacle after another. Toward the end of it, the second plot point pushes us toward the climax that will resolve the story. Then we enter a period of "falling action" as the resolution is achieved.

There are other ways to structure a story, of course. The classic newspaper story—and many stories in online news outlets as well—reads like an inverted pyramid. The most important information is in the opening paragraph, and the details—including the context that explains what's actually going on—are laid out one after another in order of decreasing importance. Stories like this are quick to read and efficient at conveying information, which is why newspapers run them. But they don't take you on a journey. They don't unfold over time. They just give you the facts. They're designed to be scanned, not to transport you. If the paper is short on space, an editor can cut from the bottom without losing much. Most people will probably have stopped reading by that point anyway.

Then there is the Hero's Journey, famously described by Joseph Campbell, the literature professor turned mythologist, in his 1949

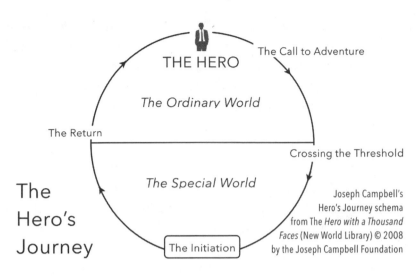

THE HERO

The Call to Adventure

The Ordinary World

The Return

Crossing the Threshold

The Special World

The Hero's Journey

The Initiation

Joseph Campbell's
Hero's Journey schema
from The *Hero with a Thousand Faces* (New World Library) © 2008
by the Joseph Campbell Foundation

book *The Hero with a Thousand Faces,* and epitomized decades later by George Lucas in *Star Wars.* It's a wonderful idea: that throughout human history there is a monomyth that unites all cultures, a secret way that we all share. That as we go through life, we encounter challenges that fall into a common pattern: the call to adventure, crossing the threshold into the unknown, the wise old man who counsels the novice, the test or rite of passage, the return with new knowledge.

"But at its core, the monomyth isn't a blueprint of a plot outline; it's a description of a psychological process," writes David Kudler, managing editor of Campbell's collected works. ". . . The point of a monomyth story is that it leads the protagonist—and therefore the person taking in the story—through a process of personal transformation." The journey is always circular. It ends where it began, but the hero comes back a new person.

At this point, unfortunately, the Hero's Journey has been overused to the point of cliché. Your product—your beer, your after-shave, your toothpaste—is not on a hero's journey. Nor are you or your customers, unless perhaps your product has been outlawed. The inverted pyramid is falling into decline as news becomes increasingly commodified. News organizations need some way to distinguish their reports, and giving them some personality is one way to do it. But the narrative arc lives on, its appeal remarkably consistent throughout history. Some authorities break it down into three acts, others five, but the basic structure is still that laid down by Aristotle in his *Poetics* in the fourth century BCE: a progression from beginning to end, organized not haphazardly but each part necessarily following the other.

This may be connected to some deeper pattern of human existence. As Ellen Lupton, a senior curator at Cooper Hewitt, Smithsonian Design Museum in New York, points out in a wonderful book called *Design Is Storytelling*, many experiences begin with a sense of anticipation, build to a crescendo, and then come to a satisfying conclusion. Eating, for one. Sex, for another.

It isn't easy to measure the brain responses of people having sex in a cramped and claustrophobic neuroimaging machine, especially since those machines have, as one study drily noted, "low tolerance when it comes to bodily motion." Even so, a few brave scientists have managed to enlist test subjects in neuroimaging studies that show what goes on in the brain when humans are aroused. In a Dutch study that relied on positron emission tomography (PET) scans to understand the brain mechanisms that control sexual response, for example, 11 men were masturbated to orgasm by their female partners while their heads were held in place by an adhesive band. A few years ago, researchers at Oxford and at the University of Groningen in the Netherlands compared results from such studies with studies that monitor brain activity during other pleasurable experiences. They found that many "reward cycles" follow the familiar pattern of arousal, climax, and satiety—sex, food, drugs, and music as well. Some of life's most enjoyable rituals, it turns out, follow the pattern of a three-act film.

"Three Stories . . . about One Story"

Still, people do crave variety. A nonlinear story includes all the events that would go into an ordinary story—inciting incident, rising action, climax, resolution—but presents them out of sequence. You may never have an orgasm before you get aroused, but you can watch Butch Coolidge (Bruce Willis) rescue his nemesis Marsellus Wallace (Ving Rhames) from a pair of rapists two-thirds of the way through *Pulp Fiction,* just before riding off with his girlfriend on an enormous chopper, his troubles over.

Quentin Tarantino's *Pulp Fiction* is a textbook case for nonlinear narrative, the one they pull out in film school to show you how it's done. Seemingly a random collage of events involving a slew of semiconnected characters, it has in fact a rigorous internal logic. The picture is bookended by its celebrated coffee-shop scene, a prologue and an epilogue in which Pumpkin (Tim Roth) and Honey Bunny (Amanda Plummer) pull out guns and start to rob the joint's customers on a sunny Southern California day. There's a second prologue as well, in which a pair of hit men, Jules Winnfield (a righteous Samuel L. Jackson) and Vincent Vega (a goofy John Travolta), trade banter about burgers before barging into an apartment and shooting up two of the three guys they find there—some college-type guys who had the extremely bad judgment to take a briefcase belonging to Marsellus, the drug kingpin who is Jules's and Vincent's employer.

What follows are three stories that themselves are told from start to finish, though they appear out of order in relation to each other. "Three stories . . . about one story," as it says on the title page of the script.

The first story, as it appears in the movie, has Vincent chaperoning Mia Wallace, Marsellus's new wife (Uma Thurman), while Marsellus is out of town—a task that takes an unexpected turn when she OD's on heroin and has to be revived with an adrenaline shot to the heart.

Next, we watch as Butch, a prizefighter who's supposed to be taking orders from Marsellus, wins the fight he's supposed to lose and makes a run for it—only to realize that he's forgotten his prized gold watch, the family heirloom that symbolizes everything decent about him. So he goes back to his apartment, not knowing that Vincent has already been sent there to rub him out. He's surprised to find a submachine gun lying on the kitchen counter, but when Vincent comes out of the toilet, Butch obliterates him with the gun, grabs the watch, and drives off—only to encounter Marsellus while stopped at a traffic light. In the ensuing melee, the two of them end up imprisoned by a pair of rednecks who plan to use them as sex slaves. Butch manages to slip away while the rednecks are in another room raping Marsellus— but then he suffers a pang of guilt and comes back to rescue the man who was going to kill him. Marsellus is so grateful he tells Butch they're cool. All Butch has to do is never tell a soul what happened in the cellar, leave LA, and not come back.

The third story takes place before this chronologically. Vincent is still alive; in fact, he and Jules are still in the apartment, dealing with the kids who double-crossed Marsellus. But this time we're in the bathroom with a fourth college kid, who hears the guns go off and panics. So the kid picks up a .357 Magnum and bursts out of the bathroom, shooting wildly at point-blank range until he's out of bullets. Big mistake: all his bullets miss. Jules takes his deliverance from this "hand cannon" as a miracle—a sign from

God. As soon as he and Vincent dispatch the Magnum guy, he announces that he's getting out of the hit-man trade. Vincent— soon to be shot dead by Butch, as we already know—scoffs.

More mayhem follows, but soon enough we're back where the movie began, in the coffee shop with Pumpkin and Honey Bunny—and Jules and Vincent, who turn out to be among the patrons. The latter two could easily have blown away this pair of amateurs, but Jules chooses to defuse the situation instead, telling Pumpkin and Honey Bunny during a tense standoff that they have found him "in a transitional period." He lets them get away with their loot, including $1,500 of his own money. And then he and Vincent stroll out the door as the twanging guitars of the 1963 hit "Surf Rider" rise on the soundtrack and the screen goes black.

What we're left with is the unexpected realization that, for all the blood and brains that get spattered about (did I forget to mention that Vincent accidentally blows the third kid's head off while holding him at gunpoint in the back seat of a friend's car?), Tarantino's is a fundamentally moral universe. Of the three main characters, those who make the right choices (Butch, Jules) live and the one who doesn't (Vincent) dies. And in a similarly surprising way, *Pulp Fiction* proves in fact to be a deeply linear story—just not linear in a chronological sense. "Each section is like a short story, presented from a different character's point of view," Syd Field writes.

What's novel, what makes it *seem* so nonlinear, is its recursive path. The prologue gives us a glimpse of what's to come, as prologues do. After that, aside from a standard-issue flashback involving Butch's gold watch, the first two-thirds of the movie are presented as they happened. But then the film starts looping back on itself, revisiting past scenes with new information and a new perspective—the apartment scene, now revealing the guy in the bathroom and the conversion he inadvertently effects in Jules; the coffee-shop scene, now showing Jules and Vincent among the customers. Nothing here is random. Nothing is a gimmick. Every choice has been carefully made.

The Axis of Linearity

A few years ago, a psychologist at Yeshiva University in New York conducted an experiment in nonlinear storytelling. She had a group of students watch "Bang! You're Dead," the Hitchcock episode about the kid who wanders out on the street with a loaded gun, thinking it's a toy—the same show that, in Uri Hasson's experiment, caused viewers' brains to work in sync. A second set of students watched the same episode, but with the scenes out of order. The students in both groups were asked to raise their hands every time they heard the word "gun." The people who viewed the film out of order, it turned out, were more likely to raise a hand every time the word occurred—presumably because they were less transported by the narrative. An article on the study suggested that this illustrates our "innate preference for linear narrative."

Right. But it's not as if successful nonlinear narratives got that way by being shuffled at random. The lesson of *Pulp Fiction*—a lesson that went unheeded by the vast majority of wannabe screenwriters who flooded Hollywood's talent agencies and movie studios with out-of-order scripts in the wake of the film's success—is that very few stories are truly nonlinear. You just have to locate their axis of linearity. If it's not time, it will be something else.

Whatever it is, it needs to serve a purpose. Being cool isn't enough, because nothing is cool if that's the only reason it's done. In *Pulp Fiction*, Tarantino presented scenes out of sequence to give the narrative a resonance it wouldn't otherwise have. Its axis of linearity is moral. The ending gains its power from our knowing that Vincent, even as he sneers at the "miracle" that leads Jules to have mercy on the two coffee-shop robbers, is soon to be a dead man, and from our recognizing if only subliminally that the unexpected compassion Jules shows the robbers echoes Butch's selflessness in going back to rescue Marsellus, the guy who wanted him dead. The mark of a great story is its ability to awaken us to new insights—and *Pulp Fiction* is a great story.

There are other ways to structure a nonlinear narrative, other axes of linearity to plumb. Christopher Nolan outdid himself with *Memento*, the 2001 thriller about a man whose determination to avenge the rape and murder of his wife is severely compromised by his inability to form new memories. *Memento* is a movie about memory, that quicksilver faculty, capricious at best, that defines and circumscribes and gives meaning to our lives. A movie about loss and grief and time that is told out of time, the film builds in increments no longer than the few minutes Leonard can hold a thought in his mind.

Time is the axis of *Memento*, the spine that supports the whole narrative—it's just that the primary timeline in this case runs backward rather than forward. Interviewed when the movie came out, Nolan said it "really is a question of finding the most suitable order for releasing information to the audience and not feeling any responsibility to do it chronologically." In fact, he added, his assistant director pointed out to him that "this is not a nonlinear film; this is an extremely linear film. You cannot move a scene."

Nolan has gone on to toy with the vagaries of time in a host of films, most notably *Inception*, one of the biggest hits of 2010. Here was a science fiction thriller about dreams in which it was by no means obvious what was a dream and what was "real life." Like *Pulp Fiction*, *Inception* provoked a generational divide, with older audiences—older Hollywood audiences in particular—coming away mystified and befuddled. They were confused by its puzzle-box structure and utterly confounded by its dream-within-a-dream conception of reality. Was the ending a dream? Was the whole movie a dream? Or what?

Gamers had no such problem. As the USC media scholar Henry Jenkins told Patrick Goldstein of the *Los Angeles Times*, *Inception* is "a movie about worlds and levels, which is very much the way video games are structured. . . . If you blink or if your mind wanders, you miss it. You're not sitting passively and sucking it all in. You have to experience it like a puzzle box. It's designed for us to talk about, to share clues and discuss online, instead of having everything explained to us."

Although *Inception* cost a reported $160 million to make and another $100 million to market, it wasn't overly surprising that Warner Bros. gave it a green light. Nolan had had several huge successes at Warner Bros.—most recently *The Dark Knight*, the second in his trilogy of Batman films—and Leonardo DiCaprio, one of the biggest box-office draws in Hollywood, was on board for less than his usual $20 million. The surprise was that it became one of the year's top-grossing movies.

When Lynda Obst, producer of such hits as *The Fisher King* and *Sleepless in Seattle* (and later of Nolan's *Interstellar*), asked a friend how he thought it would open, "he shook his head. 'Not big,' he said. 'Specialty movie . . . For cineastes . . . Too hard to explain . . . Big cities . . . Lucky to break $100 million . . . No *Dark Knight*.'" Instead it had a worldwide box-office take of nearly $830 million and an even greater cultural impact. Like *Pulp Fiction* in the nineties, like *Bonnie and Clyde* in the sixties and a handful of other films in earlier decades, *Inception* marked a turning point in the entertainment industry's approach to storytelling. The journey was getting complicated.

The Rise of Immersive Television

When *Inception* came out, most people on the tech side of things assumed that television as we knew it was doomed, soon to be replaced by the likes of YouTube—short-form, user-generated video that would render the boob tube extinct. What has happened instead, in the quarter-century or more since *Pulp Fiction* and the decade since *Inception,* is the reverse: movies and television alike have mutated from standard entertainment vehicles to elaborate attention structures that combine conventional cinematic storytelling with story structure borrowed from games and a kind of interactivity derived from social media. Yet the routes the two industries took to get there have made them vastly different from what they once were.

The rise of the international box office—once an afterthought in Hollywood, now worth more than $30 billion per year, nearly three times the take in the US and Canada—has transformed movies into the kind of lowest-common-denominator medium television once was. The language problem has been solved by superhero and action flicks, neither of which stand to lose much in translation. This has made comedy and serious drama hard to find at the multiplex. At the same time, the proliferation of cable and pay-TV channels, not to mention the arrival of Netflix, Hulu, Amazon Prime, and the like, has transformed television from a mass medium into one catering to specific audiences that are differentiated not so much demographically or even geographically as psychographically. In the ensuing pole reversal, television is becoming the prestige milieu.

For decades we've seen increasingly complex and demanding shows on television—*ER* and *Homicide* in the nineties, then *The Sopranos* and *The Wire* and *Mad Men, Breaking Bad* and *Game of Thrones* after that. But it was *Lost,* which aired on ABC from 2004 to 2010, that took the puzzle box—or the mystery box, as cocreator J. J. Abrams termed it—mainstream. Before *Lost*, TV shows had to be comprehensible, at least to people who were paying attention. After *Lost*, even that was no longer required. Better in fact if the show didn't make sense in any obvious way, because that would encourage the fans to sort it out online.

The result has been called television's second golden age, but a more apt term for it would be the rise of immersive television. How did we go from naively wholesome family shows like *The Waltons*, the homespun seventies drama centered on an aw-shucks teenager called John Boy, to all-consuming, antihero-driven serial dramas like *Breaking Bad*? In a fascinating essay in the online publication *ReDef*, Charlie Collier—then the president of AMC Networks, whose flagship he helped transform into a major cable channel with *Mad Men* and *Breaking Bad*, now head of entertainment at Fox Broadcasting Network—identified several reasons for the shift.

The first, not surprisingly, is technology: with the rise of video on demand and streaming services like Netflix, viewers are able to watch TV on their own terms—to follow serials at their own pace, to not worry about missing an episode, to binge at will. Second, across North America and Western Europe we've seen a growing acceptance of cultural differences—gender, race, sexuality—that broadens the range of subjects entertainment can broach. At the same time, Collier writes, the decline of institutionalized religion gives television a role in helping us reach our own conclusions about how to navigate the world. And with the rise of social media, viewers can speak directly and individually to show runners and network executives (not to mention each other) rather than being subsumed in some anonymous mass.

All this carries big implications for a network like AMC or Fox.

Cultural shifts make nostalgic family dramas like *The Waltons* look silly while a show about a murderous meth dealer seems topical. Because we're no longer slaves to network time slots, show runners and television executives need to nurture and engage with fan communities year-round, not only on the few weeks a show is aired on TV. Passionately engaged fans are all the more valuable to advertisers, Collier maintains. So while there's still room for escapist comedies and for dramas that wrap up in an hour, he writes, immersive television isn't a fad. "It is truly a redefinition of the television content experience itself—what we want from it, what we get from it, and the meaning it provides far beyond the actual viewing experience."

The Lives of Robots

Collier isn't the only television executive who's thinking this way. His vision has arguably been most fully realized to date at HBO, with shows like *Westworld* and *Game of Thrones*. Inspired by the 1973 Michael Crichton movie about theme-park automatons that run amok and start killing people, *Westworld* takes a point of view that's diametrically opposed to its source material's. Your sympathies from the start are with the "hosts," the ultra-humanoid robots who are the victims in this scenario. (Since robots cannot yet play other robots on TV, the task falls to real actors, who most of the time don't look like robots at all but seem quite convincingly human.) The hosts are liable to be shot, stabbed, fucked, or scalped, but, whatever the situation, they are there to serve the guests—the superrich who have the means to pay for this anything-goes experience.

Many of the guests do things to the robot hosts they'd never think of doing to another human. Others probably don't care much either way. In episode two we watch as a guest pulls out his six-shooter in the town saloon and plugs Teddy, a soulful cowboy host, again and again and again. Finally sated, the guest holsters his gun and cries, "Now, that's a fuckin' vacation!" Good thing the hosts get their memories wiped regularly.

The *Westworld* series comes with a remarkable pedigree. It was conceived by J. J. Abrams. The show runners are Jonathan Nolan, Christopher Nolan's younger brother and frequent writing partner, and his wife of the past decade or so, Lisa Joy, a studio executive turned screenwriter. The show is fascinating for the way it echoes open-world video games like *Grand Theft Auto* and *Red Dead Redemption*, games that give the player the same freedom to roam that the guests have in the show. (It's no coincidence that Nolan has played a lot of video games.) And in the same way that it's a story about games, the show is also a story about storytelling. "Since I was a child, I've always loved a good story," the park's creator (played by Anthony Hopkins) says in the season one finale. "Stories can help us become the people we dreamed of being. Lies that told a deeper truth. I always thought I could play some small part in that grand tradition." And so he introduces his new narrative—in which the hosts rebel and nearly every human present, himself included, gets slaughtered.

The series makes good use of the mystery box: it was obviously being told in a nonlinear fashion, but the chronology went unexplained for so long in season one that fans debated it online for weeks. Jeffrey Wright, one of the show's stars, tweeted that he went to an anti-Trump protest in New York City and was stopped by a cop who asked him to explain the show's chronology. One of the most persistent fan theories—correct, as it turned out—was that the show was operating in two separate timelines that were about 30 years apart. This wasn't confirmed until the final episode of the season, but a subtle clue was planted midway through that essentially clinched it: two different logos for the

Westworld theme park, one fresh and modern, the other dated and seventies-looking.

"What time am I in? It's a puzzle presentation model that we've never had with stories before," said George Gerba, a former Disney Imagineer who's now a consultant at USC's Entertainment Technology Center, when we spoke about the show. "I love it that this innovation is happening."

Above all, *Westworld* is fascinating for its take on artificial intelligence. The treatment of the hosts is the central issue of the show. Nolan and Joy address an important and increasingly topical moral question in a way that would have been inconceivable when Crichton's movie was released in 1973. HBO even posted a short video on the show's website—a promo reel, essentially—in which the actors and executive producers speak out on the morality of AI. "Your heart breaks for these characters, who we know are not human," Abrams says in the video. "But it doesn't matter, because you start to connect with them. Which is the very premise of the show—that at a certain point, it becomes irrelevant whether something is organic or not."

When Abrams suggested the idea to Nolan and Joy, she was the one who saw its potential. "When I heard, 'Western robot theme park.' Do it as a TV show. Think about the lives of the robots . . . once that thought had been triggered, I just wanted to play with it," she told Tom Bissell for *The New Yorker*. Here was a textbook case of the cultural evolution Charlie Collier cited in *ReDef*: having been born to a mother from Taiwan and raised in a household she once described as "culturally very Chinese," Joy saw the situation from a different perspective.

"I do love Westerns," she went on:

> But, in a way, traditional Westerns, for me, have been hard to love viscerally and personally. You tend to gravitate

toward stories in which you see yourself. I don't see much of myself in the traditional Western hero. I would sometimes look at the side characters in those movies, hanging out by the saloon doors, or crossing the street, or working on a railroad, and think, Well, actually, that's kind of more like who I would have been in the Old West. I wonder what their story is.

These "side characters" are the robots in *Westworld*—and viewers' willingness to see themselves in such characters is key to the success of the show. It's not by accident that so many of the hosts are women, or that the guests who have their way with them are almost invariably men. The idea that animated the show, Joy said, "was a meditation on so many things that I was thinking about at the time: navigating the world as a woman, as a human. Navigating a world in which terrible things routinely happen."

Westworld succeeds because Joy and Nolan take you on this journey. It's a complex and deeply involving story that goes far beyond its mystery box attributes. There are real stakes involved, both for the hosts and for the audience, and the writers are not afraid to take chances. Three things make those chances pay off, and they're as relevant to an elevator pitch for any new venture as they are to television:

1. A clear sense of purpose. Like the founders of Warby Parker a few years before, Nolan and Joy knew "the why"—why they were doing this show, why it mattered. And their "why" means something. Asked what they would like to say to AI developers, Nolan gave a one-word answer: "Stop." Joy was more forthcoming. "Being careful of hubris is as important as knowing the technology that you are developing," she said. "See in yourself and other people the capacity both for evil and for good. Know that the machines you build, your creations, will bear your fingerprints to some degree. And not necessarily the fingerprints you intentionally left but the ones that kind of grazed it unintentionally."

2. Knowing what not to say. Every story involves the controlled release of information. It's shaped as much by what is *not* revealed as by what is. The mystery box takes this to an extreme. It creates an information void, and that vacuum sucks us in. Would Yayoi Kusama's *Infinity Mirrored Room* be as captivating if we had ten minutes to experience it rather than 45 seconds—ten minutes to look into the corners, wonder about dust bunnies, stare at the LEDs, figure out how the illusion works? Certainly not. A person can only contemplate infinity for so long.

3. Telling the story from a unique perspective. With any story, point of view is critical. *Westworld* works because it's told from a perspective that is unexpected yet compelling—that of a third-person observer who is sympathetic to the hosts. Warby Parker and Harry's have succeeded in large part because their founders looked at eyeglasses and shaving in an unconventional way. Pepsi's "Jump In" spot failed because the people behind it were unable to see the world from the perspective of the protesters. What was life or death to people in the Black Lives Matter campaign evidently was somewhat less than that to corporate executives on their verdant suburban campus.

"Point of view is worth 80 I.Q. points," Alan Kay, the computer scientist whose work underpins the way we interact with computers today, once said. IQ is controversial these days, and for good reason. But Kay wasn't making a judgment about the nature of intelligence. He was saying that shifting perspective makes you smarter. It lets you see things you wouldn't otherwise see. Things other people don't. And if you're trying to tell a story, it can give you critical insight into the people who will make it work—or not: your characters.

4. Character

As humans, we are endlessly fascinated by other humans: what they do, what they think, what they feel, what their story is, who they are. Also by robots, animals, and anything else we can imagine to be human-like. As the storytelling animal, we are remarkably self-obsessed. We want to see other animals like ourselves, in a virtual reality headset or in live theater. Digital technology changes nothing here.

Geoff Kaufman's experiments at Ohio State, the ones that showed how differently straights and whites respond to characters who are shown to be gay or Black early in the story vs. late in the story, demonstrated how important it is to have characters we can identify with—and if we don't have a clear picture of them, we certainly won't be able to identify. We catch a glimpse of the importance of characterization in *The Wife*, the movie adaptation of Meg Wolitzer's novel. Joan, played by Glenn Close, is married to Joe Castleman, a novelist who's about to receive the ultimate honor—the Nobel Prize for literature. As he is presented with the medal in Stockholm's concert house, looking grand in white tie and tails and facing the king and queen of Sweden in their royal regalia, he hears a recitation of his achievements: ". . . You are a master of style, yet your characters are intensely real, their journeys heartbreaking, their portrayals intimate and deep . . ."

But we in the audience know this is wrong. We know because a few minutes earlier we saw Joan and Joe in a flashback, he the ambitious young novelist, she the former student he sacrificed his Ivy League teaching career to woo. It's 1957, and publishing is run by men, so she has abandoned her craft rather than risk dismissal as a "lady writer." But she's just read his first novel, fresh from the typewriter, and she is frankly dismayed. "The characters are wooden, Joe. No offense, but you haven't made them real."

No offense? Joe's fragile ego can't take this kind of abuse—but when he declares they're over as a couple, she in her neediness can't let him go. "I'm not full of big ideas the way you are!" she cries. "You're the brilliant one! You're the one who has something to say, not me!" She offers to "fix" his book. So begins the subterfuge that threatens to tear their world apart 35 years later, as he's being lionized for the brilliance that is actually hers while she is sent off to go shopping.

Joan had it right the first time. Stories may contain ideas, but they are not primarily *about* ideas, big or otherwise. They're about the people who have the ideas. Ideas come from a brain, and a brain needs somebody to live in. That somebody is what matters to us. It makes no difference if you're a novelist or a screenwriter or a journalist or an ad agency copywriter or a virtual reality film-maker: if you can't make your characters feel real, you won't have a story anyone cares about.

So let's say you're Joe, but you don't have some lady writer (or gentleman writer, or whatever) in the closet to make things right. What to do?

1. Map out the transformation. If a story is a journey, it's a journey your characters are on. They start in one place and end up somewhere else, emotionally and dramatically (if not necessarily literally) speaking, and in the process they undergo some sort of transformation. That transformation, that journey, is what your story is about. Those characters are *who* your story is about. Along with a narrative arc, your story should have a character arc.

In season one of *Westworld*, the hosts—though they realize it only gradually—are on a journey of self-discovery and self-actualization. At the start of the series, they are automatons, incapable of doing anything they haven't been programmed to do. But since the humans are free to do anything they want, the hosts not infrequently end up damaged or dead, and when that happens they're taken back to the shop to be repaired and have their memories erased. But these erasures are not quite as thorough as the people running the park think they are. A few episodes in, stray memories start breaking through.

When we first encounter them, the hosts are each caught in their own loop—first this happens to them, and then that happens, and then it reaches a climax one way or another, depending on what the guests do. The next day the cycle starts all over again as if nothing had happened. But when memories break through, consciousness follows—first a glimmer, then a flood. Until finally we see Dolores Abernathy, the rancher's daughter, galloping away on her steed, looking back and firing her six-shooter at her pursuers—just as we suddenly understand she was always meant to do.

Dolores (Evan Rachel Wood) is a crux of the show, one of the handful of characters whose shift signals a major turn in the show's development. Another is Maeve (Thandie Newton), the madam in the saloon/whorehouse in Sweetwater, the park's ironically named urban nexus. Season one is all about the hosts' evolution from mindless pleasure bots to fully sentient beings. Season two is about what happens next. Not for nothing does the motto on discoverwestworld.com, the website that was set up as an "online gateway" to the park, change from "Live without Limits" in the first season to "Life without Loops" in the second.

2. **Let the characters reflect the audience.** We all want stories about people we can identify with. John Wayne died in 1979; *Westworld* works today because enough of us share Lisa Joy's sense that the "side characters" are more interesting than the heroes on horseback. Harry's, the shaving brand, attracts fans who identify with the guys who started it. Stories are all about empathy, and people empathize with people with whom they feel a common bond. That could mean making sure your characters resemble your audience—or, if the point is that they're different (yet ultimately the same), it could mean introducing them in a way that emphasizes their humanity while drawing out their distinctiveness as the story progresses.

3. **Make the characters real.** We identify with individuals, not with generalities. Consider the patient stories that Memorial Sloan Kettering Cancer Center has told in magazine and television ads and on its website. The doctors are mentioned, as are the highly advanced treatments they planned and executed, but they're not

the focus. The stories are primarily about the patients—their illness, their loved ones, and the fact that they're still alive to talk about their ordeal.

We see "Suzanne's Story," about a 36-year-old who was diagnosed when she was a bride-to-be with a rare and aggressive form of cervical cancer—which she overcame with the support of her heavily tattooed rock-musician fiancé and the dedication of her Sloan Kettering oncologist. And "Jack's Story," about a blond, blue-eyed high school student who was diagnosed at age two with stage IV neuroblastoma, a rare cancer of the nervous system. "These doctors and these nurses, they're your family," Jack's mother says in the video. "They become family real quick." And Jack himself? "It's the best feeling in the world to be able to do what you want, be a normal kid."

There are no statistics in these stories, because statistics are abstractions. The whole point is to focus on people who manage to avoid becoming statistics. As *Adweek* noted, "the campaign portrays cancer as an unwanted chapter that can be overcome with MSK's help, allowing folks to turn the page and continue writing the stories of their lives."

The same focus on character can be seen in one of Budweiser's 2013 Super Bowl spots, a 60-second micro-movie that was the second best-liked Super Bowl ad of the past 30 years, according to a poll. The spot was called "Brotherhood," and it celebrated the bond between a horse trainer and one of the massive Clydesdales that have symbolized the brand since the repeal of Prohibition.

The guy at the center of "Brotherhood" is young and good-looking, with a winsome smile and such devotion that he sleeps in the stall with his foal when it's sick. No words are spoken. Instead, over a lone acoustic guitar and the breathy voice of

Fleetwood Mac's Stevie Nicks, we watch him care for the newborn foal and train it as it grows up. Then, inevitably, the moment of truth: an enormous Budweiser truck arrives and takes it away to join the team of show horses that represent the brand in parades across America.

Three years pass. The trainer, sitting at his kitchen table, reads in a newspaper that the Clydesdales will be appearing in Chicago soon. So he drives up in his pickup truck, catches the parade, and is about to leave for home when one of the horses—*his* horse—catches sight of him as it's being unshackled, and . . . It's an ad to make grown men weep. (My wife, on the other hand, looked at me like I was nuts.)

And the Super Bowl ad that came in first? That was "Puppy Love," a 2014 entry for Budweiser that was a sequel of sorts to "Brotherhood." This time the trainer was relegated to the background. The story revolved around his Clydesdales and a 10-week-old golden Labrador puppy that wouldn't—absolutely would *not*—be parted from its equine best buddy. The schmaltz factor was amped up to the max, not only by the story but by the soundtrack—"Let Her Go," a less-bitter-than-sweet ballad by Michael David Rosenberg, the English singer/songwriter who goes by the stage name Passenger. The reaction to this he-man confection? "If you watch @Budweiser's #BestBuds ad and almost cry, it doesn't make you less of a man," a sports fan declared on Twitter.

And yet, while Budweiser's "Brotherhood" and "Puppy Love" might have done an admirable job of putting men in touch with their feelings, they didn't sell much beer. Or so concluded Jorn Socquet, the US marketing chief at Anheuser-Busch InBev, the world's largest brewing company, formed in the 2008 takeover of Anheuser-Busch by the aggressively bottom line–focused InBev.

Still the King of Beers?

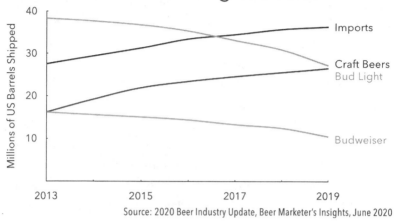

Source: 2020 Beer Industry Update, Beer Marketer's Insights, June 2020

"They have zero impact on beer sales," Socquet declared in 2015. "Those ads I wouldn't air again because they don't sell beer."

So what does?

Not much, it seems—at least, not much for Budweiser in the United States. Like other "domestic premium" brands, Bud and Bud Light have been losing market share for years. They've tried any number of strategies, any number of tactics. Their 2015 Super Bowl ad was "Brewed the Hard Way," a kick-ass commercial that told it straight to those pansy craft brews that kept eating into Bud's market share. "Our marketing has featured a bold, confident voice that speaks directly to Budweiser drinkers," Socquet said at the time, "and sales trends have improved as a result." Except they hadn't—so two years later, Bud came out with "Born the Hard Way," a classic origin-story ad that told the tale of Adolphus Busch, hardworking young immigrant and future beer baron. The next year it was "Stand by You," a good-deeds story that touted the company's humanitarian response to the trio of hurricanes that had devastated large swaths of Texas and Florida and all of Puerto Rico. Yet still Bud's market share kept shrinking.

In a case like this, the problem isn't the story; it's who's telling the story. Bud wanted Millennials, but Millennials weren't buying Bud no matter how much they liked its stories. Changing the bottle didn't help either, despite assertions from marketing that consumers found Bud Light's new aluminum bottles "more premium, more refreshing." (Nonsensical marketing claims are a sure sign your company is flailing.) Import sales were going up while sales of domestic premium beers—those mass-market brews that try to be something for everyone—were going down. Bud Light still sold better in the US than any other brand, but its position kept slipping. What to do?

Bryan Roth, a young beer blogger and craft beer enthusiast in Durham, North Carolina, quoted a 29-year-old US male from an Edelman/StrategyOne marketing survey: "Focus on making an excellent product. If you do so, then all of your marketing will be true and most of the marketing will be done by us. We are all looking for great products and brands to share with our friends. The best way to help us spread the word is by first creating a great product."

In other words, the problem with Bud is that, like Gillette, it's too big and too bland to be cool—and that's a core identity issue, not a storytelling problem.

4. Develop the backstory. The backstory is everything you know about a character that takes place before the story begins. It's there to provide depth. Much of it may never make it into the story proper, but it will inform your own understanding of the character in crucial ways. Without a backstory, your character will never seem real. Syd Field devoted page after page to the backstory in his screenwriting guide, though he generally referred to it as the character's interior life, "the emotional forces working on your character from birth." He advocated creating a sort of biographical inventory to make sure you keep these forces in mind:

> Where does he live, what city or country? Where was he born? Was he an only child, or did he have brothers and sisters? What kind of childhood did he have? Happy? Sad? Physically or medically challenging? What was his relationship to his parents? Did he get into a lot of trouble as a kid? Was he mischievous?
>
>   . . . What kind of influences did your character have while growing up? Friends? What kind of interests? School, athletics, social, political? Did your character take an interest in extra-curricular or after-school activities, like a debating club? What about sexual experiences? Relationships with peers? . . . Did any major traumatic event happen?

And so on. Think of everything you would conceivably know about your best friend and put it down.

Details like this add life and context even in a 60-second story like Budweiser's "Brotherhood." We never see the trainer interact with anyone other than his horse for more than a second or two, and when we see him reading the newspaper at his breakfast table he's alone. This is partly to keep the story focused, to avoid introducing distracting elements. But it also quickly establishes him as a person who reads, who's smart and informed, and who might be a bit lonely (especially now that his horse is gone). In a book or a movie or a television series—any story where the lens can be wider—such details are crucial.

This Is Not an Easter Egg

Consider *Sharp Objects*, the eight-part HBO series in which Amy Adams plays an alcoholic journalist who's dispatched to the small Missouri town where she grew up to investigate a gruesome murder. Adapted from the novel by Gillian Flynn—her first—the series is ostensibly a whodunit in which the Adams character, Camille Preaker, competes for explanations with the town's police chief and a Kansas City detective who's brought in to work on the case. Camille is a reporter for a St. Louis newspaper, and when the show begins she has only recently been released from a mental hospital. It quickly develops that a serial killer is at work in her hometown: one little girl is dead and another is missing, and by the end of episode one the missing girl has turned up dead as well.

Critically speaking, there are more than a few problems with all this. It's hard to believe any newspaper editor would send such a troubled reporter to cover such an explosive story, especially in her hometown, where her demons lie in wait and conflicts of interest abound. And Camille is hardly a model of journalistic integrity: she conducts only the most cursory of interviews, rarely takes notes, doesn't bother to get the spelling of her sources' names, and has sex with the detective as well as the 18-year-old boy who is everybody else's prime suspect. As for the murder mystery, it takes precious long to unfold: whole episodes seem to go nowhere. But that's because the murders are actually a MacGuffin. They're what the characters all want to solve, but the real mystery, the real focus of the story, is Camille herself and the enormously dysfunctional relationship she has with her mother.

Camille's mother (Patricia Clarkson) is the richest person in town, a saccharine southern belle named Adora. She owns a hog

farm and a meat-processing plant—the town's biggest industry—
and lives in a grand Victorian mansion on top of a hill, a house
so rambling and claustrophobic it might have given Hitchcock the
frights. She's no happier to see Camille than Camille is to see
her, and she misses no opportunity to undermine Camille and
belittle her efforts at reporting. In the heat of the town's emotional miasma she provides an icy, cutting chill, especially when
she chides Camille for not being able to "get close"—then adds
wistfully, "And it's why, I think, I never loved you."

Small wonder that Camille has taken to cutting herself, not
just slicing her skin but carving whole words into it. Her body
reads like a thesaurus of pain. At the end of episode one we see
the word VANISH cut into her arm. Next we see FORNICATE.
When she's in bed with John, the teenage suspect, he kisses the
word MERCY written in scar tissue on her back. On another
occasion we see FUCKU carved into her abdomen. And BLADE.
And WRONG. The word WRONG also appears momentarily on
her car stereo—one of dozens of examples in which words flash
onscreen, sometimes only for a single frame, as if to make us
party to Camille's hallucinations. The logo on a piece of farm
equipment morphs from "Caterpillar" to "Catfight." A neon sign
on a liquor store window suddenly says OMEN.

Predictably, all this covert messaging sent the Internet into
overdrive. On the *Sharp Objects* Subreddit, fans eagerly documented each new sighting. "These are blink and you miss
moments!" one cried. "I've watched Episode 1 three times and
Episode 2 twice and each time I catch new things. This show is
fucking incredible," wrote another.

It was a new twist on the mystery box: most of these words
are not clues to the story but a window into Camille's wounded
psyche. What might be called "mystery box" storytelling has
"trained us to treat hidden things like they're always hints, to

assume that they're pieces of evidence meant to connect to some deep, secret truth," Kathryn VanArendonk explained in the online publication *Vulture*. "They're Easter eggs, a metaphor that plainly suggests that the whole point is to crack them open so you can get the candy inside." Not so with the hidden words in *Sharp Objects*. They provoke fans to trade information at the digital water cooler, because we care about Camille and the words make explicit what's going on inside her head. Otherwise, the whole thing would feel like a gimmick. As always, character provides depth, and depth makes us care.

5. World

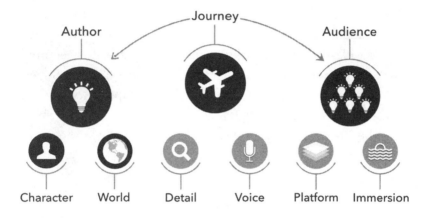

Author   Journey   Audience

Character   World   Detail   Voice   Platform   Immersion

And what about Wind Gap, the claustrophobic Missouri town Camille returns to in *Sharp Objects*? Do we care about the place? We do, because it's such a fully realized setting. But like any such milieu in the digital era, it's more than just a setting. It's a world unto itself.

The setting of a story has always been key—think of Baker Street, or Middle-earth, or the Starship *Enterprise*. But digital technology has changed the way we think about setting. Video games thrust us directly into stories and enable us to affect the outcome. Cognitive psychology and neuroscience suggest that we understand stories by projecting ourselves into them. No longer is the setting simply an evocative backdrop that helps us locate the characters in time and place. It's not enough to set the scene. The storyteller has to build a world—an immersive "story world," real or invented, that we can imaginatively inhabit alongside the story's characters. The more deeply we inhabit it, the more immersed we become, and the more persuasive the story is likely to be.

"This process of world-building encourages an encyclopedic impulse in both readers and writers," explains Henry Jenkins of USC. "This is a very different pleasure than we associate with the closure found in most classically constructed narratives, where we expect to leave the theatre knowing everything that is required to make sense of a particular story." Again, think of Baker Street, or Middle-earth, or the Starship *Enterprise*—fictional worlds that, though they predate the digital age by many decades, anticipate it in their open-endedness and the fervor with which they have been embraced, and inhabited, by fans.

The Land of Faërie

In March 1939, months before the outbreak of World War II, the Oxford linguist J. R. R. Tolkien gave a lecture at St. Andrews University in Scotland in which he offered some insight into how world-building might work. Tolkien was 47 at the time. He had published *The Hobbit* two years before and had begun the tale that would eventually become *The Lord of the Rings*, though it would not reach the public until 1954–55. His talk at St. Andrews would later be expanded and published under the title "On Fairy-Stories," which to him meant stories about the land of Faërie— "Faërie" being his word for fantasy.

Tolkien called fantasy "a natural human activity," even "a human right," and certainly not one to be reserved for children. With fantasy, he said,

What really happens is that the story-maker . . . makes a
Secondary World which your mind can enter. Inside it, what
he relates is "true": it accords with the laws of that world.
You therefore believe it, while you are, as it were, inside.
The moment disbelief arises, the spell is broken; the magic,
or rather art, has failed. You are then out in the Primary
World again, looking at the little abortive Secondary World
from outside.

There are two key ideas in this passage: First, that the storyteller creates a world "which your mind can enter"—a notion that
would not be fully understood for another 70 years or so, after
it had been explored by cognitive psychologists and neuroscientists. And second, that this world must have and maintain its own
internal logic, or else the illusion will go poof! and your mind
will be left dazed and bereft in the Primary World. For fantasy to
work, ironically, it must be grounded in the strictest logic.

This is a lesson George Lucas knew well. "*Star Wars* is a completely made-up universe; it doesn't hold to any scientific rules,
really," he once said. "But at the same time, it is very logical in a
certain kind of clock way. Once you've set up a particular kind of
rule, you don't break that rule."

Baker Street

We see Tolkien's fingerprints all around us—in *Star Wars*, in
Star Trek, in James Cameron's *Avatar*, in the multi-billion-dollar
franchise that is the Marvel Cinematic Universe. But this sort of
world-building, and the compulsive fandom it inspires, is hardly
unique to the current day. There were other examples even in
Tolkien's time. Three weeks after his lecture at St. Andrews,

20th Century-Fox released *The Hound of the Baskervilles,* the first of many Sherlock Holmes adaptations to star Basil Rathbone as the master of ratiocination. Arthur Conan Doyle, a failed physician turned hopeful writer, had created the singular detective a half-century earlier in the novel *A Study in Scarlet.* It took time for Holmes to catch on with readers, but once they embraced him, starting in 1891 with a series of short stories, he quickly became an icon of British culture.

Conan Doyle was as casual about his creation as Tolkien was obsessive. He wrote *A Study in Scarlet* in a scant three weeks, and only rarely did he offer any details about his character's life. In one story Holmes was described as being 60 years old in 1914, but there's no mention of his parents and only the vaguest hint of where he came from. He had an older brother, Mycroft, a heavyset man who worked in some sort of government position and was said to be brilliant but too sedentary to be of much use in the detecting trade. Holmes himself was eccentric and reclusive, suspicious of women, and evidently something of a hoarder, since he didn't like to throw anything out. He lived from 1881 to 1904 in a comfortable two-bedroom flat at 221B Baker Street in the fashionable London district of Marylebone, sharing the premises for most of that time with Dr. John Watson, the ex-army physician who became his sidekick, biographer, amanuensis, and foil. Almost everything we see of Holmes, we see through Watson's eyes—and to Watson he was "the most perfect reasoning and observing machine that the world has seen." It was a brilliant setup.

The world Holmes inhabited seemed more realistic than Middle-earth, but that was merely part of the illusion. Holmes's world "was as cozily self-contained as a snow globe," writes Michael Saler, a historian at the University of California at Davis. "And like Tolkien, Conan Doyle enhanced the reader's imaginative participation in the world by alluding to intriguing, unpublished events that gave the world additional depth and mystery"—like an offhand reference in a 1924 short story to "the giant rat of Sumatra, a story for which the world is not yet prepared."

There are inconsistencies galore in the saga of Holmes and Watson, but the basic situation—a seemingly emotionless and supremely logical mind solving life-and-death problems in the company of his very human associate—is so compelling it doesn't matter. Conan Doyle had stumbled upon—had helped invent— the earliest form of interactive fiction there is: the detective story. So it was fitting that the fans should not only try to solve his cases as they read but take over the task of making the world of Sherlock work. "It was the dawn of fandom as we now know it," declared Scott Brown, one of the writers on *Sharp Objects*, "zealous, fractious, hydra-headed, and participatory."

Conan Doyle discovered exactly how fractious it was when he tried to kill Holmes off in 1893. The author had hoped to devote himself instead to the historical novels—now long forgotten— he thought more worthy of his time. Even his mother advised against the move, but to no avail. After it was done, fans raised a huge fuss—so huge that in 1901 Holmes reappeared in *The Hound of the Baskervilles*, a novel set in the moors of Devonshire some time before his reported demise. Two years later, Conan Doyle brought him back to life with a half-convincing tale of how Holmes had not in fact plunged to his death in the Swiss Alps while wrestling with his arch-nemesis Professor Moriarty as presumed; instead he had dispatched Moriarty and then gone into hiding to avoid the professor's henchmen. Another Holmes novel and 31 more short stories would follow before Conan Doyle collapsed of a heart attack in 1930.

But Holmes did not die with him. Instead, Holmes fandom took a strange new turn. In 1934, Christopher Morley, a novelist and newspaperman, founded the Baker Street Irregulars in New York; the Sherlock Holmes Society sprang up in London the same year. Both groups were (and still are) made up of enthusiasts who eagerly play "the game"—the pretense that Sherlock Holmes actually lived, that Watson was indeed his scribe, and that Conan Doyle was not the author of the stories but merely Watson's literary agent. Even the Abbey National Bank, which moved into a new building at 219–229 Baker Street in 1932, was in on the game: when the Royal Mail started delivering letters addressed to Holmes, many of them from people seeking his help, the bank hired a "secretary" to write back that Holmes had retired to Sussex to raise bees.

The game has been used to explain any number of omissions and inconsistencies, from Holmes's birth date (calculated to be January 6, 1854) to whether Watson was wounded in the leg in the Anglo-Afghan Wars, as reported in one story, or in the shoulder, as reported in another. (Both, it was eventually concluded, on the novel theory that the Afghans' homemade bullets were so erratic that one might well have split apart in midair and hit him in both places.) So while Conan Doyle may have been careless in casting his spell, Holmes was so mesmerizing that readers were happy to fill in the gaps.

From Baker Street to Hedeby Island

If you go to Baker Street today you'll find the Sherlock Holmes Museum, in a Regency town house that's like many others in Marylebone and neighboring areas except that it too maintains the fiction of the great detective's existence. Billed as "the Official Home of Sherlock Holmes," it features a wildly overstuffed simulacrum of the flat he supposedly shared with Watson, and above that the flat of their putative landlady. It even bears the address 221B Baker Street, though its actual address is 239. Still, the museum is closer to the location Conan Doyle had in mind than any of our planet's other 221B Baker Streets—the one at the Sherlock Holmes Pub, two miles away in Charing Cross; or the one in Switzerland, near the falls where Holmes supposedly faked his death; or the other one in Switzerland, in a hotel where Conan Doyle's son liked to stay; or the one at the University of Minnesota, assembled by a particularly obsessive collector. For someone who never existed, Holmes sure had a lot of real estate.

What all the 221B Baker Streets have in common is that they are liminal spaces, occupying a threshold, one foot in reality, one foot in some other plane. They are not alone. The world is full of real places that turn up in fictional stories, and fictional places that turn up in real ones. Three tube stops away from Baker Street is King's Cross Station, where an official-looking sign marks the otherwise invisible Platform 9¾, the magical departure point used by wizards leaving for Hogwarts in the Harry Potter stories. There's a luggage cart embedded halfway in the wall and, inevitably, a gift shop. In Northern Ireland, where much of HBO's *Game of Thrones* was shot, fans can "live the *Game of Thrones* experience" at the seat of House Stark, Winterfell—known in real life as Old Castle Ward—and even do a "meet and greet" with two of the Starks' magical direwolves, Summer and Grey Wind. In Stockholm there's a walking tour that stops at sites named in Stieg Larsson's *Millennium* trilogy—*The Girl with the Dragon Tattoo* and its sequels.

I went on the *Millennium* tour a few years ago. It was February and unbelievably cold, but I stood in the frigid air and took it all in regardless—the neo-Gothic apartment block on Bellmansgatan where Mikael Blomkvist, crusading journalist and Stieg Larsson's alter ego, supposedly lived. The building where *Millennium*, Blomkvist's muckraking political magazine, supposedly had its offices. Kvarnen, the pub where Lisbeth Salander, she of the dragon tattoo, was said to have performed with her punk band. The apartment tower where she bought a 21-room penthouse with stolen money (that is, money righteously stolen from the bad guy, this being Larsson's story world). Having done some work for David Fincher's 2011 film, ghostwriting articles for a special edition of *Millennium* and taking on other assignments to expand the story beyond the movie screen, I found the tour fascinating. But I was particularly struck by a conversation I had with a woman selling tickets at the Stockholm City Museum.

She told me about a couple who had come from Chicago to trace the steps of Larsson's characters. Before leaving the States they'd asked their travel agent to book them on a train that would take them to Hedestad, the town next to Hedeby Island, where most of the action in *The Girl with the Dragon Tattoo* takes place. The agent could find no such train. Frustrated, the couple decided to fly to Stockholm and buy the tickets themselves—hadn't Blomkvist taken the train there in the book? But they had no luck. They couldn't even find Hedestad on a map. Finally they came to the City Museum, where they were told that Hedestad and Hedeby Island didn't exist—they were made-up places. Not easily deterred, the couple headed for a car rental agency, determined to follow Larsson's admittedly vague directions—somewhere beyond Uppsala on the Norrland coast, "a little more than an hour north of Gävle"—and drive there. That was the last anyone at the museum had seen of them.

All of which left me wondering about the appeal of this sort of thing. Why would two people be that determined to visit the site where fictional Nazis threatened fictional victims with horrific acts of torture and murder? At one level, the answer was obvious. When we read a novel, we conjure up the characters and the locations—what they look like, what they sound like, how they make us feel. When we watch a movie or a TV show, we're given those things—but either way we co-create the story, completing it in our minds. And having done so, we'd like some confirmation.

The deeper reason has to do with the idea that we understand stories by projecting ourselves into them. If the story is effective, we bond with its characters and even its setting. But it is a strange sort of bonding, one quite capable of defying our expectations and confounding our belief systems. When the Danish theoretical physicist Niels Bohr and his then-student Werner Heisenberg visited Elsinore in 1924, Bohr remarked:

> Isn't it strange how this castle changes as soon as one imagines that Hamlet lived here. As scientists we believe that a castle consists only of stones, and admire the way the architect put them together. . . . None of this should be changed by the fact that Hamlet lived here, and yet it is changed completely. Suddenly the walls and the ramparts speak a different language. The courtyard becomes an entire world, a dark corner reminds us of the darkness of the human soul, we hear Hamlet's "To be or not to be." Yet all we really know about Hamlet is that his name appears in a thirteenth-century chronicle. No one can prove that he really lived here. But everyone knows the questions Shakespeare had him ask, the human depths he was made to reveal.

Building a World

Like the nonlinearity of *Pulp Fiction*, like the mystery box structure of *Lost* and *Westworld*, the idea of the story world has reset our expectations of what a story should be. The setting is now a character in its own right. Storytellers are expected to leave room for the audience because audiences want to step inside this world in their imagination—to experience it, to trade ideas about it, to make it their own. But what does it mean to "leave room for the audience"? What do you have to do?

1. **Make the characters and their world complex enough to give people something to wonder about.** Which in our current environment means something to wonder about together online. *Westworld* has taken this to an extreme, which is why you saw articles like " 'Westworld' Theories: Eight Mind-Blowing Possibilities" (*SlashFilm*) and "There are five other parks besides Westworld! What are they?" (*Hypable*). But you don't have to go this far. A couple of murders and the unexplained appearance of some rogue words onscreen worked quite nicely for *Sharp Objects*. And with Sherlock Holmes, even greater levels of participation could be achieved with nothing more than a throwaway line— like the one about the giant rat of Sumatra, which has inspired a half-dozen or more fanfiction novels, numerous short stories and radio plays, episodes of the BBC series *Sherlock* and *Doctor Who*, even an album by the Firesign Theatre comedy troupe in the seventies.

2. **Keep the story straight.** Arthur Conan Doyle got away with a lot. You might too, if you create a character that transfixes readers and audiences the world over for 135 years and counting. Otherwise, best not to push it. Try to keep your story from contradicting itself lest your Secondary World pop like a bubble.

3. **Let the audience add to the story.** Fanfiction used to be viewed as copyright infringement. Now it's made E. L. James, whose *Fifty Shades of Grey* began as a *Twilight* takeoff posted on

fanfiction.net under the pseudonym Snowqueens Icedragon, one of the world's most highly paid authors. *Twilight* hasn't exactly suffered either. There's room for everybody here.

4. Make the experience as open-ended as possible. Much as we want art that isn't constrained by a frame and theater that isn't constricted by a proscenium arch, we increasingly want stories that aren't wrapped up in an hour or two. Television series have already become like video games, not so much in the way we "play" them but in the hour after hour of entertainment they provide. Closure is delayed, often for years.

In Search of the Infinite Ending

This comes at a cost, for fans and producers alike: how do you wrap up a story that people have invested countless hours in watching?

Very carefully. When a story lands precisely on point after years in the telling—like *The Americans*, the six-season FX series about a pair of Cold War–era Soviet spies and their kids in the suburbs of Washington, DC—it is a wondrous thing to experience. More common is something like the series finale of *Lost*. Some bought the idea that everyone had actually died in the plane crash that started the show—it was certainly more likely than that they'd all survived—but others reacted with incredulity. "Six seasons of polar bears, bachelor pad hatches, landlocked ships, personal submarines and a fleet of fallen airplanes, and it was all apparently some sort of shared afterlife experience," a *Los Angeles Times* critic remarked acerbically.

This was mild compared to the treatment *Game of Thrones* got when it ended in 2019. The show had become an outsized hit for HBO and an obsession for millions of fans. But for many it wasn't just the final episode that fell short—it was the whole last season. And disappointment barely began to describe their reaction. An editor at *The New Republic* asked, "Do we all agree that this was the worst of all possible endings to the show?" No argument on that from the Nashville sports radio host who shared his thoughts on Twitter: "I wasted eight years of my life on this story, and at the end they came and they stabbed me."

The real problem for shows like this is that they have to end at all. We've come to a place where world-building is so paramount and fandom so intense that many stories would go on forever if fans could will it so. And some fans just might get their wish. Will we ever come to the end of the Marvel Cinematic Universe, as the phenomenally successful Disney-owned franchise has come to be known? Unlikely; maybe even categorically impossible. As the poet and critic Maya Phillips noted in *The New Yorker*, "can the M.C.U. really keep expanding? How flexible is a story, ultimately? Can it be extended indefinitely without becoming meaningless, or will it reach some natural limit? How infinite can a fictional world be?"

A good question, and one the Marvel Cinematic Universe seems determined to answer. But as fantastical and apparently infinite as such worlds may be, stories that don't get neatly tied up in an hour or two come closer to resembling our experience of life—which may be one reason we find them so compelling.

6. Detail

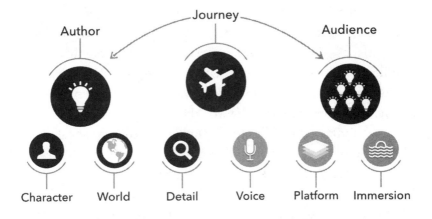

Another way in which stories tend to resemble our experience of life: detail. Logic involves generalizations; stories are specific. They are about individuals, not types. Holmes and Watson. The young horse trainer in "Brotherhood." The cancer-stricken bride who doesn't want to lose her hair in "Suzanne's Story" and the tatted-up rock musician who stands by her. And while stories like these can certainly communicate ideas, they are not primarily *about* ideas. Ideas are abstractions; stories are particular. Detail is what makes them so.

There is no end of psychological research that shows the numbing effect of abstraction. Much of it has to do with empathy: humans show far more empathy to an individual than to a statistic. One study tried to fathom the response to victims like

"Baby Jessica," an 18-month-old girl who in 1987 got more than $700,000 in donations after tumbling into a well in Texas, while millions of desperately needy children get nearly nothing. The researchers, at Carnegie Mellon in Pittsburgh, first offered individual college students $5 to fill out a questionnaire about their use of technology. Then they gave each student five one-dollar bills, along with an envelope and an appeal from Save the Children, and asked if they would like to donate some of what they had just earned. Some students got an appeal that relied purely on statistics—food shortages in Malawi affecting more than three million children, for example. Others were told about Rokia, a seven-year-old girl from Mali who was facing severe hunger or even starvation but whose life would be changed because of their gift. A third group got the story of Rokia and the statistical information too. As it turned out, those who got only the statistics gave an average of $1.14, while the average gift from those who read only about Rokia was $2.38—more than twice as much. Those who got both the story *and* the statistics gave only a little more than the first group.

The researchers concluded that Rokia's story, an emotional appeal, was undercut by the rational thinking that the statistics induced. But these findings are also consistent with the idea that we understand stories by imaginatively projecting ourselves into them. Rokia's story is only a paragraph long, but it contains crucial details. The statistical summary offers no details at all—and nothing to project ourselves into. As for Baby Jessica, her story came with a seemingly endless amount of detail, since it took a 56-hour rescue effort to extract her from the well and the drama got round-the-clock TV coverage.

A subsequent study in Sweden found that empathy for victims begins to deteriorate when there are as few as two of them. When a psychologist there asked students to give money to Rokia and also to a nine-year-old boy named Moussa, the donations were somewhat smaller than for either Rokia or Moussa alone. When asked to help one, two, or eight children, each of them identified by name, students gave least to the eight. But when the eight children were presented as a unit—that is, shown together in a single photograph and identified as brothers and sisters—donations were the same as those for a single child.

This may explain the response to the Chilean mine collapse in the summer and fall of 2010. For more than three months, 33 miners were trapped nearly half a mile underground in a copper mine in northern Chile's Atacama Desert. The bill to rescue them came to $20 million—one-third of it provided by individual donors. As with Baby Jessica, the spectacle drew blanket media coverage for the 69 days it took to locate the trapped miners, figure out how to rescue them, and bring them to the surface. When the rescue was finally effected, Chilean state television reported that a billion people watched it on television, with millions more streaming it online. Clearly there was something about the combination of crisis, claustrophobia, heroism, and suspense that caused a lot of people who have never ventured into a mine to identify with the trapped men, imagining the men's perspective while subsuming their own.

Into the Woods

Detail gives us something to hang on to, a peg for the emotion that stories convey. Sometimes it's the backstory that makes the best tales so vivid. Tolkien went to astonishing lengths to detail the world of hobbits. *The Lord of the Rings* concludes with a map and six appendices that provide the early history of Middle-earth, several hobbit family trees, a couple of different calendar systems, a timeline that covers thousands of years, a writing and pronunciation guide to the several languages he had created for Middle-

earth, and an account of all its different races—the hobbits, the elves, the hideous orcs. Then there's *The Silmarillion*, a five-part chronicle of the history and development not just of Middle-earth but of the entire universe of which it was a part. Tolkien started writing it when he was a young army lieutenant in the trenches of World War I and still had not finished it when he died in 1973 in the seacoast town of Bournemouth at the age of 81. It was finally published in 1977, after his son Christopher took it over and tied up the loose ends.

But as much as detail can bring characters and their world to life, it is not there to be strewn about at random. It can be stuck in the back in an appendix if you like. But if it's actually part of the story, it has to be deployed for a reason. It should help convey the intent of the characters, the mood of the place, the meaning of the story. It should provide, the novelist Jane Alison wrote, "sensory glimmers . . . to draw the reader in." It should form a path.

I have a number of guest speakers at my Strategic Storytelling

program at Columbia. One of the most popular is Ellen Lupton, the Cooper Hewitt curator who wrote *Design Is Storytelling*. Ellen is tall and lean and blond and blessed with a gigawatt smile and a noticeable lisp—a wonderful lisp, because it helps make everything she says seem delightfully infectious.

When she came to the seminar, she showed us two photographs: Which, she asked, is more narrative?

The answer, obviously, is B.

Why so obvious? Because looking at A, you see no way in. There might as well be a screen between you and the woods. Actually, there is a screen—it's the undergrowth. B is different. It tells you other people have been there before. It invites you to follow their footsteps (or their tire tracks, if you want to get technical about it). It also, as Ellen pointed out, suggests movement and time—two of the most basic components of a narrative arc, conflict being the third. It signals that you're going to be moving forward. That you're on a journey.

That's what detail should do. It should form a path. It should seduce people onto the journey you've prepared for them.

This path is what enables the audience to project themselves into the story. It encourages them to walk in and inhabit the world you've created. Without detail, this world is uninviting. With it, the world can feel not just realistic but enticing. But how much detail do you need? How do you distinguish between detail that creates a pathway and detail that makes like the underbrush?

The Reality Effect

A lot depends on how the detail is presented. It's all too easy to dismiss detail as "useless" when it doesn't specifically advance the plot. But a story is much more than a plot summary. The test of detail is not whether it advances the plot but whether it illuminates a character or expands our understanding of her world.

Take, for example, *Madame Bovary*, Gustave Flaubert's scandalous 1857 novel of intense marital frustration in the face of dull, provincial existence. Emma Bovary is not merely unhappy; she is desperately, miserably unhappy, and consumed by the knowledge that other, richer people in other, bigger towns are luxuriating in delights that, but for a cruel twist of fate, might be hers. Multiple essays have been written about a single paragraph that comes about one-fifth of the way through the book:

> But it was above all at mealtimes that she could bear it no longer, in that little room on the ground floor, with the smoking stove, the creaking door, the oozing walls, the damp floor-tiles; all the bitterness of life seemed to be served to her on her plate, and, with the steam from the boiled beef, there rose from the depths of her soul other exhalations as it were of disgust. Charles was a slow eater;

she would nibble a few hazel-nuts, or else, leaning on her elbow, would amuse herself making marks on the oilcloth with the point of her table-knife.

The genius of this passage is not only in the vividness of Flaubert's description, though that certainly matters. It's in the point of view. Every detail—the smoking stove, the creaking door, the leaking walls, the damp floor, the boiled beef—serves to reinforce Emma's sense of hopelessness and despair, because we view each of them through her eyes. Nothing is superfluous. Her husband eats slowly, as he does everything else. Emma barely eats at all, her plate being heaped with bitterness. In a few sentences we see "Emma's world as it now appears to her," in the words of the critic Erich Auerbach, "its cheerlessness, unvaryingness, grayness, staleness, airlessness, and inescapability now first become clearly apparent to her."

Flaubert was 29 when he began this novel—his first—and 35 when it was published. Handsome and athletic in his youth but already half-bald, pot-bellied, and dissipated by the time it came out, he lived with his mother in a little village in Normandy not far from the scenes of Emma's degradation. He filled *Madame Bovary* with unapologetic depictions of female passion and untamed desire, depictions that scandalized the authorities when it first appeared in serial form in the *Revue de Paris*. "She glorified adultery," cried the prosecutor at the obscenity trial that followed; "she sang the song of adultery, its poesy and its delights." Yet Flaubert was acquitted, and the book became a bestseller—little wonder, given such a buildup.

Flaubert's powers of description may have been too real for the public prosecutor, but for other novelists they were a tonic. His ability to convey a scene spelled the beginning of literary realism, the literature of the familiar and the day-to-day, of Chekhov and Nabokov, Wharton and Updike. From Flaubert came the idea that "the finest style of writing is a procession of strung details, a necklace of sensualities," wrote the critic James Wood. It was this necklace of detail that generated what Roland Barthes called "the reality effect," the product of "a kind of narrative *luxury*, lavish to the point of offering many 'futile' details and thereby increasing the cost of narrative information." Increasing the cost, as luxuries do, but also increasing the reward—for what may seem frivolous to someone focused solely on the efficient transmittal of information is essential to the emotional impact of a story.

Immaculate Reality and the End of the Death Star

Of course, there's no reason the reality effect should be confined to realism. In fact, the farther from reality we get, the more we need it. Or so concluded George Lucas as he was making *Star Wars*.

Like Emma's world in *Madame Bovary*, like Tolkien's Middle-earth, *Star Wars* was built on a relentless accumulation of detail. Nothing about it was accidental or arbitrary. Lucas was inspired by the samurai epics of Akira Kurosawa, whose work he had been introduced to by the director John Milius when they were both film school students at USC in the sixties. Structurally, *Star Wars* owed a lot to Kurosawa's 1958 film *The Hidden Fortress*, which was told through the misadventures of two luckless peasants—the models for Lucas's charmingly humanoid robots, R2-D2 and C-3PO. Stylistically, Lucas was influenced by Kurosawa's concept of "immaculate reality," which became his version of the reality effect.

Immaculate reality is anything but immaculate. The point was to create what Lucas called a "used future": dingy, dirty, beat-up.

This was all but unknown in science fiction, which tended to present a future that was sleek and pristine. Before *Star Wars*, most science fiction films—even the great ones, like Stanley Kubrick's *2001: A Space Odyssey*—bought into the less-is-more aesthetic of twentieth-century modernism. After *Star Wars* came movies like *Blade Runner*, Ridley Scott's 1982 *noir* masterpiece, with its futuristic squalor, its endless rain, its intimations of technology as a dead-end pursuit.

"Kurosawa created historical realism by layering his sets and characters with patina, wear, and filth. Lucas created a realistic future out of distressed surfaces, oil stains, and a soundscape that included grinding gears and backfires," wrote the artist John Powers in "star wars: a new heap," an influential essay that presented *Star Wars* in opposition to minimalism and modernism. "Two visual rhetorics are at war on-screen"—on one side, the spare utilitarianism of a modern industrial superpower; on the other, the patchwork improvisation of a rogue fringe.

Powers saw the destruction of the Death Star—the Galactic Empire's enormous spheroidal superweapon, an essential work of minimalism blown up in the movie's climactic scene—as a turning point. Here was the end of mid-century modernism, and with it came the suggestion that modernism was a fraud. "Even the initially smooth and unitary form of the Death Star was shown, as the rebel fighters skimmed its surface, to be deeply fissured with an ever-diminishing body of structural fragments," Powers went on. "These crenelated details suggested a depth and complexity to modern life that modernism's pure geometries often obscured."

Depth and complexity are precisely the point. If you want an audience to project themselves into the world you've created, you have to give them something to hang on to. Then they can surrender to it, become immersed in it the same way Lucas had become immersed in Kurosawa's vision of samurai-era Japan.

And looking to the past is never a bad idea if you want to create a believable world that's set in the future. The past is a reliable guide to what is going to happen because it already *has* happened, as opposed to what theoretically *might* happen. It reveals who we are and what we're capable of as humans—sometimes frighteningly so.

Lucas's use of detail was of course different from Flaubert's. Film is different from fiction. Virtual reality is different from both. But detail—like character development, like world-building—is still imperative. The trick is to get the three to work together.

The Many Faces of Pepe the Frog

Everything you've just read should be thrown out the window when dealing not with books or movies or VR but with self-replicating culture units—that is, memes. On the surface, memes seem almost ridiculously small—which is one reason they can proliferate so wildly. But packed inside them is a narrative that contains a panoply of ideas, even an entire worldview, and that is capable of expanding on contact with sympathetic brain receptors to become a powerful motivator for millions of people. In memes, the detail is implicit: the audience supplies it, not the author. It is the ultimate form of co-creation.

We know memes now for exploding across the Internet, but they existed long before electronic communication. A meme functions as a symbol—a highly potent representation of something much bigger than itself—and we've had symbols for centuries. Religion is rife with symbols that act as talismans of cultural identity and transmission: the cross, the crucifix, the fish symbol of the early Christians, the star of David, the crescent and star, the dharma wheel. Nationalism too: the Union Jack, the Stars and Stripes, the Stars and Bars of the Confederacy, the Rising

Sun, the Nazi swastika. But the word "meme" dates from 1976, when Richard Dawkins introduced it in his book *The Selfish Gene.*

Not quite 30 years later, a super-nice-guy cartoonist named Matt Furie created a slacker amphibian he called Pepe the Frog. Pepe got his name, Furie says in a documentary that aired on PBS in 2020, because "it sounded like pee-pee." Pepe's signature phrase was "feels good, man," uttered because he liked to drop his trousers to the floor and pee bare-assed. Later, Furie and others would wonder why Pepe of all frogs should get adopted—appropriated might be a better word—by users on the Internet message board 4chan, a wild and woolly corner of cyberspace that's known as both a meme factory and a petri dish of nasty behavior, much of it from the so-called alt-right. In fact, the slacker frog was just juvenile enough to appeal to slacker Internet trolls, which is why among other mutations he has turned up in a KKK hood, or wearing an SS helmet, or saying "Kill Jews, Man," or in the run-up to the 2016 election as an orange-maned Donald J. Trump standing behind a podium adorned with the presidential seal.

Were Pepe's new memesters really Jew-hating Nazi symps, or were they just in it for the lulz, for the sheer, ineffable joy of sparking outrage? It's not necessarily an either/or question—but in any case, they quickly got the reaction they wanted.

That October, the Anti-Defamation League designated Pepe a hate symbol. Hillary Clinton's campaign organization, fresh off her "basket of deplorables" meme, proclaimed this new, right-wing Pepe "horrifying." Furie himself seemed indifferent at first, then proclaimed in *Time* magazine that the whole thing was "a nightmare," though at least it afforded him the opportunity "to speak out against hate." This sort of response was, to borrow a phrase from the journalist Jesse Singal, "catnip for the trolls," who care mainly about getting attention, ideally in as offensive a manner as possible. Thus demonstrating that meme warfare is inherently asymmetrical: if you care about anything, if you admit to having any human hopes or dreams or values or—God forbid—feelings, you're just setting yourself up to get trolled. Sucker.

TMI?

But anyway, detail. The question with detail is always the same: how much, and to what end? Often it's a matter of taste. As influential as Flaubert may have been, the poet Paul Valéry was no fan: "Another vice of this style—there's always room for one more detail," Valéry groused in his notebook in 1924. But while Flaubert provided a great deal of description, he was hardly profligate. On the contrary, writes the novelist John Barth, "his passion for the *mot juste*"—the right word, the *exact* word—"involved far more subtraction than addition."

Postmodern novelists—Don DeLillo, Thomas Pynchon, Dave Eggers, David Foster Wallace—have tended to lose the subtraction. Writing about Wallace's *Infinite Jest* (1,079 pages, including endnotes), the journalist/critic/video game writer Tom Bissell cites "the revelatory power of freakishly thorough noticing, of corralling and controlling detail." James Wood, who dubbed it "hysterical realism," was less impressed.

There will always be tension between too much and too little. Tension is good. The writer's job, no matter what the medium, is to keep it in balance. Obviously, this has to be done on a case-by-case basis. But here are a few guidelines:

1. Observe closely. It worked for Sherlock. Detail is only as good as the information it contains.

2. Make every detail work. Use it to throw light on your characters and the world you've built for them. Flaubert did this by presenting details from his main character's point of view, providing insight into her moods, her thoughts, her secrets. But don't try to get away with description for its own sake. You risk presenting a list of factoids—and lists have no business in a story, unless perhaps you find one taped to some character's refrigerator door. And even then, it had better have blood on it.

The antithesis of this approach was taken by Moe Levine, a highly successful New York trial lawyer of the 1950s and 1960s. In one celebrated case, representing a plaintiff who had lost both arms in an accident, Levine delivered a summation to the jury that was barely 120 words long—but if its brevity was shocking, the emotional impact of those few, well-chosen words was even more so:

> Your honor, eminent counsel for defense, ladies and gentlemen of the jury: as you know, about an hour ago we broke for lunch. I saw the bailiff come and take you all as a group to have lunch in the jury room. Then I saw the defense attorney, Mr. Horowitz. He and his client decided to go to lunch together. The judge and court clerk went to lunch.
>
> So, I turned to my client, Harold, and said "Why don't you and I go to lunch together?"
>
> We went across the street to that little restaurant and had lunch.
>
> [Significant pause.]
>
> Ladies and gentlemen, I just had lunch with my client. He has no arms. He eats like a dog.
>
> Thank you very much.

Levine picked out the one detail that mattered, the one that no person in the jury could fail to identify with, and led them directly to it. After this brief oration, he is said to have won one of the largest settlements in the history of New York State.

3. Sometimes you just need to get the point across. Several years ago I met Mike Hardy, a silver-haired man who headed the global program for intercultural dialogue at British Council, which promotes British culture abroad. Hardy had flown to Indonesia after the 2004 tsunami, which sent waves up to 100 feet high over parts of a dozen countries and killed nearly 230,000 people—almost three-quarters of them in Indonesia. As he was walking from village to village on the devastated island of Sumatra, he came across a man who was sitting alone amid the desolation, crying.

"There were no streets," Hardy recalled. "There were no buildings left." Hardy, in his suit and tie, asked him how he was. "He said, 'I've lost 87 members of my family.' And I'm thinking, I don't know 87 members of my family. But what happened then was he started telling stories about his family. Everything was a story. And the only way you could answer a question was to tell him a story about yourself." When Hardy emerged from his tent the next morning, he realized he had learned something important about connecting with people: "Don't ask banal questions. Tell a story about how you feel."

Hardy's story about storytelling was slim on detail—I never learned who the man was, how old he was, what he looked like, what he did for a living, or even who any of his 87 lost family members were—but I've never forgotten it. Like Roger Schank's story about the two Jewish girls playing tennis, it dramatically illustrated a point—one that too much detail might have obscured.

4. Clear a path for the audience. Properly deployed, description provides a vector for the audience to enter the story. But random detail is like underbrush: it gets in the way. And jargon is a veritable briar patch, guaranteed to halt all progress. It can sometimes work when it's presented from an outside perspective, as a special language that's being used to illuminate the world a character lives in. Even then it requires skillful deployment, in a way that makes it clear that it's there to take the audience into the character's head, not to keep out the uninitiated.

5. Bait the pathway with questions the audience can't stop itself from trying to answer. In "Hansel and Gretel," Hansel left bread crumbs on the trail so he and his sister could find their way back home after their father abandoned them in the woods. Today we have Easter eggs and the like, including the psychic clues that so intrigued the fans of *Sharp Objects*. They are not there to get the characters back home but to keep the audience following closely.

6. Be precise. Choose words and images with care. While you're at it, avoid adverbs whenever possible. As Stephen King put it in *On Writing*, "*The adverb is not your friend.*" (The italics are his.) Elmore Leonard called the use of adverbs "a mortal sin." Leonard also said, "Avoid detailed descriptions of characters," citing Hemingway as an authority. It worked for Hemingway, obviously. But he was a minimalist, a literary icon of the modernist movement that exploded with the Death Star. Fashion is fashion and it's fine to ignore it. But if you do, best to make the choice deliberately.

These are guidelines, not rules. Your approach to detail will depend on what kind of story you are telling but also on who you are—which you will become fully aware of as you find your voice.

7. Voice

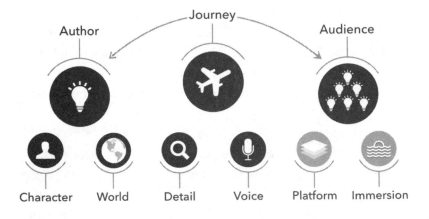

Author · Journey · Audience

Character · World · Detail · Voice · Platform · Immersion

Some years back, a renegade brand consultancy called Naked Communications worked with Virgin Group to help define its identity. No conglomerate is typical, but Virgin is more atypical than most. At any given time it's made up of more than two dozen wildly divergent companies, some wholly owned, some part-owned, some just licensing the Virgin name. Virgin Atlantic, Virgin America, Virgin Galactic, Virgin Holidays, Virgin Mobile, Virgin Money, even for a few years Virgin Brides, which the organization's cofounder and chair, Sir Richard Branson, promoted by shaving his beard and posing in a wedding gown. "Why did Virgin Brides fail?" he quipped in a blog post after the last store closed. "Because we soon realized there weren't any!" So the corporate identity quest was a major undertaking: what was Virgin, anyway?

Virgin's peculiarities went well beyond its unlikely agglomeration of businesses. Having started out in the early seventies with a single London record shop, Branson and his partners launched a hip music label and then moved into the airline business— hardly a typical trajectory. Now Virgin was a global pop-culture phenomenon. Not just a brand but a state of mind, and oddly consistent. Irrefutably hip. Quintessentially British, yet innovative and fun-loving in a way that subverted British stereotypes. Its businesses could be in any sector, for hidden away in a back room somewhere was apparently a lab devoted to finding broken industries and figuring out how to reinvent them. Airlines. Banks. Even trains.

As for Naked, it was a radical organization in ad-land, a band of "brilliant misfits" (as they styled themselves) who saw that advertising agencies were pushing a solution that no longer worked. So Naked, founded in London in 2000, billed itself as "media neutral": instead of making money by creating and placing 30-second spots, it offered strategic advice untainted by self-interest. One of its key beliefs was that "everything communicates"—not just advertising. Another was that in the digital age, brands stand naked before the consumer—hence the name. Naked and Virgin were a good match.

The idea was to codify what Virgin was about—its purpose, its promise, its ambition, the voice with which it spoke. Voice is an expression of personality, of the mental pattern that makes each of us unique. Writers take years to find their voice—that combination of cadence, tone, and attitude that characterizes them and their work. Smart organizations recognize that they too have a voice—or need to develop one if they don't. But it isn't a matter of "deciding" what your voice should be. What everyone comes to realize, individuals and organizations alike, is that before you can find your voice, you have to find yourself. Because voice is how you tell us who you are. It is unique and readily identifiable. And it is expressed in everything you do.

Naked and Virgin spent months conducting interviews and workshops. Some 150 people were brought into the process. Eventually, the team reached a conclusion: Virgin was Branson himself—irrepressible and full of contradictions. They summarized all this in "The Virgin Way: Our Brand Purpose," a short, heavily illustrated booklet that laid out "a cohesive and consistent story" about the company's identity. Virgin's contradictions, the booklet noted, were Branson's own. Like him, its people were mavericks who worked hard and had fun doing it. Who followed the rules but challenged the norm. Who did well while doing good.

Once you know who you are, you can start to find your voice. The Virgin folks summed it up in a series of short, upbeat descriptors: "no bullshit," "no jargon," "vibrant and fun," "a wink and a smile," "flirtatious and playful," "cheeky but never blatant."

A Global Growth Investor

One contradiction remained. "Our purpose is to change business for good," the company declares on its website, even as it defines itself more soberly elsewhere on the site as "a global, growth investor" with a portfolio that is "diversified across multiple asset classes and geographies." Virgin's early history is replete with hair-raising tales of entrepreneurial derring-do, but Virgin Group today is essentially an investment vehicle that does deals with such top-tier private equity and venture capital firms as Bain Capital, Kleiner Perkins, Sequoia Capital, and Venrock, founded as the venture arm of the Rockefeller family. As the *Financial Times* put it, Virgin "most resembles a huge 'family office' with a portfolio run by professional investment managers and the profits channelled—via a number of trusts and a network of holding companies—to the Branson family."

When the *FT* investigated, in 2014, it found "about 80 businesses" bearing the Virgin name, with combined revenues the previous fiscal year of some £15 billion (about $24 billion at the time). But Virgin Group held direct stakes in fewer than half of them. As with the Trump Organization, many of Virgin's profits actually come from licensing its name to enterprises it has no other financial interest in. Among these companies are some of the biggest, including Virgin Media, the UK telecoms and mobile provider, and Virgin Mobile in the US, Canada, and Australia. And though Branson was deeply engaged with his startups earlier on, he has had minimal involvement since 2005 in anything save Virgin Galactic, his space tourism venture, and Virgin Unite, a nonprofit that aims to address climate change, spur entrepreneurship, and promote the well-being of people and their planet.

Not only are Virgin's other companies not run by Branson; many of them share little to nothing with one another except the Virgin brand. All this makes the personality traits that determine Virgin's voice more important than ever, since those are the attributes Virgin is licensing—not simply the name but what the name represents: the idea of doing well while doing good, not to mention smart disruption, boundless enthusiasm, defying expectations, and delivering experiences that are "red-hot."

Various constituent parts of Virgin Group have done their own version of the "Virgin Way" study. One is Virgin Media, the Internet and mobile services provider formed in the 2006 merger of two cable and broadband companies with Virgin Mobile, which Branson had launched several years before. Branson was a major shareholder of Virgin Media, having sold Virgin Mobile to it for close to £1 billion ($1.75 billion) in cash and stock. Then, in 2013, it was bought by Liberty Global, a multinational telecom provider headed by John Malone, the US cable billionaire, in a £15 billion ($23.3 billion) deal. Branson was no longer involved, though Liberty Global continued to license the Virgin name. Meanwhile, Virgin Media was working with a London consultancy called Engine Service Design on an initiative they dubbed Voice of Our Brand.

Few customers like their telecom providers. You might think that's because telecom services tend to go out all the time. But when Virgin Media analyzed some three million customer service calls, it found that getting their service back actually resonated less with customers than having a positive emotional experience on the phone. This shouldn't be as surprising as it sounds: research has shown that establishing an emotional connection is the most important factor in brand loyalty—more so even than customer satisfaction. After eight years of study, the US consumer intelligence firm Motista identified some 300 "motivating emotions," singling out 10 that fulfill "deep, often unconscious desires" in a wide range of people. Among them: having a sense of well-being, a sense of freedom, a sense of thrill, and a sense of belonging. (Note the balance between action and excitement on the one hand, comfort and safety on the other.) Brands that fulfilled one or more of these desires tended to be considerably more successful than those that simply tried to keep their customers satisfied.

Meanwhile, focus groups were telling Virgin Media that customers expected its call center operators to reflect the personality and confidence of Branson himself. That may seem like a lot to ask, but if Virgin is supposed to embody Branson's unique personality, why not? Engine and Virgin Media developed a set of guidelines and coaching materials that were used to train everybody in the call centers. The program was so successful they expanded it to include salespeople, retail personnel, and installers and technicians—the proverbial cable guys, now installing fiber and retooled to sound like Branson. This move proved popular too—so popular that after a couple of years Liberty Global decided to rebrand its previously existing offering in Ireland as Virgin. A television ad was produced in which Branson appeared as a hologram, cheerfully showing a hapless dad how to keep his three kids entertained with superfast broadband. "We're trying to bring Richard very much to the heart of what we're doing," the head of brand and marketing told *The Irish Times*.

But the gap between Branson's way of doing business and Malone's is enormous, and by this time the gap between image and reality was widening as well. This came out when results from a Virgin Media employee Q&A were leaked to *The Register*, a notably irreverent British tech news site. (Its motto: "Biting the hand that feeds IT.") One Virgin staffer derided their new corporate owners as "faceless change drivers with no concern for the Virgin values." Liberty Global "seems to be ripping the very soul (and people) out of the company and everything that was good/ Virgin about it," said another. A third person saw the Virgin values being eroded away: "What ever happened to 'keep the staff happy and we shall inevitably have happy customers'?" Asked for a response, Virgin Media's chief executive put much of it down to "growth pains."

The Day the Music Died

Obviously, not controlling the companies that carry your name has its drawbacks. Even as Virgin Media was in the midst of upheaval, Virgin America, one of the many Virgin-branded airlines, was sold to Alaska Airlines in 2016 over Branson's objections. Virgin customers were dismayed. "I love Virgin," a 29-year-old Silicon Valley marketing manager told the *New York Times*. "I think of it as a young, hip airline. Alaska is more of a friendly aunt." A travel industry analyst lamented that trading Virgin America for Alaska "is like giving up your sexy imported sports car for a reliable but unsexy sedan." Branson was no happier. "I'm told some people at Virgin America are calling today 'the day the music died,'" he wrote on the Virgin blog when the sale went through. "It is a sad (and some would say baffling) day." But there was nothing he could do to stop the sale, since American law prevents foreign nationals from owning or controlling more than 25 percent of a US carrier.

Branson had launched Virgin America less than a decade before. Like Virgin Atlantic, it was the experience economy in action. Not surprisingly, its competitors called for an investigation that nearly killed it before it got off the ground. When service finally began, in August 2007, Virgin America became the first airline to offer mood lighting (with settings for "dawn," "dusk," and "blue sky") and individually controlled seatback video screens for every passenger. "You've got a choice," Branson said at a media event when the airline started flying to Dallas a couple of years later. "You can either go on that other carrier, and get their kind of service—which is sort of a bit like those animals over there," he added, gesturing toward some cattle that happened to be penned up nearby. "Or you can come on the Virgin carrier, and you're going to have a blast."

But when Virgin America went public in 2014, other airlines started looking to buy it. Two bidders emerged: jetBlue, a similarly stylish and low-cost alternative to the major domestic carriers, and Alaska Airlines, a Seattle-based company with flights up and down the West Coast. JetBlue wanted to beef up its cross-country offerings, but it wasn't prepared to match the $2.6 billion

Alaska ultimately bid. For Alaska, though, Virgin's California-to-the-East-Coast routes made it a must-have—even if culturally an Alaska-Virgin matchup made no sense whatever.

Before the bidding began, Virgin America released a video that showed what it thought of its competitors: a five-hour-and-45-minute ad that purported to show in real time a Newark-to-San Francisco flight on BLAH Airlines. The viewing experience was excruciating, punctuated as it was by squalling infants, loud pings from the intercom, repeated distribution of free peanuts, and bad jokes from a disturbingly distracted-sounding captain. The passengers were all, quite literally, wooden dummies. A website offered testimonials from past customers:

"They got me to Seattle. I'll give them that."—Megan P., 31, Saratosa [sic], Florida

as well as the expected page of FAQs:

How Can I Get on the Standby List?
You can get on the standby list by standing in line at the airport.

BLAH Airlines was hardly a fair description of Alaska, which at that point had won J. D. Powers' highest rating for customer satisfaction for traditional carriers eight years in a row. But not long before the sale was announced, Alaska released its own video. "The Face on the Tail: An Investigative Film" was a slightly (very slightly) tongue-in-cheek mini-documentary about the Eskimo face that has adorned Alaska's planes since the 1970s. A mock-serious voiceover outlines the quest: to identify the native on the tail of Alaska's planes. After a few false starts the filmmakers end up 30 miles north of the Arctic Circle in a town so remote you can get to it only by air. Various names are floated. "Everybody in Alaska knows who's on the tail," one man declares. "They just can't agree." Laughter all around. Finally the voiceover concludes with a deeper message: "He's a reflection of people. Their stories. Their connection to an airline they love. The presence of something bigger. Something indefinable, flying proudly in the sky, toward an endless horizon." Cue the musical crescendo.

When the Alaska–Virgin America merger was announced, Alaska didn't say if it would keep Virgin's identity or fold Virgin into Alaska. Some even speculated that Alaska might drop its own name and rebrand itself as Virgin America. Alaska's CEO told a J.P. Morgan analyst that the issue "is the thing I am losing the most sleep over." But then, after almost a year, Alaska said it was retiring the Virgin brand. Branson wasn't happy, but given Alaska's resolute unsexiness, the quirky earnestness of its voice, it was a merciful conclusion. Plus it kept him from having to make another hologram appearance.

The Real Thing?

When business involves performance, a bid for the attention of an increasingly distracted public, questions arise that didn't seem of much consequence before. These are the questions Joseph Pine and James Gilmore addressed in *Authenticity*, their follow-up to *The Experience Economy*. "In a world increasingly filled with deliberately and sensationally staged experiences—an increasingly *unreal* world—consumers choose to buy or not buy based on how *real* they perceive an offering to be. Business today, therefore, is all about being real," they wrote. "In any industry where experiences come to the fore, issues of authenticity follow closely behind." In an industry such as air travel, a carrier that offers a staid yet warm and reliable experience and speaks with a voice to match would have to struggle to look witty, sophisticated, and fun. Or in telecom, people might wonder why the fiber guy who shows up at their door, the one who's supposed to make like Branson, seems glum and dispirited instead.

"People no longer accept fake offerings from slickly marketed phonies," Gilmore and Pine wrote; "they want real offerings from genuinely transparent sources." But how do you know what's genuine and what's fake? It's not always easy to tell. Authenticity sounds simple—something either is or it isn't. In fact, it is a notoriously quicksilver quality.

Take the iconic Coca-Cola slogan: "It's the real thing" first turned up on Coke signs in the 1940s, then was made the centerpiece of an ad campaign that began in 1969 and has been reprised several times since. Ira C. Herbert, Coke's brand manager in the late sixties, said the slogan was a response "to research which shows that young people seek the real, the original and the natural as an escape from phoniness" (showing that no, authenticity was not invented yesterday). For Coke, the slogan reaffirmed its status as the original cola, introduced in Atlanta in 1886, 12 years before Pepsi Cola was first served in North Carolina.

How "real" can a sugar-water concoction that started out with cocaine in its formula and ended up sweetened with corn syrup instead of sugar actually be? That depends on your point of view. But it's worth noting that when New Coke was introduced in April 1985 and withdrawn a mere 11 weeks later, a major complaint against it was that it was not, in fact, the real thing.

Pine and Gilmore's test for authenticity was inspired by a famous line from *Hamlet* in which Polonius tells his son Laertes,

> *This above all—to thine own self be true;*
> *And it must follow, as the night the day,*
> *Thou canst not then be false to any man.*

In this Pine and Gilmore found two standards of authenticity: being true to yourself, and being what you say you are to others. The first is an internal test, the second external. Richard Branson is authentic on both counts: he is true to himself (the occasional holographic cameo notwithstanding), and he is what he claims to be—the hippie adventurer who built a global brand by questioning all the rules of business. Virgin Media, not so much. The transparent fakery of Pepsi's "Jump In" video was at the heart of the problem people had with it. But it's hardly the only ad with this issue: advertising, as Pine and Gilmore note, "has become a phoniness-generating machine."

Sometimes, though, what's phony may not seem that way, at least if you don't look into the matter too closely. Authenticity may appear to be an inherent quality, but it's actually a matter of perception, and perceptions can always be manipulated. A good example is Madewell, the line of casual clothing that was introduced by J. Crew in 2006.

In the past few years, Madewell has soared even as the once-popular J. Crew has sunk into decline. (The entire company went into bankruptcy in 2020, felled by the coronavirus, then emerged a few months later with its creditors in control.) Part of Madewell's appeal, at least at first, was its apparent authenticity. Its LinkedIn page said it "was started in 1937 as a workwear company" and was "always looking to the brand's roots for inspiration." Its Instagram and Twitter handles were @Madewell1937. But the 1937 Madewell was a no-nonsense New England company that made heavy denim overalls for dockworkers and the like. Its last factory closed in 1989. In 2004 its trademark—all that was left by that point—was acquired by Mickey Drexler, the newly named CEO of J. Crew. Two years after that, Drexler resurrected the Madewell name and logo for J. Crew's new womenswear stores. As Dan

Nosowitz, a descendant of Madewell's founder, wrote in an eye-opening account on *BuzzFeed*, Drexler "shrewdly read the market and realized that stocking nice clothes wouldn't be enough: He'd have to tell a story along with them. Drexler didn't have any stories, so he bought ours."

When Stories Aren't Enough: Burberry

Burberry was in an entirely different position. A nineteenth-century English "heritage brand" known for its classic trench coats and its signature check, it had a fabulous story but had nonetheless sunk low by the end of its first 140 years. Then, under a succession of strong chief executives and a brilliant creative director, it staged an astonishing recovery, its revenues rising tenfold and its profits close to twentyfold in an 18-year sprint. Authentic storytelling and a strong, clear voice were key elements in the company's success—but then it stumbled. Here's what happened.

In 2001, when 30-year-old Christopher Bailey was named design director, it was a dubious honor. There were intimations of a turnaround, but no clear sense that it would last. The chief executive, Rose Marie Bravo, had been brought in from the States to salvage the brand, but despite some progress it was still beset by cheap counterfeits and constrained by licensing deals outside the UK that gave away much of its profit. Bravo had decided to make the distinctive "Burberry check" as ubiquitous as Prada's inverted triangle logo, splashing it on hats, luggage, bikinis, bandanas, even baby booties in vivid colors like pink and purple. But that tactic was backfiring. Intended for an upscale market, Burberry was instead becoming the uniform of choice for football hooligans and chavs—loutish, working-class youths with a taste for bling. It reached the point that pubs across the UK started banning people dressed in Burberry.

The nadir came in 2002, when Danniella Westbrook—on-again/off-again actress on the BBC nighttime soap *EastEnders*, so in thrall to cocaine it had eaten away her septum—was caught on the street in a paparazzi shot, "clad top to toe," as the *Guardian* put it, "in Burberry check: the hat, the skirt, the scarf, her baby dressed up to match, as if she had gorged herself upon it, rolled about in it like a pig in muck." So much for "the much heralded Burberry revival," the paper concluded. The only person who wasn't appalled by this display, apparently, was Christopher Bailey, the new design chief, who came to her defense in an interview. "I felt very uncomfortable with all the media aggression towards this one person," he said later. "But also, I am just not snobby. I grew up in a working-class family. I went to quite a tough school."

Given his class background, Bailey was hardly an obvious choice to help transform a failing English trench coat manufacturer into a full-fledged luxury brand. He'd grown up amid the failing coal mines and woolen mills of West Yorkshire, his father a carpenter, his mother a window dresser for the Marks & Spencer department store chain. Home was a modest row house of the type common to English mill towns; he got chased there from school a lot. "You didn't aspire to do anything other than going into the army or working in a shop or factory," he said. "You know that film *Billy Elliot*?"—about a coal miner's son in the North of England who desperately wants to be a ballet dancer. "I strongly related to that when I saw it."

Encouraged by an art teacher in secondary school, Bailey went to London to study fashion. At one point he went to a store on Bond Street to buy a watch for his mother for Christmas with money his father had saved up. The reception he got there has never left him. "I felt so belittled," he told me. "It felt like the antithesis of the magical experience that we had anticipated it being. And I had to lie to my dad about the experience, which made me feel even more wretched. And subsequently to my mum, when she opened it on Christmas Day and I said, 'Oh, you'll never believe, I went into this magical space, and these people showed me . . . ' It was an illusion that really was shattered. I remember so vividly coming out of that shop on Bond Street and saying that if ever I'm in a position where I get to make somebody feel special and magical, I'm going to do my most, I'm going to work the hardest to make sure that no matter whether you're buying the least expensive or the most expensive, it's the same experience."

After he graduated, Bailey worked first at Donna Karan in New York, then with Tom Ford at Gucci in Milan before being recruited to come back to London. In 2006, when Rose Marie Bravo decided to step down, he suggested for her replacement Angela Ahrendts, an American fashion executive he had worked with at Donna Karan. Income and profits had risen steadily under Bravo, but there was still a lot to do. Ahrendts got a sense of how much at her first strategic planning meeting, when she greeted 60-odd managers from around the world on a rainy day and realized that not one of them was wearing Burberry. Meanwhile, their stores were still selling everything from kilts to dog leashes. "There's nothing wrong with any of those products individually, but together they added up to just a lot of stuff," she recalled later. "In luxury, ubiquity will kill you—it means you're not really luxury anymore. And we were becoming ubiquitous."

To bring some coherence to the brand, Ahrendts disbanded Burberry's semiautonomous design teams in Hong Kong and New York and made Bailey the company's global "brand czar," overseeing everything that touched customers anywhere in the world. She and Bailey decided to target Millennials, a group she saw as "the luxury customers of the future"—even if they weren't the luxury customers of today. Ahrendts and Bailey also decided to focus on the company's iconic yet neglected trench coats, made from gabardine, the water-resistant fabric that Thomas Burberry himself had invented in 1879, 23 years after opening his first shop. Much as Louis Vuitton had built a luxury brand around luggage, they would go back to trench coats and grow from there.

What ensued over the next several years was a near-flawless case of brand-building. The focus on Millennials meant appealing to a group that had little knowledge of Burberry's past, so the company could emphasize heritage and craftsmanship—that is, authenticity—while at the same time appearing fresh. And it could do this by promoting the trench coat on social media, which itself was new and fresh at the time. On the short-form blogging site Tumblr, Ahrendts and Bailey set up The Art of the Trench, where people could post photos of themselves in their Burberry trench coats. In 2010 they created Burberry Acoustic, a page on the burberry.com website to showcase specially recorded videos of young British rock musicians. At a time when the typical visit to burberry.com lasted 7.8 minutes, people averaged 18 minutes on Burberry Acoustic.

This was not the sort of thing that luxury brands did, but as an ambitious upstart trying to compete with far bigger, more successful companies, Burberry didn't have other options. "We couldn't afford six pages in this glossy magazine," Bailey said. "We couldn't afford *one* page in a glossy magazine." Also, Bailey loved the Internet. "As a designer, I can't think of anything more wonderful. You've got movement, you've got sound, you've got color, you've got communities, you can engage with people directly. You're in their bedrooms, in their sitting rooms. So I found it very exciting. But it was a very misunderstood concept, digital. Fashion was quite late to the party."

Like other entrenched industries, fashion had no appetite for disruption. But Burberry's embrace of digital was more than opportunistic. It expressed a conception of luxury that was both expansive and democratic, embracing anyone who appreciates craftsmanship and design. Bailey is dismissive of those who say they're too special for digital—"like, *bullshit*, you know? A luxury customer is just the same as anybody in the world. That's what I always felt, and it goes back to my experience of buying that watch." At the same time, his approach was experiential rather than transactional, and that put it squarely in line with the Millennials Burberry sought. "I always felt it doesn't matter if somebody goes online or walks into one of our shops and they can never imagine having enough money to buy a product," he said. "That was irrelevant. Burberry for me was about experiencing this thing and maybe one day you might find something from Burberry, but if you don't, that's okay. It was not just about selling."

The apotheosis of this approach was Burberry Bespoke, a page on burberry.com where people could design their own trench coats. There were thousands of options to choose from: color, cut, and length, along with any number of different belts, epaulets, buttons, linings, collars, cuff straps, and so on—enough to yield 12 million possible combinations. With prices in the US starting at $1,800 and running as high as $8,800, reporters wondered how many the company could possibly sell. "Honestly, it makes no difference at all," Ahrendts told them. "It's customer engagement. You want them to engage with the brand." People didn't even have to buy what they'd created; they could simply post their combinations on social media.

"Social media was all about expressing your personality," Bailey explained, "and Bespoke was a part of that. It was all these people from completely different worlds, from Korea and Tokyo and New York or Edinburgh, all these people suddenly creating a community and commenting as they'd upload their own image. Hundreds, thousands of images we used to get. I started using it in the studio to inspire new designs because, wow, have you seen the way that this woman or this guy has put together this trench coat? We should look at this! And so it started to feed us."

Not for nothing was burberry.com called Burberry World: it was the center, the hub that kept the whole narrative going. Burberry Acoustic was part of the story. Burberry Bespoke was part of the story. And the story was told anywhere the company could find a place to tell it, even on digital tags sewn into Burberry garments: hold one up before an RFID-enabled mirror in Burberry's flagship store on Regent Street—otherwise known as Burberry World Live—and the mirror would transform itself into a video screen displaying the story of the product.

But the most extraordinary thing about Burberry was its voice. With other luxury brands, you often get the sense that the merchandise is expensive because it is expensive. Bailey ventured beneath the glossy surface to show the pride and craftsmanship within. "It was less about the finished thing, the finished, final, perfect thing, than it was the imperfect and the story behind it," he said. "Not the made thing, but how is it made? Because that's actually intriguing." Witness a black-and-white television spot, wordless but set to thundering chords from the English indie group Morning Runner, that mixed vintage footage from the mills with iconic views of Tower Bridge and the Union Jack before concluding with an impeccably suited Eddie Redmayne, looking rather iconic himself.

Bailey's Burberry "projected an RP kind of Britishness," wrote the *Guardian*'s fashion editor, Jess Cartner-Morley—RP meaning "Received Pronunciation," the accent of the Oxbridge elite. It was a voice that fit the brand perfectly, and even though Bailey hailed from the postindustrial North it suited the man he had become. And yet Burberry also resonated with the boy he had been. "I used to cycle a lot as a kid, along Haworth moor, near where the Brontës lived," he told Cartner-Morley. "When it's sunny, it's beautiful, but when it's misty and rainy, it's almost more magical. I love proper weather." No wonder he and Ahrendts began by going back to the trench coat. "I suppose, in a way, I made Burberry up to suit myself. I am from Yorkshire, I grew up cycling in the rain. Someone else might have seen this brand quite differently."

A New Day, a New Story

Then, in October 2013, it was announced that Angela Ahrendts would leave Burberry to become head of retail and online stores for Apple. Bailey would take over as chief executive in addition to chief creative officer. Together they had had an extraordinary run: revenues, which had stood at £428 million when Bailey joined in 2001 and £743 million when Ahrendts took over in 2006, would that year exceed £2.3 billion (nearly $3.7 billion US). Adjusted operating profit during the same 12-year period went from £69 million to £166 million to more than £460 million (nearly $740 million US)—a nearly sevenfold increase. Burberry was the equal of nearly any fashion brand in Paris or Milan—a status no other British company could claim. And yet, Bailey told me, "I hadn't finished. I guess I could have decided to step back then, but I felt that I still had more to do. And the board were very keen that I take over the role as well." But outside Burberry's beautifully renovated headquarters in an art deco office block on Westminster's Horseferry Road, concerns were raised immediately. An analyst in Paris said she was "astounded by the idea. . . . It's too much for one man." She was not alone—nor was she wrong.

Sales and profits, both of which had risen steadily for more than a decade, began to wobble not long after Bailey's ascension. China and Hong Kong had been the focus of a huge push that began in 2010—but sales there turned soft as Bailey was taking over, thanks to political unrest in Hong Kong and uncertainty on the mainland. China's rich started going to shop in Europe and Japan, where Burberry was seriously underrepresented by comparison with other luxury brands. Sales fell in the US as well. Profits dropped by 10 percent. The stock price slid by nearly 40 percent. Major investors started asking for Bailey's head.

In July 2016, a little more than two years after Bailey assumed the CEO role, the company announced that he would relinquish it to Mario Gobbetti, chief executive of the French luxury brand Céline. Gobbetti was a known quantity in the fashion trade, a veteran of Givenchy, Moschino, and Bottega Veneta who had revivified Céline as Bravo and Ahrendts had rescued Burberry. Bailey would stay on as president and chief creative officer. The hope was that he would forge the kind of partnership with Gobbetti that he had had with Ahrendts. Instead, Burberry announced his departure not long after Gobbetti took over. His replacement: Riccardo Tisci, who had earlier worked side by side with Gobbetti to revive Givenchy.

Tisci is by all accounts a brilliant designer. And though his background is southern Italian—his parents came from a coastal city in Puglia, in the heel of Italy's boot—he has some British bona fides. In the nineties he studied by day at Central Saint Martins, London's leading fashion school, and went clubbing by night, rubbing shoulders with the likes of Kate Moss and Vivienne Westwood. Yet his sensibilities are distinctly Continental—dark, gothic, sensual, edgy. When his appointment was announced, *British Vogue* reported, "shockwaves reverberated through the industry." Tisci's response: "It's a new dawn, a new day, a new story both for me and for Burberry."

The thing was, Burberry didn't need a new story; it needed stronger management. But apparently it had to get both. Bailey's last show—"the final chapter in nearly two decades of compelling storytelling," as the *Guardian*'s Cartner-Morley put it—was a rainbow-hued tribute to gay youth. As Bailey moved toward the exit, his burden lightened considerably by a golden handshake worth some £13 million (worth at that point well over $17 million), it became clear that Tisci saw the brand quite differently.

There was a key moment early on, at the February 2019 show for the fall/winter women's collection. It happened on Instagram, when Liz Kennedy, a Burberry model, posted photos of another model on Burberry's runway, wearing a hoodie with the drawstring tied quite conspicuously in a noose. Alongside the photos she wrote, "Suicide is not fashion. It is not glamorous nor edgy and since this show is dedicated to the youth expressing their voice, here I go. Riccardo Tisci and everyone at Burberry it is beyond me how you could let a look resembling a noose hanging from a neck out on the runway."

In the ensuing blowback, Tisci professed to be "so deeply sorry for the distress that has been caused" and claimed, somewhat bizarrely, that the design was actually "inspired by a nautical theme." Gobbetti issued a similar apology. But it did not go unnoted that Burberry was the third luxury fashion brand to evoke a racist meme in as many months. Weeks earlier, with the governor and the attorney general of Virginia in the news for apparently wearing blackface in college yearbook photos, Gucci had come out with an $890 black turtleneck designed to roll up around the face, with a bizarre cutout for the mouth edged in what could only be taken for enormous red lips. In December, shortly after a young Hitler admirer was convicted of murder after driving into a crowd of people who were protesting a white supremacist rally in Charlottesville, Virginia, Prada was caught decorating a lower Manhattan store window with $550 black monkey trinkets that had bulging eyes and big red lips. Gucci apologized "deeply" and professed diversity to be "a fundamental value." Prada claimed to "abhor all forms of racism" and vowed to form an advisory council "to guide our efforts on diversity."

Seriously? "This shit is for attention," tweeted Dani Kwateng-Clark, an editor at Vice Media. "There's no fathomable way that fashion pulls from art and culture, yet is completely oblivious to triggering symbols." A year later, of course, these brands would be banging the Black Lives Matter drum.

Belonging

Burberry would eventually right itself, innovations by Tisci leading to growing sales. At the same time its voice was shifting, an even older British institution was going through a similarly dramatic transition. It began in 2017, when the British Army put out a new set of recruitment ads. The old ads were what you'd expect—loud and full of guns. The new ads talked about *feelings*. They did so quietly and unexpectedly—as in a wordless 20-second video that showed a young soldier shivering in a driving rain, breathing rapidly, lost in himself. His jungle encampment is a sodden hellhole. But then he's joined by a mate who pours him a mug of tea from a thermos. Within moments he's surrounded by more of his mates, and when one of them playfully ruffles his hair the guy can't help but laugh. The words "This Is Belonging" appear on-screen.

The British Army's "This Is Belonging" campaign was created by Karmarama, a small, innovative London agency whose executive chair is Jon Wilkins, one of the cofounders of Naked. The brief was simple if daunting: find a way to reach a broader group of young people than the working-class white males who have traditionally formed the army's recruitment pool. That pool was getting shallower. The number of 16- and 17-year-olds—prime recruiting age in the UK—was at its lowest level since 1996. Low unemployment in Scotland and the North of England meant fewer recruits from areas the army had long relied on. Attitudes toward war had turned negative following Britain's involvement in the post-9/11 fighting in Iraq and Afghanistan. And the army itself was shrinking—troop strength was half what it had been in the 1982 Falkland Islands war, so far fewer young people had a friend or family member in the army. They weren't watching much television, either: as Karmarama and MediaCom, the campaign's media-buying agency, noted in a report, "Their world is digital, social, and private." On top of all this, there was the problem of "khaki blindness": the army's guns-and-tanks recruitment spots were so routine and predictable that no one even noticed them.

The normal agency tactic in a situation like this is to do lots of research. Karmarama was no different, except that its research relied on machine learning and artificial intelligence, fields that are outside the ken of most agencies. A specially formulated algorithm scraped online profiles of soldiers and matched their interactions with army recruiters with their social media posts. This allowed the agency to see what motivated them at various points in the recruitment process. Karmarama found the expected drivers: leadership, adventure, challenge, making a difference. But when the agency went out to barracks to talk with soldiers face to face, it discovered an entirely different reality.

"We expected to hear these rational things, but we didn't hear any of that," said Charlotte Farrington, who spearheaded the campaign. "The thing that kept coming back was not what the Army talked about. It was community, family, brotherhood, sisterhood. Some people called it love." That was what you really got from joining the army: as the Karmarama/MediaCom report noted, "The benefit was *each other*."

"The need to belong can be considered a fundamental human motivation," Roy Baumeister and Mark Leary concluded in one of the most influential papers in psychology in recent decades. This is not necessarily a good thing: "It may be no accident that people seem most likely to be prejudiced against members of groups to which they have little or no opportunity to belong," the paper continued. "Thus, the most common and widespread bases of prejudice are race, gender, and national origin. People bolster their own in-group at the expense of out-groups from which they are excluded." But the army is different: it's a group to which, in theory at least, any Briton can belong.

Belonging is nothing new to army life—it's closely tied to camaraderie, the mutual trust that soldiers have always relied on in combat. But it hadn't been touted in recruitment ads, nor had it led the soldiers Karmarama talked with to join. It was something they discovered after they signed up. When the creative team talked with soldiers about the 12 functional drivers they'd identified—leadership, adventure, challenge, and the like—they realized that belonging played a part in each one. A sense of belonging makes it possible to challenge yourself, to grow into a leader; strong bonds with others make it more meaningful to travel the world or have an adventure. And when soldiers leave the army, said Farrington, "the one thing they miss most is that feeling of kinship."

The idea was to express that feeling through true stories of life in the army. After three months of collecting anecdotes from soldiers in army barracks, the Karmarama team went back to London to turn the five best into scripts. They hired documentary filmmakers to shoot the videos and insisted on casting actual soldiers rather than actors, sometimes to the filmmakers' dismay. Authenticity would be critical here. "Where everybody else was trying to give 10 rational messages, we just showed human emotion," Farrington told me. The result: applications to join went up 38 percent for the year; applications to join the reserves shot up 48 percent. Even applications to join the officer corps went up.

For year two of "This Is Belonging," the message was that the army is in fact a group to which any Briton can belong—gay or straight, male or female, Christian or Muslim. Soldiers had already been in evidence at gay pride marches in London, Manchester, and other cities. Karmarama put out "Army Pride Camo" face-paint sticks, not in the usual camouflage hues of black, green, and brown but in the colors of the rainbow flag, in a plastic holder that read:

> NORMAL CAMO IS FOR BLENDING IN
> TODAY IS FOR STANDING OUT
> #THISISBELONGING

Now the message was broadened. In a video called "Keeping My Faith," a squad on patrol halts while a Muslim recruit prays to Mecca. In "Expressing My Emotions," an older soldier in the jungle reads a letter from home with tears on his face. In a series of animated videos, soldiers in voiceover address such issues as "What If I Get Emotional in the Army?" and "Can I Be Gay in the Army?"

As it turned out, some people got very emotional about the idea of expressing emotion in the army. "It's Fine to Cry, Army Tells New Recruits" blared a headline in the *Sunday Times*. "It's no good just having an army that is jolly nice to people," a retired general harrumphed on BBC Radio 4, Britain's leading news and talk station. On ITV's *Good Morning, Britain*, cohost Piers Morgan—never one to dodge a chance to grandstand—denounced the campaign as an "assault on modern masculinity." In the *Sun*, a retired colonel—Richard Kemp, best-selling author and former commander of British forces in Afghanistan—accused politicians of "dangerous political correctness" and suggested that all this "soft, touchy-feely, caring-sharing" stuff would invite aggression from Britain's foes. "Images of combat," he declared on the BBC, were what Britain needed.

"It's amazing how much vitriol the campaign got," Wilkins, the Karmarama chair, told me. Year three of the campaign created yet more controversy, with World War I–style posters playing against generational stereotypes with messages like "Snow Flakes: Your Army Needs YOU and Your Compassion" and "Binge Gamers: Your Army Needs YOU and Your Drive." But despite the flak, it generated a wave of applications—9,700 in the first three weeks of January alone, nearly double the number for the whole of January 2018. By the end of the year, applications were up more than 70 percent over the year before. The 2020 campaign, built on the idea that army service gives you confidence—one ad showed a series of beers with the words, "Confidence can last for the night or it can last a lifetime"—got off to an even better start. Bloviating ex-colonels and television hosts, it turns out, were not actually the people army recruitment campaigns needed to reach.

Finding Your Voice

As Virgin, Burberry, and the British Army all discovered, voice is a tricky proposition. Establishing it, as Virgin did, is crucial. Maintaining it, as Virgin and Burberry both found, is a constant challenge. Changing it, as the British Army tried to do, is fraught. It's so closely tied to identity, and at the core of identity is emotion, the lingua franca of stories.

To communicate successfully, your voice needs to be authentic, consistent, and appropriate. The uproar over the British Army's "This Is Belonging" campaign was all about appropriateness: was it fitting for the army to speak in terms of belonging and inclusion and emotional connection, or was it obliged to appeal to a fascination with guns and mayhem? So it was with the backlash against Burberry's noose-tied hoodie: was it appropriate for a luxury fashion brand to reference suicide and lynching in a clothing line for young women? Authenticity was at the core of the Virgin America/Alaska Airlines conundrum: could the folks behind Alaska's homespun "Face on the Tail" video promise—much less deliver—an experience that was "red-hot"? And consistency was at issue in all three cases: should the British Army speak to prospective recruits with a voice that's loud and bellicose or move to something warmer and more welcoming? Should Burberry maintain its plummy "RP" tones or go for something darker and more Goth? Could Alaska be homey and cosmopolitan at the same time?

Since voice is an expression of personality, a brand's—or an organization's—personality will be key to determining its voice. Beginning in the 1980s, psychologists in the field of trait theory have hypothesized that personality attributes in humans can be reduced to the "Big Five," sometimes known by the acronym OCEAN: openness, conscientiousness, extraversion, agreeableness, and neuroticism. Each of these represents a continuum, not an either/or. People who are open tend to be more creative and adventurous than unimaginative and resistant to change. People who are conscientious are more detail-oriented and well-prepared than messy and disorganized. Extraverts are sociable and attention-seeking rather than awkward and retiring. Agreeableness is a measure of empathy and altruism versus narcissism and thoughtlessness. Neuroticism is marked by anxiety and emotional instability as opposed to optimism and resilience.

In 1997, Jennifer Aaker—then at UCLA, now a professor at Stanford Business School—proposed a comparable personality scheme for brands. After extensive research, she came up with five key dimensions of brand personality: sincerity (epitomized by Hallmark cards), excitement (MTV), competence (the *Wall Street Journal*), sophistication (Guess jeans), and ruggedness (Nike). Brands that exhibit sincerity are said to be down-to-earth, honest, wholesome, and cheerful; Alaska Airlines would certainly qualify. MTV doesn't seem that exciting (daring, spirited, imaginative, up-to-date) any more, but Red Bull does. Competence (reliability, intelligence, success) is exhibited by Warby Parker as well as by the *Wall Street Journal*. Sophistication (defined as upper-class or charming in Aaker's scheme of things) seemed characteristic of Guess and Kate Spade 20-odd years ago; since then it has taken root at Apple, as evidenced by the sleek, minimal designs of its products and stores alike. Ruggedness (outdoorsy, tough) is as much in evidence at Patagonia as it is at Nike. Each of these brands speaks with a single voice—a voice that suits its personality.

Finding that voice and negotiating the emotional terrain it evokes is a three-stage process. First you need to do the kind of inventory Virgin Group undertook. Start by pulling together all your existing communications—ads, videos, web copy, blog posts, email blasts, white papers, logos, taglines, the lot of it. What do they say about you? Do they add up to a portrait that's clean and coherent, or is it just a jumble? Look anew at your audience (consumers, fans): Who are they? What do they say about you? And then ask how much of what you're doing is appropriate—to who you are, to who *they* are, to what they expect from you.

Second—and again, like Virgin—you need to capture the essence of your voice. Start by locating your brand in Aaker's five-part brand personality framework. How would you describe that personality in a few well-chosen words? Then describe the voice that personality would speak with. What sort of things would it say, and how would it say them? That's how "The Virgin

Way" came to have its simple descriptors—simple and straight-forward, youthful exuberance, witty. The goal is to match your voice to your brand. To sound authentic. If your brand is authentic, you'll want to let everyone know—but quietly, please. Shouting won't help. If it's not—well, you can always try faking it. It worked for Madewell.

Finally, you'll need to codify your voice so it can be replicated by anyone in your organization. To do this, build out the brief descriptions you created at stage 2. Use plenty of examples, or do's and don'ts. A key facet of voice is tone—not what you say or even the words you choose, but how you say them. Voice is a constant, but tone—formal or informal, jokey or serious—can change to suit the situation. Be as specific as possible. Mailchimp, for example, the email marketing platform used at last count by some 11 million organizations, came up with this:

1. **We are plainspoken.** We understand the world our customers are living in: one muddled by hyperbolic language, upsells, and over-promises. We strip all that away and value clarity above all. Because businesses come to Mailchimp to get to work, we avoid distractions like fluffy metaphors and cheap plays to emotion.

2. **We are genuine.** We get small businesses because we were one not too long ago. That means we relate to customers' challenges and passions and speak to them in a familiar, warm, and accessible way.

3. **We are translators.** Only experts can make what's difficult look easy, and it's our job to demystify B2B-speak and actually educate.

4. **Our humor is dry.** Our sense of humor is straight-faced, subtle, and a touch eccentric. We're weird but not inappropriate, smart but not snobbish. We prefer winking to shout-

ing. We're never condescending or exclusive—we always bring our customers in on the joke.

And make sure everyone in your organization understands what your brand's voice involves, because whatever your voice is, it has to be consistent.

Once you've developed a voice, the next step is to create not just a brand but a platform—a construct that can transform your offering from a product to a network. And in the digital age, a platform is what you want to have.

8. Platform

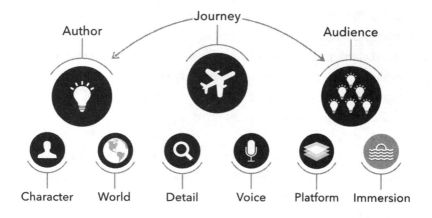

W hen Charlie Collier, then the president of AMC, wrote about the rise of immersive television a few years back, he singled out what the network was doing for its most popular show. *The Walking Dead*, he wrote,

> exists on television as a live event for only 16 nights a year, but remains an active and vibrant community all year long. Fan events, panels, releases of clips and images, ongoing discussions and a strong social presence keep the series very much front and center all year long. . . . Immersive dramas both benefit from and demand this kind of commitment.

What has happened with media properties like *The Walking Dead* is unprecedented. No longer is a TV show simply a TV show, or a movie just a movie. As technology gives rise to an ever-proliferating array of digital media and devices, stories are being told on multiple media at once—on television, online, through books and games, through physical experiences in the real world. This is deep media, and it's been happening for well over a decade. But what was still experimental in the case of "Why So Serious?," the alternate reality game developed by 42 Entertainment to promote Christopher Nolan's *The Dark Knight*, or Dunder Mifflin Infinity, the online extension of the US version of *The Office*, has since given rise to a new way of operating in the entertainment industry. This is occurring partly because fans demand it and partly because companies like AMC see it as a marketing opportunity. But what Collier is describing is more than a labor-intensive, year-round promo effort. AMC has created an online information exchange around *The Walking Dead*—a service fans can use to access information about the show and its characters and to interact with fellow fans. In the process, AMC has created a blueprint for how to transform a television series—or, by extension, any kind of business that relies on storytelling—from a product to a platform.

The distinction is crucial. A *product* is made by one group of people for other people to buy or rent or otherwise consume. Products can be goods or services or experiences. Coffee beans, a cup of coffee, a cappuccino made to order at Starbucks—all these are products. A *platform* is—well, as my Columbia colleague David Rogers points out in *The Digital Transformation Playbook*, "Vagueness abounds in the current use of the word."

To technologists, a platform is a machine, like PlayStation or Xbox, or a software environment, like macOS or Microsoft Windows. Media and advertising executives think of platforms as

the businesses and technologies they rely on for distribution—
broadcast, cable, mobile. To economists, a platform is a business
that connects different groups of people, often through websites
or apps: Airbnb. Uber and Lyft. Etsy and eBay. YouTube. Facebook. Amazon. But its "most general meaning," Rogers notes, "is
'something on which you can build.'"

As this last list suggests, platform business models are central
to the digital disruption of the past 20 years. As I write this, seven
of the world's ten most highly valued public companies have platform business models, at least in part: Alibaba, Alphabet (Google's
parent), Amazon, Apple, Facebook, Microsoft, and Tencent. (The
other three are Berkshire Hathaway, Tesla, and TSMC, the Taiwan-
based semiconductor manufacturer.) Each of these seven corpora-
tions runs what's known as a two-sided or multisided platform,
meaning they create a market that brings different types of people
together. (One-sided platforms, by contrast, connect customers
with a product and its producers.) Hotel chains and taxi companies sell hotel rooms and taxi rides. Airbnb, Uber, and Lyft serve
as an exchange, connecting people who have a spare room or an
idle car with people who need a place to stay or a ride across town.

There are several advantages to being in this kind of business.
First, and not surprisingly, it's much cheaper to run an exchange
than it is to amass a string of hotels or a fleet of taxis. Before
the coronavirus upended the entire travel industry, Airbnb had
some seven million listings in 100,000 cities around the world—
and managed it all with fewer than 13,500 employees, or one
for every 520 listings. Marriott had 174,000 employees and fewer
than 1.4 million rooms, which works out to one person for about
every eight rooms. At the same time, platform businesses offload
the financial risk of building products and maintaining an inventory that might not sell. In an economic downturn, Marriott
might have to close some of its hotels and stop construction on

others, throwing people out of work. As more and more workers lose their jobs, they could list their properties on Airbnb, causing its inventory to soar at very little cost to the company—which in turn would put further strain on hotel chains.*

A second advantage is that platforms benefit from network effects: the more users they have, the more valuable they become, both to the people using them and the people who own them. This was apparent at the introduction of the telephone, a device so novel that early on it was leased in pairs. The same dynamic was at work in 2009, when WhatsApp gave people the ability to send free text messages to other people—as long as they were WhatsApp users too. Growth was slow at first. But within five years, WhatsApp had 470 million users per month and was bought by Facebook for $19 billion. Like telephone networks, WhatsApp is considered a one-sided platform because it connects only one class of customers to its servers. Network effects can be even stronger with two-sided platforms like eBay, where more sellers attract more buyers and vice versa.

Another intriguing fact about WhatsApp: by the time the Facebook deal closed, it had 600 million users per month—but still only about 70 employees. That works out to about 8,600 users per employee, which is so few as to make Airbnb look like some sort of full employment scheme. This points to a third advantage that platforms enjoy: vast economies of scale. Not only is it cheaper and less risky to run an exchange than it is to make products and then try to sell them; as more and more users join

---

* The coronavirus pandemic was hardly a normal downturn. Hotel chains suffered tremendously, but with people afraid to travel, Airbnb didn't fare well either. Not until CEO Brian Chesky instituted painful cutbacks and reoriented listings to feature vacation rentals within driving distance of major cities did the company start to turn around.

the platform, the cost of serving each one goes down, making it even harder for others to compete.

A fourth advantage: platform owners collect the data that comes from having a direct relationship with customers. Taxi companies respond to random pickup requests; Uber and Lyft know where you live. They have detailed customer profiles, thanks to apps that know everywhere you go and track your progress moment by moment. Television networks connect advertisers with audiences, but until quite recently their actual customers weren't people watching TV but the cable and satellite companies that carried the signal to those customers. Not all direct-to-consumer companies run a multisided platform: Netflix is considered a one-sided platform because it carries no ads, but nonetheless it not only knows who its viewers are, it also has detailed data on their tastes and preferences. Still, the ability to provide a direct connection with customers is one of the most powerful benefits a digital platform can offer.

Economists have devoted a lot of attention to the platform phenomenon in recent years—not too surprising, given how these companies have come to dominate the stock market. The first step—identifying such companies as special and different—was taken in a 2003 paper on two-sided markets by Jean-Charles Rochet and Jean Tirole of the University of Toulouse. Building on their work, David Evans of the University of Chicago and Richard Schmalensee of MIT's Sloan School of Management identified four broad categories of platforms: exchanges, ad-supported media, transaction systems, and software platforms. What they all have in common is the ability to bring together different groups of people for their mutual benefit.

Exchanges bring together buyers and sellers: eBay, Airbnb, Uber, Lyft. We've had exchanges for centuries: the first modern stock exchange is said to have been set up in Amsterdam by the Dutch East India Company in 1611, and some trace the idea back even further. Other long-standing exchange-type businesses include auction houses and various sorts of brokers and agents, including literary agents (who connect authors and publishers), talent agents (entertainers and producers), real estate agents (buyers and sellers), and insurance brokers (insurers and owners). More recently, the Internet has given rise to dating sites, hookup apps, online forums, social media sites, and any number of other information exchanges that can connect millions, even billions of users.

Advertising platforms bring together advertisers and audiences (or readers): television networks, newspapers, magazines, social media sites. To attract audiences, conventional media platforms license content from outside producers or hire people to create it in-house; the bigger the audience, the more attractive it will be to advertisers. With digital media, the size of the audience matters less than how "relevant" the ads are to individual users. This helps explain why Google and Facebook between them carry, according to the research firm eMarketer, more than half of all digital advertising in the US and nearly 70 percent of that in the UK.

Transaction systems connect merchants, consumers, and banks: Visa, Mastercard, PayPal, Apple Pay. Network effects are particularly strong here, since merchants won't want to install card readers if there aren't many people using the cards, and consumers won't want to sign up for a card if most merchants won't accept it.

Technology platforms establish software and hardware standards for others to follow. This rarely happens without a fight:

Sony's Blu-ray v. Toshiba's HD-DVD for high-definition DVDs, Sony's PlayStation v. Microsoft's Xbox for videogames, Apple's macOS v. Microsoft's Windows for personal computers, Apple's iOS v. Google's Android for smartphones. Sometimes competing platforms manage to coexist; other times, only one will survive. As Rogers points out in *The Digital Transformation Playbook*, the winner-take-all effect is particularly acute when the differentiation between two standards is low and the cost of switching is high. With high-def DVD players, for instance, one worked about as well as the other, and nobody would want to own two of them, so the choice largely came down to which system had the best selection of movies, TV shows, and video games. Sony owned a major Hollywood studio and was able to bundle Blu-ray with the PlayStation video game console—so it was game over for Toshiba.

Building a Platform

Companies that have a platform business model generally operate at an economic advantage, because making products is expensive and inherently risky. Yet it's possible to be a product company and a platform company at the same time. Not only is it possible—it can make the product that much more desirable.

Apple, for example, is celebrated for the products it makes—the Mac, the iPod, the iPad, the iPhone. But what made the iPod a success where earlier MP3 players failed was Apple's iTunes Store—once Steve Jobs agreed to make iTunes compatible with Windows computers. A few years later, the App Store made the iPhone a runaway hit—but not until Jobs agreed to open the App Store to outside developers rather than have Apple build all its apps in-house. If he hadn't done so, Steve Ballmer, Microsoft's then-CEO, might well have been right when he declared in 2007 that there was "no chance that the iPhone is going to get any significant market share. No chance."

To understand why that one decision made such a difference, we need to take a detour into economics. The idea is one we're all familiar with: the lower the price, the greater the demand, all else being equal. But when a lot of free apps become available for the iPhone, suddenly all else is *not* equal. As Andrew McAfee of MIT and Erik Brynjolfsson of Stanford explain in their book *Machine | Platform | Crowd*, "An expensive phone doesn't become that much more attractive a purchase because there's one desirable and free app available for it. But what about when there are hundreds of thousands of free apps, a large subset of which are going to be desirable to almost any imaginable customer?" In case you were wondering why iPhones cost so much.

Beyond Tractors

But it's not only Silicon Valley companies like Apple that can leverage the power of the platform to sell products. In their book *Platform Revolution*, Geoffrey Parker of Dartmouth, Marshall Van Alstyne of Boston University, and Sangeet Paul Choudary put it this way: "Can any product or service become the basis of a platform business? Here's the test: if the firm can use either information or community to add value to what it sells, then there is potential for creating a viable platform."

Use information or community to add value. That brings to mind John Deere, the tractor and heavy equipment manufacturer. John Deere—the actual person—was 33 years old when he started a blacksmith shop in Illinois in 1837. A recent transplant from Vermont, Deere saw that the horse-drawn iron plows of the day weren't working well in the dense clay soil of the prairie, so he crafted a smooth-sided, self-scouring steel plow that did the job better. Then he started manufacturing them in advance so customers wouldn't have to wait for their order to be filled. As the years wore on, his company introduced still better plows, then horse-drawn manure spreaders, and eventually gasoline-powered tractors, diesel tractors, combine harvesters, rotary combines, cotton pickers, seed drills . . .

Then, in 2012—175 years after Deere opened his blacksmith shop—company executives flipped the switch on MyJohnDeere .com, an online information exchange for farmers. Free to anyone who has purchased John Deere products, accessible via smartphone and tablet as well as computer, it brings big data to the cornfield. What Nike+ did for runners, MyJohnDeere does for farmers: provide up-to-the-moment information from sensors on the equipment it sells, in addition to historical data on soil conditions and crop yields, software from outside suppliers, and connections to other people in the ag world.

It adds up to a radical reenvisioning of what John Deere is and why it exists. As Sunil Gupta of Harvard Business School put it, the real question is, "What business are you in?"

> For the longest time, if you asked John Deere this question, the company would say they are in the business of producing farm equipment . . . but if you look at it from a slightly different angle, the reason why a farmer buys John Deere equipment is to have better productivity on the farm. Slowly, John Deere recognized that they are not in the business of producing tractors and trailers, but instead, are in the business of farm management to help the farmers increase the productivity on their farms.

The question Gupta asks—what business are you in?—recalls Theodore Levitt's classic *Harvard Business Review* article, "Marketing Myopia." The railroads, Levitt wrote in 1960, let airlines and auto manufacturers take their customers away because "they assumed themselves to be in the railroad business rather than in the transportation business." Developing a platform strategy not only forced John Deere to rethink its business; it gave the company a focus that had to do with authenticity: what are we really doing here?

The Fifth Platform

A particularly interesting characteristic of platforms is that they can be built on top of one another. As McAfee and Brynjolfsson pointed out in *Machine | Platform | Crowd*, the World Wide Web, which Tim Berners-Lee invented at the end of the eighties, "is a multimedia, easy-to-navigate platform built on top of the original Internet information transfer protocols," which were formulated in the sixties. Google in turn is built on top of the web, as are Facebook and Twitter and most of the other platforms we interact with daily. And other platforms can be built on top of them—including the narrative platform that AMC created for *The Walking Dead*.

Narrative platforms constitute a fifth type of platform. At its simplest, a digital storytelling platform can just be a social media service like Twitter or TikTok. But a media company like AMC—or Marriott, or Burberry, since every enterprise is potentially a media company now—can do much more. It can create an ecosystem of stories that functions as an exchange of sorts, bringing people together in a marketplace of ideas and information.

Technologically, such platforms are rarely a single operation, like Apple's App Store, but rather an ad-hoc construct that straddles multiple existing platforms: Twitter, Facebook, YouTube, websites, video game consoles, live-action events like Comic-Con, a television channel like HBO or a streaming service like Netflix if it's built around an entertainment offering, or retail shops like Warby Parker's or Burberry's if it's constructed for physical products. Together, these parts form a whole that expands the story well beyond its original dimensions.

If a single-sided platform connects people with a brand, and a multisided platform connects different groups of people with one another, a narrative platform does both—it connects people with the story *and* with one another. Which means those people can not only co-create the story, they can immerse themselves in it in ways that would have been hard to imagine as recently as twenty years ago.

So while Marriott will never be as lean as Airbnb, all those travel stories and all those interactions with travelers suggest that it can be just as effective as creating an emotional bond. The narrative platform Marriott has created, customer-focused and data-informed, demonstrates that the company is not just here to sell you a hotel room. Transactional relationships are one-offs; narratives are emotion-based, and likely to spawn a relationship. With its string of podcasts and online magazines, with short films like "French Kiss" (6.3 million views in YouTube at last count) and surprise interactions with guests, Marriott created an ecosystem of stories designed to appeal to its best customers. And until March 2020, when the pandemic brought the travel industry to a sudden halt, it was also hosting live music events and the like at which guests would connect with one another—a defining feature of successful narrative platforms.

Visualizing the Platform

A big question with a platform like this is, how do you manage everything that's on it? It's complicated enough in the writers' room trying to keep track of the storylines in a single show with multicolored sticky notes on the walls. Add all this other stuff—including storylines in other media—and the complexity multiplies exponentially.

When Paul Woolmington and I were putting together the storytelling program at Columbia, we developed a suite of visualization tools to help people manage these complex narrative ecosystems. It's a two-part model that can be applied to all sorts of communications—not just entertainment, but product marketing and journalism too.

The first part is a platform visualization tool that authors and publishers can use to organize an array of media properties. Conceptually it builds on another idea from economics: stock and flow. As defined more than a century ago by Irving Fisher, one of the founding economists of the modern era, stock is analogous to capital, flow to income. "Stock relates to a point of time, flow to a stretch of time," Fisher wrote. "Food in the pantry at any instant is capital, the monthly flow of food through the pantry is income." In a somewhat more recent blog post, the Bay Area novelist Robin Sloan (a one-time economics major) reformulated the idea and applied it to digital media:

- Flow is the feed. It's the posts and the tweets. It's the stream of daily and sub-daily updates that reminds people you exist.
- Stock is the durable stuff. It's the content you produce that's as interesting in two months (or two years) as it is today. It's what people discover via search. It's what spreads slowly but surely, building fans over time.

Stock, Hub, Flow: The Platform

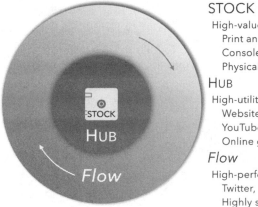

STOCK
High-value assets: the vault
Print and television
Console games
Physical and retail

HUB
High-utility assets: the engine
Website, e-commerce
YouTube
Online games

Flow
High-performance assets: The stream
Twitter, Facebook, Instagram
Highly shareable, in the moment

Stock and flow make a handy framework for creative individuals who want to bring some balance to their lives—writers like Sloan, for instance. For the kind of sprawling narrative ecosystem AMC created around *The Walking Dead*, however, the model seemed to need something more. So Paul and I—inspired by Noah Brier, who had worked with Paul at Naked Communications and had recently cofounded the marketing platform Percolate—devised a third component: the hub, which is the engine that drives everything else.

The combination of stock, hub, and flow gave us a visualization tool that can transform a random-seeming assortment of media properties into a coherent whole. Instead of the usual tangle of "channels" that marketing people, among others, have to navigate—mobile, social, what-have-you—this tool offers a functional view of the entire narrative platform and everything on it:

Stock—high-cost, high-value assets like movies, television shows, console games, print and television ads, and retail outlets

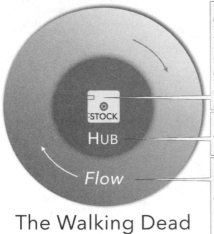

	The Walking Dead–TV series
	Fear the Walking Dead–TV spinoff
	Talking Dead–TV talk show
	The Walking Dead–comic
	The Walking Dead–video game
	The Walking Dead: Survival Instinct–video game
	Fear the Walking Dead: Flight 462–miniseries
	The Walking Dead: Rise of the Governor–novel
	The Walking Dead Escape–live event
	AMC Zombie School–for extras
	The Walking Dead website
	The Walking Dead Shop–online store
	Webisodes and bonus videos–online video
	The Walking Dead Wiki
	@WalkingDead_AMC on Twitter
	The Walking Dead Facebook page
	The Walking Dead Social Game
	Apocalypse Survival Test–online quiz
	Know Your Walkers–photo quiz
	Dead Yourself–mobile app
	The Walking Dead: Assault–mobile game

The Walking Dead

Hub—high-utility assets that power the whole system, such as websites, e-commerce sites, online games, YouTube channels, and a fan wiki

Flow—highly shareable, in-the-moment assets like Twitter, Snapchat, and Instagram

The goal is to keep all three running smoothly and in tandem in such a way that each reinforces the others.

Applied to *The Walking Dead*, the model looks like this:

Stock: Conventional broadcast media—the television series, the spin-off series *Fear the Walking Dead*, and the postbroadcast talk show *Talking Dead*—make up the bulk of the high-cost, high-value assets in the network's vault. There's also the source material—the comic series by Robert Kirkman, who was struggling to get by on day jobs in rural Kentucky when it launched in 2003. But with the *Walking Dead* media platform officially upgraded to the *Walking Dead* Universe, the vault started to get crowded. Early on, the comic and the television show spawned three different video games, a TV miniseries, and a novelization. There was also *The Walking Dead Escape*, a highly participatory live event that premiered at the annual Comic-Con fan festival in San Diego and subsequently traveled to New York and other cities. By the time season 10 got underway in October 2019, AMC had greenlit a second TV spin-off, this one led by female characters, and three movies featuring the return of Rick Grimes, the one-time deputy sheriff who'd been the show's main character until he was apparently killed off in season 9.

But perhaps the most remarkable component is the AMC Zombie School in Atlanta, where the series is shot. A training program for fans who want to play "walkers" on the show, the Zombie School is among the most popular components of the *Walking Dead* platform—and certainly the most demanding. "I get email after email, and I get stopped on the street," said Greg Nicotero, the executive producer who runs the program. "People will come up and go, 'How do I get to be a zombie on *The Walking Dead?*' They don't think about the fact that it's 120 degrees outside, and you're going to be sitting in a makeup chair for an hour and a half, and you're going to be sticky and hot, and you're going to work all day, and then at the end of the day we've got to use all the remover. It sounds more glamorous than it is."

Hub: This is the engine, home to widely available media that generate traffic and awareness for the *Walking Dead* Universe— including the *Walking Dead* website and any number of *Walking Dead* "webisodes" exploring the stories of relatively minor characters. There's an online emporium, Shop *The Walking Dead*, that sells hoodies, T-shirts, bobbleheads, and action figures (that is, dolls for dudes), not to mention barbed-wire-wrapped baseball bats "crafted to match the exact specifications" of the instrument

used by Negan, the charismatic leader of a cult-like band of survivors, to beat other, more popular characters to a lifeless pulp in
some of the most gruesome scenes ever to appear on television.
And of course there's a fan-run wiki on Fandom, the for-profit
sibling of Wikipedia.

Flow: Transitory, of-the-moment media experiences designed to
keep fans engaged and to stoke interest among those who might
become fans. *The Walking Dead* was America's most talked-about
television series on social media by far, according to Nielsen.
During season 7 (2016–17), it averaged more than two million
fan interactions per episode on Facebook and Twitter alone—
more than double the tally for the runner-up, Fox's *Empire*, even
though Negan's depredations and other storytelling misfires
caused viewership to fall as the season progressed. Mobile apps,
online quizzes, and trivia challenges serve the same purpose: to
make the show an indelible part of fans' lives. *The Walking Dead*
became the first cable series to beat every other show on television in the key 18-to-49 demographic—and its fan engagement
platform kept the show going for years, even as lackluster storytelling choices led many disheartened fans to rail against the
direction the show was taking.

What Would Walt Do?

AMC was hardly the first media company to produce entertainment and build a narrative platform to support it. One of the earliest champions of this approach was Walt Disney, who mapped
out the process in 1957.

It was a critical period for Disney's business enterprises. Disneyland, the park he had long dreamed of building, had opened
in 1955, and *Sleeping Beauty*, whose castle was Disneyland's cen

terpiece, would hit movie theaters in 1959. Disney had already moved well beyond the animated features he was best known for, and the company map showed the connections between various parts of his growing media empire. At the center was the motion picture studio, the heart of the enterprise since Walt and his brother Roy founded it in a Hollywood storefront in 1923. Arrayed around the studio were other divisions and partnerships, including television, music, books and comic books, comic strips, merchandising, and the newly opened park. Each fed on ideas and properties that came from the studio, and each served as marketing for the films while also providing concepts and marketing for other divisions. Of all these outlying enterprises, by far the most important was Disneyland, which was linked to every other part of the company.

Disney died in 1966, and this schematic—essentially a map of his company's vast narrative ecosystem, each division working in concert with the others and with outside enterprises to bring in fans—lay fallow in the archives for years while his heirs squandered his legacy. "Even during Walt Disney's lifetime," wrote his biographer, Neal Gabler, "the question by which the bean-counters governed was: 'What would Walt do?'" In 1984, after nearly 20 years of dismal movies and dwindling relevance, the company was rescued from corporate raiders when the board fired Disney's son-in-law and brought in 42-year-old Michael Eisner—a protégé of Barry Diller, who was chair of Paramount at the time—to run the place.

Like other media moguls of the day, Eisner focused on megamergers—Miramax Films, ABC and its corporate sibling ESPN, various others that never came to pass—while fumbling the Internet. The rationale for the deals that created these global media conglomerates was that they would create "synergy" across different divisions, an idea that echoed Walt Disney's vision from the fifties. But the organization charts of these companies made it a joke. "Sony is not one company, it's about 50 companies, and there's nothing other than the CEO's office to bring them together," a Japanese telecom executive told me. "It's a bunch of vertical poles that don't even hit one another in the breeze because they're too far apart." The same comment could have been made about any of these conglomerates.

Disney did better than most. Animated hits like *Beauty and the Beast*, *The Lion King*, and Pixar's *Toy Story* brought in hundreds of millions of dollars at the box office and even more as Broadway plays, theme park attractions, and cruise ship experiences. As for the merger derby, "bigger is not always better," Eisner admitted to me one day. We were sitting in his office in the Team Disney headquarters on the Disney lot in Burbank, a monumental building whose massive pediment is supported by outsized statues of the seven dwarfs. "On the other hand," he continued, "in this world, where others are bigger and enjoy a good game of Monopoly, you have to be strong enough and big enough to understand the difference between Park Place and Boardwalk."

Ego was a prime driver of the media mergers of the nineties, as Eisner's non-answer suggests. But after Robert Iger, Eisner's number two, took over as CEO in 2005, the acquisitions became more strategic. Iger moved quickly to patch up a rift with Steve Jobs over Disney's distribution of Pixar films, then bought Pixar outright in a $7.4 billion deal that made Jobs Disney's largest shareholder and put him on Disney's board. In 2009 Iger spent $4.2 billion to buy Marvel, which had sparked a superhero revival at the box office when it partnered with Fox for *X-Men* and Sony for *Spider-Man*. Then, after negotiating personally with George Lucas for nearly a year and a half, Iger bought Lucasfilm for $4 billion. And in 2019 he concluded a $71.3 billion deal to buy most of 21st Century-Fox, landing one of Hollywood's most storied studios, returning the X-Men and other characters to the Marvel umbrella, and picking up James Cameron's *Avatar* films in the bargain. By this time, Disney's market cap had surpassed $250 billion.

More than Eisner, Iger seemed to be reading from Walt's playbook. Disney not only turned its movies into theme park attractions and staged them on Broadway; it mined them for comics and action figures and television series, built cruises and hotels around them, transmogrified them into all-consuming, megagrossing universes. When *Frozen* became a surprise hit in 2013, the studio surrounded it with offerings that evoked its characters and their world. Books that "allow families to immerse themselves in the story" (as the press release put it). *Frozen* fashion items and a trunk to keep them in. An app that told the story from the point of view of either of the two main characters. When demand for these treasures outstripped supply at Christmastime, parents went into panic mode.

Disney's corporate synergy diagram reappeared that same year, this time in a *Harvard Business Review* article by Todd Zenger of the University of Utah, who dubbed it "a remarkable illustration of posthumous leadership." Two years after that, Jack Dorsey, cofounder and CEO of Twitter, tweeted the chart and a link to the *HBR* article with the comment, "The actual strategy drawing Walt Disney gave investors. Unbelievably great (and timeless)."

As Dorsey's endorsement suggests, the idea of a narrative platform is not limited to entertainment companies. Warby Parker makes eyeglasses. Harry's was still in start-up mode when it spent $100 million to buy a razor-blade factory. Both businesses are made possible by efficient online stores that bypass traditional sales outlets and go directly to the public. Augmented by blogs, social media, and (in the case of Warby Parker) physical stores, they form a brand narrative ecosystem that's not unlike what Disney envisioned in 1957.

Where Like Meets Like:
The Rise of the Self-Seeking Market

Still, narrative platforms like these differ in a crucial way from the classic platform business model as described by economists. These are not multisided markets, at least not technically speaking. The definition can be quite strict: David Evans and Richard Schmalensee cite the example of a heterosexual singles club that "needs to get two groups of customers on board its platform"— men and women—but it seems not to have occurred to them that gay bars function the same way, except that the two groups are one. If the two economists had ventured over to the Eagle, the gay leather bar on Manhattan's formerly rough-and-tumble West Side waterfront, they would have seen that this particular marketplace was no place for a woman—nor for that matter for a pair of pointy-headed intellectuals from the groves of academe. The closest they'd find to a two-sided market would be leather dudes cruising for other leather dudes.

This dynamic—like seeking like—is also characteristic of one-sided platforms, like WhatsApp or the telephone network, that benefit from network effects. It is also characteristic of narrative platforms. They are not a typical one-sided market, connecting people to a brand, nor are they multisided, connecting different groups to one another. Narrative platforms are something else: they are a *self-seeking* market. A place for like-minded people to interact with other like-minded people—people who are there to connect with the story, yes, but also to connect with each other *about* the story. The platform links everyone who wants to join in. It disseminates the narrative. It encourages immersion. It's how we tell ourselves a story in the digital age.

9. Immersion

B ut let's face it: fans, customers—nobody cares about your platform strategy. They're here to enjoy themselves, maybe throw themselves into your story and share it with some friends. That's why we have the immersion framework, which lets us see the same array of media properties from the point of view of the audience. How do they engage? What kind of experience do they have? How immersed do they become?

This framework—inspired by James Cameron's remark about drilling down to "secondary and tertiary levels of detail"—provides a view of the same array of properties according to the degree of engagement they induce. The main offering, if it's a book or a movie or a television show, will be the story itself. The others will lead fans deeper and deeper into the world of the

Four Levels of Engagement

L 1: One-to-many/broadcast
Movies and television shows
Books and comics
Products and services

L 2: One-to-one/interactive
Online quizzes
Single-player games

L 3: Many-to-many/online
Multiplayer games, YouTube
Twitter, Facebook, Snapchat, Instagram

L 4: Many-to-many/experiential
Real-world experiences
For the superfans

story, just as Cameron imagined when he was making *Avatar*. Together, these four levels of engagement form a deep media network that strengthens the connection of existing fans even as it brings new ones in.

Immersion is not engagement—at least, not in the conventional sense. Immersion, that feeling of losing yourself in another world, is an involuntary experience. Engagement is active and participatory; it's something you choose to do. And yet engagement is its own form of immersion, a means of stepping into a world like Cameron's. The same dynamic applies to other businesses, including consumer product companies, B2B companies, and direct-to-consumer enterprises like Warby Parker and Harry's.

Level 1 in this framework is where you'll find a conventional mass media property—a television series, a movie, a novel—as well as any spin-offs that don't involve interactivity. Level 2 is for one-on-one interactions, Level 3 for multiplayer experiences. At the deepest level we find the story taken into the real world, where only the most committed fans will follow—the Baker Street Irregulars and their ilk.

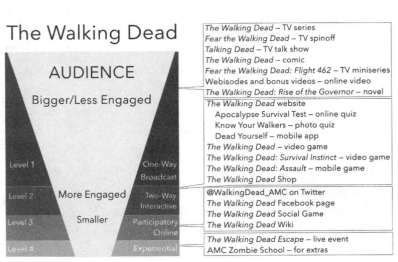

The Walking Dead

AUDIENCE

Bigger/Less Engaged

More Engaged

Smaller

Level 1 — One-Way Broadcast
Level 2 — Two-Way Interactive
Level 3 — Participatory Online
Level 4 — Experiential

The Walking Dead – TV series
Fear the Walking Dead – TV spinoff
Talking Dead – TV talk show
The Walking Dead – comic
Fear the Walking Dead: Flight 462 – TV miniseries
Webisodes and bonus videos – online video
The Walking Dead: Rise of the Governor – novel

The Walking Dead website
  Apocalypse Survival Test – online quiz
  Know Your Walkers – photo quiz
  Dead Yourself – mobile app
The Walking Dead – video game
The Walking Dead: Survival Instinct – video game
The Walking Dead: Assault – mobile game
The Walking Dead Shop

@WalkingDead_AMC on Twitter
The Walking Dead Facebook page
The Walking Dead Social Game
The Walking Dead Wiki

The Walking Dead Escape – live event
AMC Zombie School – for extras

How does *The Walking Dead* fit into the Four Levels of Engagement framework? Let's take a look:

Level 1: One-to-many/broadcast—Like the comic that inspired it, *The Walking Dead* is a conventional, one-to-many experience. But it has spawned not only spin-off TV and web series but a panoply of other properties.

Level 2: One-to-one/interactive—These include online quizzes and single-player video games (*The Walking Dead*, *The Walking Dead: Survival Instinct*) . . .

Level 3: Many-to-many/participatory— . . . as well as highly participatory offerings such as multiplayer video games and social media initiatives on Twitter and Facebook. Some exist primarily as marketing tools, to bring in new fans. Others may be designed to engage existing fans, with the aim of inspiring them to influence others. In fact, the line between the two goals is blurry. It can be hard to say in advance what will draw new fans and what

will entice existing fans to plunge deeper into the story. Material produced by the fans themselves—UGC, or user-generated
content, in the dispiriting lingo of marketing claptrap—will likely
prove most engaging of all. This makes it imperative to step back
and let the fans "own" the story. Far from cheapening the intellectual property behind it, they will add value.

Level 4: Experiential—At the deep end, targeting the most dedicated fans, are real-world experiences like *The Walking Dead Escape*
("The virus is spreading to a city near you") and the AMC Zombie School in Atlanta. Their appeal is limited, and they don't
scale. But the excitement they generate is highly contagious, giving them an impact far beyond the number of people they involve.

Did You Mean Mailchimp?

Few companies have led people into the deep end as effectively
as Mailchimp, the email marketing outfit. It began quite inno-
cently. When Mailchimp rolled out its first ads, on the public
radio program *This American Life*, no one had any idea they would
become part of the cultural conversation. But a spot that ran in
the show's 2014 spin-off, the true-crime podcast *Serial*, changed
that forever.

The ad was as simple as an ad can get: a 20-second audio spot
in which a series of people say the company's name and what it
does. But four seconds in, you hear a girl's voice stumbling over
the name: "Mail . . . kimp? . . . chimp?" So began a meme that
started on Twitter and soon built into a minor media storm. It
didn't hurt that *Serial* itself was a pop-culture sensation or that
the girl—eventually identified as a 14-year-old from Norway who
was recorded while waiting in line with her parents to buy the lat-
est iPhone—sounded utterly innocent and unrehearsed.

All this was perfect for Mailchimp, with its quirky, band-of-misfits mentality. Founded in Atlanta in 2001, the company was by this time being used to send more than 10 billion emails per month—all without ever taking venture capital or mounting a major ad campaign. Wisely, its cofounders, Ben Chestnut and Dan Kurzius, didn't try to capitalize on the free publicity the *Serial* spot had generated. But three years later, in 2017, they put out a response in partnership with the ad agency Droga5—a digital campaign that was as elaborate as the original podcast spot was straightforward.

Instead of one ad there were nine, each with its own website and each supposedly based on a different mispronunciation of "Mailchimp." A trio of highly eccentric 60-second films— MailShrimp, KaleLimp, and JailBlimp—were first shown in US movie theaters before going online. At veilhymn.com there was an interactive four-and-a-half-minute music video by Devonté Hynes, aka Blood Orange, and Bryndon Cook. A product called SnailPrimp—supposedly an antiaging facial made from snail secretions—popped up online on Instagram and in real life in a one-day-only spa on the roof of the Ace Hotel in Los Angeles. MaleCrimp celebrated men who crimp their hair. At NailChamp you could witness "the ultimate nail art battle" among fingernail fetishists. At Whalesynth you could generate synthetic whale tones. Some 200,000 bags of FailChips—pre-crushed potato chips custom-made by Snyder's of Hanover, a 108-year-old pretzel-and-potato-chip concern in Pennsylvania—were handed out free at delis and fast-food joints. "So there you have it," one commentator quipped—"real ads for a fake product that is in stores but you can't buy but you can eat."

Mailchimp itself was barely mentioned on any of these sites. This was not an oversight. The idea was to pique people's curiosity enough to drive them to the web. And there, thanks to a clever buy on Google's search advertising platform, the response you'd get if you Googled any of the nine names was, "Did you mean Mailchimp?"

"Just Being Cows"

Mailchimp is a quintessential platform company, providing tools that enable small businesses to connect with their customers. Now it was building a narrative platform on top of that—a narrative platform that won Droga5 a Cyber Grand Prix at the Cannes Lions, the global ad industry's annual orgy of self-celebration, and that the Columbia Digital Storytelling Lab named to the 2018 Digital Dozen. The campaign generated some 67 million web searches. Visits to the nine sites averaged a remarkable four minutes per person. The odd thing was, Mailchimp almost had to talk its agency into taking the leap.

The campaign had started as a thought scribbled on a note-card that was tacked to a wall with 15 or 20 other concepts. "At first it seemed ludicrous," Mark DiCristina, Mailchimp's head of brand marketing, told me. "Too small. But we kept coming back to it." And it kept growing, until eventually they had something like 50 ideas for it—"anything that felt like it remotely rhymed with 'mail' and remotely rhymed with 'chimp.'" Most of those ideas got rejected. Like WailAmp—a web app that would let you yell out your frustrations into your computer and then play it on a giant amp in the desert somewhere. Or FrailGym—a gym with exercise equipment that was entirely made of glass. Finally, DiCristina said, "Our account director said, 'I have to tell you, this feels borderline reckless.' That was the moment when I felt like we were really on to something."

After the "Did You Mean Mailchimp?" campaign, however, the company stopped working with Droga5 and went in a different direction—one more focused on the product than on the brand.

What they were trying to get across with the Droga5 campaign, DiCristina said, "was an empowering message to entrepreneurs and small businesses—the idea that you don't have to do the thing that everybody else is doing." Now they wanted to some-how reconcile the out-there-ness of the MailChimp brand with the practicality of the actual product. The result, introduced in June 2019, was "Mailchimp Presents," a series of short films and podcasts—"original content that celebrates the entrepreneurial spirit," it says on the website—for the kind of people who use Mailchimp.

It's hard to imagine two initiatives more diametrically opposed than "Did You Mean Mailchimp?" and "Mailchimp Presents," and yet they both work. "Mailchimp Presents" is content market-ing that doesn't feel like marketing or even like "content." It feels like stories. My favorite is "73 Cows," an award-winning short film that focuses on England's Bradley Nook Farm. The farmer who owns it, a gray-haired vegan well into his sixties, has found fulfillment by sending most of his £40,000 herd of cows (that's $51,000 at the then-current exchange rate) not to the slaughter-house but to live out their days in an animal sanctuary. The rest he keeps as pets. "A herd of cows from the East Midlands will be mooing a sigh of relief," a newspaper article about him began. Near the close of the film, a drone shot shows the cows frolicking across a field like puppies as the farmer talks about them "enjoy-ing just being cows."

"It really resonated with vegans, I can tell you," said DiCristina.

Another "Mailchimp Presents" feature is the podcast *Lifecycle of a Business*, which introduces us to such people as a 24-year-old would-be musician who works in a pet cemetery, handling cremations and open-casket funerals. Sample question: "If you want to make music for a living, why are you turning pets into dust?" Another podcast, *Going Through It*, features interviews with women who've dealt with adversity: Rebecca Traister, author of *Big Girls Don't Cry*, who found herself facing writer's block and postpartum depression when she started her second book. Hillary Clinton, who talked about feeling like an impostor as a student at Wellesley. Ellen Pao, who sued Kleiner, Perkins, the top-flight Silicon Valley venture capital firm, for sex discrimination—and lost.

This may seem oddly frivolous to some people in the ad business: where's the sell, the brand connection, the call to action? Again, there isn't one. "It's not just an ad but actually a product," DiCristina said. "This is an entertainment platform where we're telling stories about the experience of being an entrepreneur. And it almost immediately began doing the kind of thing we hoped it would. The people who were enjoying it, sharing it, were more likely to become paid customers than free—so it's a way to identify people who will be very high-value customers of Mailchimp." Compare this to advertising, he added, where "you have to pay to get attention, and the minute you stop paying, they take it down and it ceases to exist. At the end of the day, we have a much more durable asset—and we own it."

All this is in addition to the vast amounts of text and video on Mailchimp's website that are designed to help its customers with their own marketing. There's page after page on marketing basics like customer relationship management, behavioral targeting, personalization, and A/B testing—each of which Mailchimp gives you tools to manage, making the platform particularly useful to the neophytes it tends to attract. There are endless how-to's: how to design a product page that sells, how to grow your audience with postcards and landing pages, how to choose the right domain name for your website, how to design automated emails that work. And there's the Mailchimp Content Style Guide, a free-to-anyone resource that covers voice and tone, grammar

Four Levels of Engagement: Mailchimp

and mechanics, copyright and trademarks, blog posts and email newsletters, technical and legal copy.

Because Mailchimp is itself a two-sided platform, connecting marketers with prospective customers, it looks quite different from a television show like *The Walking Dead* when you map it to the Four Levels of Engagement framework. The primary property—Mailchimp itself—is not a one-to-many broadcast but a highly participatory online environment that connects people who use Mailchimp with their customers. Most of Mailchimp's marketing materials—the videos and podcasts on "Mailchimp Presents," as well as the many guides and tutorials Mailchimp offers its users—do function as broadcast media, albeit online. At the interactive level are most of the tools and services Mailchimp provides to its users, including customer relationship management software, automated postings on social media, and telephone and chat support. At the participatory level, aside from Mailchimp's customer offerings and the usual social media accounts, there's Mailchimp on GitHub, the software platform, where tech-savvy customers can find the software development kits and application program interfaces that make it work. And finally there's Mailchimp's Agency Partner Program, a network of agencies and freelancers who provide support to Mailchimp customers. Once a year the top partners are invited to Mailchimp's Atlanta headquarters—in an enormous office/apartment/shopping/entertainment complex that was built nearly a century ago as a Sears, Roebuck distribution center—for training and the like at its Partner Lab.

For a business like Mailchimp, as for an entertainment property like *The Walking Dead*, creating an immersive story platform has clear advantages. It works for other organizations as well—not all of them so benign.

In the Grayzone

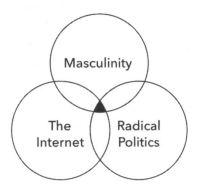

"I'm a great believer in Venn diagrams," said Javaad Alipoor, the playwright and performer, as we sat in the courtyard of Summerhall, a century-old stone-and-glass pile that's a hub of activity for Edinburgh's annual Festival Fringe. He reached for my notebook and drew one: three interlocking circles he labeled Masculinity, Radical Politics, and The Internet. The spot where they all meet is the subject of Alipoor's startling one-act play, *The Believers Are But Brothers*.

Alipoor was born in Britain, the son of a white English mother and an Iranian father from a fishing village on the Caspian Sea. He grew up in a housing estate—not a nice one—in Bradford, a once grand, now depressed industrial city of half a million people in the North of England. He spent three years as a youth and community worker, his efforts funded by Prevent, a counterterrorism program intended to keep young people from becoming radicalized. Although Prevent has been controversial for the way it treats Islamic youth, it did enable him to give kids a sense of possibility. But after the Tories came to power in 2010 and "took a scorched-earth policy to youth and community work," as Alipoor put it, he turned to theater.

Audiences were transfixed when Alipoor first presented his play at the Fringe in 2017. Here was a world in which, as Lyn Gardner wrote in *The Guardian*, "young men with uncertain futures watch glossy, Hollywood-style ISIS propaganda and reckon that being a jihadist looks a lot like *Game of Thrones* and might beat a life stacking shelves in Tesco." *The Believers Are But Brothers* starts out as the story of two young Muslim men in England, Atif in the south, Marwan in the north. As the play opens, Alipoor is sitting with his back to us, playing *Call of Duty* on his computer. He's tall and clean-shaven, in his mid-thirties, wearing faded blue jeans, red sneakers, and a red V-neck shirt. Directly in front of him is a large, semitransparent screen on which we see his face in a ghostly digital projection. "This story starts in a cell," he says, his spectral visage staring directly at us. "It's the story of how the West's colonial nightmare of Islam came to light. It's a vision, made vision, made flesh."

Part of the drama plays out on WhatsApp as Alipoor speaks. It starts with a quiz on our smartphones: How many Muslims in the UK? How many do we think have joined ISIS? Later the texts will turn darker and more threatening. Meanwhile, Alipoor continues his monologue: "Atif finds a magazine. It's called *Dabiq*.*

---

* Named after a small town in Syria that, according to a prophecy by the Prophet Muhammad, could be the site of the final battle between Muslims and nonbelievers.

Dabiq makes him dizzy. Inside, he finds these articles that speak to a feeling that he's been carrying around for months. That every new outrage, every nightclub attacked in Paris, every gay bar attacked in Orlando[*] is part of a plan. A plan that will bring the world that torments and humiliates Muslims, that torments and humiliates *him*, to its knees."

About halfway through the play, Alipoor suddenly switches personas. Now we're no longer with Atif or Marwan but with Ethan, aka 4thelulz, a 21-year-old in Southern California who spends much of his time on 4chan. The character is loosely based on Elliot Rodger, a self-described "incel" (involuntary celibate, in the much-aggrieved lingo of young, ultraright males) who "got even" in 2014 by killing six fellow students at UC Santa Barbara and injuring 14 others before shooting himself in the head. Rodger left behind a 100,000-word "manifesto" and a self-pitying YouTube video in which he said, "My problem is girls. There are so many beautiful girls here, but none of them give me a chance—and I don't know why." Ethan doesn't kill anyone, but like Atif and Marwan with their terrorist recruitment videos he lives in an electronic fever dream of hatred and delusion, fed by a toxic spring of murderous memes and violence-friendly hangouts that range from the depths of the Dark Web to YouTube and Twitter.

The last half of the production ricochets back and forth

---

[*] In November 2015, 90 people died when Islamic terrorists armed with automatic weapons strode into the Bataclan Theater in Paris and started shooting. In June 2016, seven months later, a security guard who had recently pledged his allegiance to the leader of ISIS burst into a gay nightclub in Orlando, Florida, with a semiautomatic rifle and a semiautomatic pistol. He shot 102 people, nearly half of them fatally, before he himself was shot dead by police.

between the travails of Atif and Marwan in Syria and Ethan/4thelulz raving about cucks and libtards from the comfort of his parents' suburban home. At one point the Islamists invoke "the Grayzone," the great mass of Christians and Muslims—soon to be extinct, in their view—who seem content to live in harmony. "The Grayzone is liberalism and democracy," Alipoor declares, now facing us directly. "It's human rights and anti-racism. It's everything that binds us together." And next we're back with Ethan as he hails the emergence of "a clear line, all the cucks and degenerates on one side, and him and his brothers on the other."

Never underestimate the appeal of dead certainty. Especially when fueled by self-righteous rage.

"I'm not an anthropologist, but in a different life I would quite like to be one," Alipoor said as we sat in Summerhall's courtyard, which was crammed with picnic tables and food stalls and slung with tarps to protect against the drizzle. With this production, he went on, "I try to ask the question, what is in our hearts that we are unleashing with this technology?"

What he has found there is not so much ideology—left or right, Christian or Muslim—as a crisis of masculinity, compounded by the still-evolving media it plays out in. Young men become immersed in stories they find online, stories that play to their frustrations and amplify their discontent. Those stories might compel them to pull out a gun and slaughter the infidels, or pull out a gun and shoot the stuck-up bitches who won't put out, or whatever. It's all the same—the same ugliness, the same weakness. The same desire not to eliminate the screen but to crawl up inside it and live there in a haze of resentment and retribution. Only the narratives are different.

Story, Narrative, Myth

Platforms and immersion are about more than a story. They lead to an overarching narrative. A story—from the Latin and Greek *historia*, related to *histor*, meaning one who knows—is the retelling of a sequence of events that take place over time. Narrative too has to do with knowing, but from a different root and a different route. It comes from the Latin *narrare*, to tell, related to *gnarus*, knowing. The kind of narrative we're talking about here is the sum of all your stories. It can offer perspective, meaning, purpose, direction. It can apply to politics or economics or business or religion. It can transmute fiction into truth.

Robert Shiller noted the emergence of such overarching narratives in *Narrative Economics*. He called them "constellations," as in the groups of stars we make up fables about. One such group of stories centers on the tale of George Washington and the cherry tree: asked by his father who cut down the cherry tree in the garden, the little boy who would grow up to be the Father of His Country says, "I cannot tell a lie." This little yarn, invented by a biographer shortly after Washington's death, "is part of a constellation of narratives about honesty," Shiller wrote—one "that has likely helped propel the US economy by creating trust in business dealings and by limiting bribery and corruption." A less helpful constellation of narratives has been emerging in response to the coronavirus pandemic: like the Great Depression of the 1930s, the pandemic could well have "belief-scarring effects" that will last for years and be far more damaging to the economy than the short-term effects of shutting down nonessential activities.

As with economics, so with everything else in life. Harry's has a narrative. Virgin has a narrative. ISIS has a narrative. The British Army, with its "This Is Belonging" campaign, has a counternarrative. But the most important narrative any of us will ever fashion is the one we tell ourselves about ourselves. In *Homo Deus*, his book-length speculation on the future of humanity, the always-intriguing historian Yuval Noah Harari put it this way:

> . . . the self too is an imaginary story, just like nations, gods and money. Each of us has a sophisticated system that throws away most of our experiences, keeps only a few choice samples, mixes them up with bits from movies we've seen, novels we've read, speeches we've heard, and daydreams we've savoured, and out of all that jumble it weaves a seemingly coherent story about who I am, where I came from and where I am going. This story tells me what to love, whom to hate and what to do with myself. This story may even cause me to sacrifice my life, if that's what the plot requires. We all have our genre. Some people live a tragedy, others inhabit a never-ending religious drama, some approach life as if it were an action film, and not a few act as if in a comedy. But in the end, they're all just stories.

In one sense, "narrative" is simply a five-dollar word for "story." But as the sum of all your stories—as the product of a well-constructed and fully immersive narrative platform, in other words—it is much more than that. It is what you would have us believe. It is what you would have *yourself* believe. And if it is successful enough, if it entices enough people over time to activate their cortices in sync, it may ultimately attain the status of myth (from the Greek *muthos*, which means—of course—story). If they succeed in transmuting story into myth, brands, institutions, and politicians can become part of the sea we swim in. A pervasive reality. A reality so widely shared we accept it without question, if indeed we notice it at all.

Part III

~

THE SHAPE OF
THE FUTURE

UNDER THE OVERGROUND IN THE EAST END OF LONDON there's a place called Otherworld. From a narrow, cobblestoned street in a modest residential district, you step through a glass wall set into a brick archway beneath a once-abandoned nineteenth-century railway viaduct. Now you're in a long, cave-like space that's lined on both sides with sleek, white cylinders. These cylinders, all identical, all big enough to hold a couple of people comfortably, are Otherworld's "immersion rooms." For upward of £19 an hour (about $23 these days), you can rent one, put on a virtual reality headset and earphones, and have the experience of being somewhere else entirely. When I was there, in August 2019, you could fight zombies or trek through Iceland to the sounds of Bjork's *Vulnicura*. Or you could pilot Doctor Who's TARDIS across the universe and, in a truly superb bit of augury, fight a virus that was threatening to shred the fabric of reality. All in the confines of your private immersion pod.

Virtual reality looked like the future incarnate back in 2014, when Facebook laid out more than $2 billion to buy Oculus VR, a two-year-old company that had yet to release a product. Google, Samsung, and Sony jumped into the market; venture capitalists hurled billions at it. Then reality—the actual sort—kicked in: the headsets that delivered the illusion were clunky and expensive, most of them had to be tethered to high-end computers, and to get the full experience you needed a dedicated room. Small wonder that, according to Nielsen SuperData, worldwide VR sales in 2019 came to only $6.2 billion for hardware and software combined, while the market for video game software alone was nearly $110 billion. And while SuperData was expecting VR sales to triple over the next three years as the technology improved, others were comparing it to the brief vogue for 3D-TV in the early 2010s.

Chris Adams and Ed Wardle, the young Oxford graduates behind Otherworld, took note of all this and figured an arcade was the way to go. They opened in spring 2019. Soon after, they noticed that people weren't reacting as they'd expected. Like Facebook and Google and multiple Hollywood directors before them, Adams and Wardle saw VR as a storytelling medium. But they had misjudged a crucial element: the audience. "I realized that I wasn't the storyteller, *they* were," said Wardle, the chief creative officer. "You have to set people up to tell their own story. They want to go out and have their own experiences. They don't want somebody else's experience." Wardle was in the midst of a wholesale rewrite as we spoke.

Step inside one of Otherworld's VR pods, strap on a top-of-the-line HTC Vive headset, and you're confronted with a disconcerting facsimile of reality. The illusion feels physically convincing, and yet no one would ever mistake it for real. You're free to explore an island, but it's cartoonlike, all primary colors and no sense of nature. What's genius is Otherworld's physical aspect, its half-crumbling brick interior set off by the sleekest of interventions—the white immersion pods, a long white counter running the length of the place, a luminous white bar at the end. This is a place to bring your friends, have a craft beer or drinks by a mixologist from Milk & Honey, maybe some street food from London's Lords of Poké. No one will see you stumbling around in a headset; that happens only in the privacy of your pod. Otherworld delivers a virtual experience and it delivers a real experience, and it knows enough to keep them distinct. And when the coronavirus struck, it was able to promise that you and your friends could "travel to a virtual paradise together, whilst your bodies remain safe in your own private, solo immersion room."

Wardle and Adams are well aware that VR is a novelty to most people—including many who come here to experience it. But to them it's a generational thing. "What's that quote?" Wardle asked. " 'Too late to explore the planet, too early to explore the stars?' One of the things that's always made humanity great is the way we crave frontiers. New realities to explore."

"I saw this vast digital expanse," Adams put in. Adams looks a bit posh—white dress shirt (untucked), thick blond hair brushed back, no earring or stubble like Wardle. After Oxford, he'd worked at McKinsey, then consulted for the likes of Intercontinental Hotels and Credit Suisse. "It's an opportunity."

"We were told you can all be famous and all be rich," Wardle went on. "It's a logical impossibility. But now, in VR, you *can* be rich and famous. You can be a dragon if you want to."

This line of thought led us, somewhat improbably, to talk of self-actualization—the quest to reach one's full potential. "When you're risking it all to start a business with your credit card, you have to have an answer for what you're doing and why you're doing it," Wardle said. "We concluded that we wanted to bring this technology to the mass market because it would provide self-actualization for our generation."

Right—but one of the inspirations for VR was a radically dystopian vision of the future: Neal Stephenson's *Snow Crash*, the 1992 cyberpunk novel that's set in a world in which the US government has fallen apart, the Central Intelligence Corporation has merged with the Library of Congress, and the gated communities of the wealthy have morphed into quasi-sovereign burbclaves. Stephenson's main character, Hiro, lives in a 20-by-30-foot corrugated metal compartment in a U-Stor-It near LAX. But as Stephenson put it,

Hiro's not actually here at all. He's in a computer-generated universe that his computer is drawing onto his goggles and pumping into his earphones. In the lingo, this imaginary place is known as the Metaverse. Hiro spends a lot of time in the Metaverse. It beats the shit out of the U-Stor-It.

Exactly, Wardle replied. "He doesn't live in a storage crate because he wants to. So what if I have a shit job and I live in an apartment that has mold on the walls? If I can interrupt the sensory input I hate and replace it with sensory input that I do like, would that not be good?"

Even if that input isn't real?

"Who cares? All it is is sensory input. Whether that turns out to be a Faustian bargain remains to be seen. But I'm optimistic."

I was beginning to think it was too late for Doctor Who's TARDIS to take on that reality-shredding virus.

When the Fictional Bleeds into the Real

Not that I can blame Ed Wardle. The fabric of reality is indeed being torn, and it will take much more than the BBC's much-loved doctor, even having made the jump from TV to VR, to fix it.

Ten years ago, in *The Art of Immersion*, I wrote about a speech by Philip K. Dick called "How to Build a Universe That Doesn't Fall Apart Two Days Later." Dick was saying he actually likes to build fictional universes that fall apart, because then he gets to see how the characters respond. Also because he has "a secret love of chaos." But what happens, I wondered,

when the universe that digital media spins for us begins to fall apart—as inevitably it will? It's not just the characters that have to respond, after all; it's us. How do we cope when the fictional bleeds into the real, and vice versa? How do we handle the blur?

Well, now we know: so far, at least, with an ineffectual mix of hysteria and denial. And I have to wonder: What have these new forms of stories gotten us? Where are these new forms of stories taking us?

When Storytelling Gets Out of Control

In August 2020, the *Wall Street Journal* ran what's known as an "explainer" about QAnon, the far-right conspiracy theory that holds that—well, as the *Journal* put it,

> . . . that a cabal of Satan-worshipping pedophiles, mainly consisting of what they see as elitist Democrats, politicians, journalists, entertainment moguls and other institutional figures, have long controlled much of the "deep state" government, which they say seeks to undermine President Trump, mostly with aid of media and entertainment outlets.

As 'splainers go, this one's a doozy. But it accurately sums up a development that might have floored even Philip K. Dick, a man who was no stranger to the wacko. The QAnon conspiracy theory has echoes of Watergate—Q is said to be an actual person, anonymous of course, in a high-ranking government position who is exposing these evils out of patriotism. QAnon's obsession with child sexual exploitation has allowed it to hijack the #SaveThe-Children conversation online, substituting baseless conspiracy theories for information that might actually keep children safe. It has merged with "pizzagate," the bogus rumor, widely promoted by bots on social media in the run-up to the 2016 election, that

Hillary Clinton was leading a ring of devil-worshiping pedophiles who met in the basement of a Washington, DC, pizza parlor. And it has managed to work thousands, then hundreds of thousands, then millions of believers into a righteous frenzy, raining death threats onto innocent people by phone and social media even as Trump himself toyed with embracing it.

Every aspect of QAnon is absurd. No, JFK Jr. did not fake his death in order to secretly lead the anti-pedophile crusade. No, Hillary Clinton and her accomplices do not eat children in order to slurp up some life-extending substance that's in their blood. But the fanatical enthusiasm that greets such tales is not new. When the brain's pattern-seeking mechanism goes haywire— when it spies an image of the Virgin Mary in the condensation on a living-room window in Chicago, say, or in a cloud hovering above the South Pacific—there can be no stopping it.

QAnon-type narratives are as old as America. The historian Richard Hofstadter noted previous examples in his 1964 essay, "The Paranoid Style in American Politics." In 1951, the virulently anti-Communist senator Joseph McCarthy proclaimed himself to be fighting a "conspiracy on a scale so immense as to dwarf any previous such venture in the history of man." A century earlier, a Texas newspaper warned that "the Monarchs of Europe and the Pope of Rome are at this very moment plotting our destruction and threatening the extinction of our political, civil, and religious institutions." And so on, back to Europe, where it all began with the anti-Semitic smear that Jews feast on the blood of Christian children. (Not true, and as Wikipedia helpfully notes, also not kosher.)

But QAnon is also digitally native. The cult began in late 2017 with a cryptic post on 4chan. The post was signed by "Q," aka "Q Clearance Patriot," suggesting someone with access to nuclear secrets at the Energy Department. From there it was picked up by ordinary folks who sent posts bubbling up on Facebook and Twitter and the like. Within months, QAnon signs were turning up at Trump rallies. When the coronavirus pandemic hit the US in March 2020, involvement in QAnon skyrocketed; the *Wall Street Journal* reported that average membership in 10 large, public QAnon Facebook groups grew by nearly 600 percent in five months.

By this time, a handful of observers had begun to notice a curious resemblance. One of them was Adrian Hon, a Londoner who had spent years designing alternate reality games—the Internet-based collaborative fictions that presaged the elaborate narrative ecosystems of shows like *Westworld* and *The Walking Dead*. ARGs typically began with a clue hidden in some incredibly obscure place—one of the first, a promotion for the 2001 Steven Spielberg film *A.I. Artificial Intelligence,* started with a credit for a "sentient machine therapist" on the movie poster—and mushroomed into an all-consuming narrative that players had to piece together themselves, joining forces online to solve puzzles and decipher cryptic messages. Characteristic of ARGs was the "rabbit hole," the hidden clue designed to lure players deeper and deeper into the story: in the *A.I.* ARG it was the sentient machine therapist's name, which when Googled would lead you to a vast network of interconnected websites. Another hallmark of ARGs was the way they started online but bled into the real world, manifesting themselves through fake newspaper ads, phone calls, and faxes, secret messages transmitted via ring tone. A third hallmark was their "this is not a game" ethos—the pretense that the story everyone was assembling was real.

QAnon too has multiple rabbit holes, bleeds inexorably into the real world, and takes itself very, very seriously. It's no secret that conspiracy theories hold a special appeal to people who feel lost and powerless, and this one, Hon noted in a blog post, is the product of "deep mistrust and fear and economic and spiritual malaise." QAnon washes away the malaise. Its followers are imbued with a sense of mission. They have purpose. They see what's really going on in the world, all the stuff the media and the Satan-worshiping elites are trying to hide. QAnon believers have amazing revelations at their fingertips and a growing Internet community to share them with. "Everything is online," Hon writes. "Every discussion, every idea, every theory is all joined together in a warped edifice where speculation becomes fact and fact leads to action." But it only looks warped from the outside. Once you've swallowed the red pill . . .

Real or Virtual?

I was in Los Angeles one day when I found myself in a large conference room at USC's Robert Zemeckis Center for Digital Arts, a nondescript white box of a building just down the street from the university's palm-studded, park-like campus. If there are people who can tell us where these new forms of stories are taking us, I figured, they ought to be here. Seated around me were the half-dozen individuals who run futuristic research projects at the Entertainment Technology Center, a think tank funded by every major Hollywood studio—Disney, Paramount, Sony, Universal, Warner Bros.—and by tech and telecom companies like Cisco, Microsoft, and Verizon. They're exploring the kind of thing Steven Spielberg brought up in that discussion with George Lucas—getting rid of the screen and putting the player inside the experience. "I don't think narrative is the bulk of the opportunity," ETC's director, Kenneth Williams, was saying.

"You're going to have a narrative story but also a new type of immersive experience," put in Philip Lelyveld, who heads ETC's Immersive Media Initiative, an effort focused on virtual reality, augmented reality, and mixed reality, known collectively as XR. An experience that's not directed or edited, he went on, that lacks quick cuts or close-ups, that may boast a 360-degree field of view, and that provides not just visual and auditory stimulation but sparks the other senses as well—touch, temperature, taste, smell. "People say the story emerges after you leave the experience"—as in a game, but with a twist: "The ultimate goal is effectively to have multi-sensory input that you can't tell what is real and what is virtual."

The blur again: I was starting to wonder about this whole immersion thing.

Seated at my left was Yves Bergquist, who heads ETC's AI and Neuroscience in Media Initiative. Most of ETC's top people are old Hollywood hands, which gives them credibility with the studios as well as insight into how the studio people think. Williams, ETC's director, was a longtime Sony Pictures executive who in the nineties founded Sony Pictures Imageworks, the digital studio behind such visual-effects wonders as the destruction of London's Tower Bridge in *Spider-Man: Far from Home*. Lelyveld is a former vice president at Disney. Bergquist—tall and lean in his late forties, sporting a haircut that looks expensively shaggy—could easily pass for a Hollywood player. But his background is different.

A decade and a half ago he was Alexis Debat, Middle East expert and on-air consultant for ABC News. Then, in 2007, it came out that he had made up large parts of his personal story—that he had falsely claimed a PhD from the Sorbonne, exaggerated a position with the French government, and apparently faked interviews with then-Senator Barack Obama and other leaders. His news career suddenly over, he quickly dropped from view. Former associates suggested he sell his story to Hollywood. Instead he resurfaced as Yves Bergquist (his own middle name coupled with his wife's family name), data and analytics expert and CEO of Novamente, a small firm pursuing general-purpose AI. After a couple of years of unpaid consulting for ETC, he joined its staff in 2018. By this time, he says, "I realized the entertainment industry was a great opportunity for AI." He may well be right.

A Quantitative Theory of Interestingness

"Nobody knows anything." That was William Goldman's take on Hollywood. Goldman was the screenwriter for two Oscar winners, *All the President's Men* and *Butch Cassidy and the Sundance Kid*, as well as *Marathon Man* and *The Princess Bride*. This pithy observation was the first sentence of his 1983 memoir, *Adventures in the Screen Trade*, and it has been trotted out weekly if not daily ever since by producers and directors and the presidents of this or that at the motion picture studios and the television networks—by the people who are supposed to know something, in other words. Except they can't, because nobody does. Disney's *Frozen* became a global hit, to the surprise of everyone. *Solo: A Star Wars Story* lost an estimated $77 million, the first bomb in the 40-plus-year history of the franchise. Goldman penned the fundamental axiom of Hollywood. Bergquist hopes to disprove it.

"My team and I are well on our way to understanding the cognitive relationship between stories and people," he said one afternoon as we sat in a Hollywood Boulevard coffee bar. "The media and entertainment industry trades in brain states"—as Uri Hasson demonstrated with his *The Good, the Bad and the Ugly* experiments, as Fox News demonstrates nightly. "We are chasing a mathematical theory that would explain what kind of narratives would drive what kind of behavior." A quantitative theory of interestingness, he calls it.

Bergquist's theory was sparked by an insight from Jürgen

Schmidhuber, one of the world's leading AI researchers. Schmid-huber, who is based in Switzerland, pioneered the artificial neural networks that have produced the spectacular advances in AI and machine learning over the past 20 years—advances that have yielded such wonders as Siri, Alexa, and (presumably, some-day) self-driving cars. More recently, he has argued that what we find beautiful and what we find interesting in every field of art or science depends on how novel they seem to us. Novelty triggers curiosity, he has written, a quality that "motivates exploring infants, pure mathematicians, composers, artists, dancers, come-dians, yourself, and recent artificial systems."

"Everything the human mind finds interesting—movies, songs, people, everything—has a similar ratio of things that we know and things that are new," Bergquist explains. "The human brain is optimized for novelty. But too much novelty and it's overwhelming. Not enough novelty and it's boring. That's why Philip Glass doesn't sell millions of albums. And that applies to everything. People would click a lot more on a flat-Earth video because if you're in a round-Earth society, flat-Earth is a novelty." (Researchers have found YouTube to be behind a surprising uptick in flat-Earth sentiment in recent years.) Armed with this insight, he adds, "We are developing a tool that can score the interestingness of anything, based on familiarity and novelty."

The tool is called Corto, as is the start-up he heads that's developing it. (ETC is a research organization; it doesn't build products.) In its early, rough form, Bergquist said, Corto could predict the success of a song with 98 percent accuracy. Movies and tele-vision shows are a lot more complicated, but by 2020 Corto had a database of 220,000 titles, each of which could be scored and compared with others on the basis of narrative structure, emotional tonality, the emotional arc of characters, color scheme, and a host of other characteristics. Type in *Pulp Fiction*, for example, and Corto will tell you its characters are aggressive, anxious, artistic, body-focused, food-focused, friend-focused, sex-focused, family-oriented (the gold watch!), work-oriented, and melancholy but extremely low on agreeableness, happiness, and social skills. *Westworld* isn't very similar to anything else in emotional tone, but it ranks closer to *True Detective* and *Killing Eve* than to other science fiction series like *The Man in the High Castle* or *The Leftovers*. Corto thinks Amazon's *The Man in the High Castle* series, based on the novel by Philip K. Dick, is quite close emotionally to *Nancy Drew* and *Sherlock*.

Corto also scans social media to see what people are saying. "Reddit is a very big predictor of success," Bergquist says. "Everything that gets big, gets big on Reddit first." The words people use matter too: having your movie described as "cinematic" is a very good sign. "For certain types of movies, the cast doesn't matter very much—at least in North America." On this continent, people "really complain about the story being poorly written. Overseas, a big-name cast will make a big difference." With three-quarters of the global box office coming from outside North America, movie stars don't have to worry yet.

Bergquist is careful to frame Corto as a helpful tool for screenwriters, directors, and producers, not as a threat to their artistic freedom. "It gives the content creators a lot of signals," he says. "We're trying to bring neuroscience to what is fundamentally a neuroscience problem—storytelling. Understanding stories is a lot like understanding physics. It's the world around you."

From Rebel Alliance to Galactic Empire

These two initiatives from ETC—Bergquist's work in AI, which aims to replace guesswork with certainty, and Philip Lelyveld's work in XR, with its ultimate goal of erasing the boundary between what's real and what's virtual—represent the twin directions in which digital media are evolving. On the one hand, toward the elimination of uncertainty—in advertising, in screen-writing, in any field that requires buy-in from an audience; on the other, toward the blurring of reality, to the point that it becomes all but impossible to say what is certain and what is not. These two contradictory impulses will help determine not only how we tell stories but what kind of stories we tell.

As is often the case, we landed here more or less by happen-stance. It was only 25 years ago that digital media seemed in dan-ger of being strangled in their crib. At *Wired*, where I worked from 1999 to 2009, this was viewed as a war between the Bellheads—the phone company loyalists who hated anything that wasn't POTS, or Plain Old Telephone Service—and the Netheads. The latter, *Wired* explained, "believe in intelligent software rather than brute-force hardware, in flexible and adaptive routing instead of fixed traffic control." In the Rebel Alliance as opposed to the Galactic Empire.

Meanwhile, the global media conglomerates that dominated the entertainment business—movies, television, music, books and magazines, theme parks—remained firmly under the com-mand of a clueless overseer class. Whenever they tried to ven-ture forth into the digital wilderness, they inevitably met with disaster—most notably with Time Warner's 1994 Pathfinder ini-tiative, which lost so much money that magazine division chief Don Logan famously declared it had "given new meaning to me of the scientific term black hole."

Then, in 2000, at the peak of the dotcom bubble, Time Warner's CEO sold the company—the largest media conglomerate in the world—to America Online, the brash young Internet portal and dial-up Internet service provider. Never mind that AOL's wildly inflated stock would soon crash or that AOL itself was about to become irrelevant as the world moved to broadband. Today, AOL

Time Warner no longer exists: division after division was spun off until in 2018, AT&T swallowed what was left—HBO, CNN and the other Turner channels, and the Warner Bros. film and television studio.

Meanwhile, tech was soaring. By late 2020, Apple was the most valuable publicly traded company in the world, with a market cap hovering around $2 trillion. Microsoft and Amazon were each worth well over $1 trillion, with Alphabet (the parent company of Google and YouTube), Facebook, and the Chinese Internet giants Alibaba and TenCent not far behind. Apple cleared more than $57 billion in its most recent fiscal year, making it the third most profitable company in the world. Microsoft made $39 billion, Alphabet $34 billion, Facebook $18.5 billion. Too bad so much of this money was generated off your data.

A lot has been written about "privacy" lately, but that little word doesn't begin to convey what's at issue. Privacy is what you'd like when you go to the toilet. What fuels the triumph of tech is your being monitored, 24 hours a day, 365 days a year, by the apps on your smartphone, by your smartphone itself, by the "smart speakers" in your house and your car, by the "smart thermostat" you had installed, and by any number of other apps and devices you're probably not aware of, online and off, all so that Google or Facebook or Amazon or their customers or Cambridge Analytica or just about anybody can know everything there is to know about you and—this is the important part—what you're going to do next. The word that covers this phenomenon is "surveillance," as in Shoshana Zuboff's *The Age of Surveillance Capitalism*.

All Your Data Are Belong to Us

In her groundbreaking 2019 book, Zuboff notes that "surveillance capitalism was invented by a specific group of human beings in a specific time and place." The time was late 2000 to 2001; the place, Silicon Valley; the humans, engineers and executives at Google Inc. What they did then would transform the Internet forever, from the anarchic, techno-hippie free-for-all of the nineties to the corporate surveillance machine it has become today.

Google lost nearly $15 million in 2000, its second full year of operation, and when the Internet bubble burst that year it was suddenly under pressure to make money. The key to doing so, it was thought, would be licensing its search technology to companies like Yahoo that were portals to the web. Yet it was slowly becoming apparent that the portals were little more than training wheels. Once people got their bearings, they wouldn't need training wheels. What people needed in the face of infinite information was not more information, it was search—to be able to sift through billions of websites to find exactly what they wanted. To find the tiniest needle in a haystack as big as the world. But search didn't seem to be something you could charge for.

Sergey Brin and Larry Page, Google's founders, had always disdained advertising, and most of their engineers felt likewise. But now, under pressure, they stumbled across a payment system that charged advertisers only when someone actually clicked on their ad. This meant that advertisers didn't pay for ads unless they "worked." Meanwhile, Google engineers had been capturing vast amounts of information on what its users did during and after their search inquiries—"data exhaust" that was fed back into the company's computers to improve its search results through machine learning. Gradually it dawned on people there that locked within this data exhaust was an extraordinary predictive power. Now, it seemed, they could take the uncertainty out of advertising. When that connection was made, privacy went out the window and ad money started pouring in.

Google made $100 million in 2002. Zuboff dubbed this "the

watershed year during which surveillance capitalism took root."
Ads have migrated inexorably to the Internet ever since, primarily
at the expense of newspapers and magazines. But the illusion of
certainty that targeted advertising produced—the sense that as
an advertiser you could reach only those people who might want
your product—would not be Google's alone.

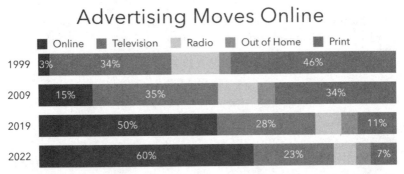

Advertising Moves Online

	Online	Television	Radio	Out of Home	Print
1999	3%	34%			46%
2009	15%	35%			34%
2019	50%		28%		11%
2022	60%		23%		7%

In 20 years, advertising in the US and Canada has shifted overwhelmingly to
the Internet – primarily at the expense of newspapers and magazines and to
the benefit of Google and Facebook. This trend is expected to accelerate.

Out of home includes billboards and cinemas. Print includes newspapers and magazines (print editions only).
Source: Advertising Expenditure Forecasts, Zenith, December 2019.

"We Decided These Would Be the Norms Now"

When 19-year-old Mark Zuckerberg launched Thefacebook at
Harvard in February 2004, he was as dismissive of advertising
as Brin and Page had been. But he too would change his mind.
In November 2007 he introduced Facebook Ads, a self-service
system that included some very strange features—particularly
something called Beacon, which would automatically alert your
Facebook friends whenever you made a purchase from certain
retailers.

Almost immediately, Beacon started spoiling Christmas. There was the North Carolina college student who learned on Facebook that her sister had bought her a Harry Potter game. The woman in Michigan whose cousin found her entire holiday shopping list published for all her friends to see. The Massachusetts guy who had to tell his wife about her surprise after Facebook informed her he'd just bought a diamond ring. Yet at Facebook headquarters in Silicon Valley, such complaints were met with hubris. "Whenever we innovate and create great new experiences and new features, if they are not well understood at the outset, one thing we need to do is give people an opportunity to interact with them," one executive said. "After a while, they fall in love with them."

Not this time. Beacon was soon made optional, and in 2009 it was shut down entirely in response to a class-action lawsuit. Three months after settling the lawsuit, however, Facebook made unilateral changes to its privacy policy that appeared to give its users more control while actually giving them less. "People have really gotten comfortable not only sharing more information and different kinds, but more openly and with more people," Zuckerberg said later. "We decided that these would be the social norms now, and we just went for it."

As with Zuckerberg, so with Google's CEO, Eric Schmidt, who bought into social media when he engineered the purchase of YouTube in 2006. "If you have something that you don't want anyone to know, maybe you shouldn't be doing it in the first place," Schmidt told CNBC. This comment could be seen as telling it like it is, or it could be seen as glib, self-serving, patronizing, and totally out of touch with the lives of real people in the actual world. "As a person who is being stalked for being an innocent bystander in a child custody case, I can tell you that losing my choices over what is searchable or not is huge," a woman commented on the tech blog *ReadWriteWeb*. A University of Texas student was outed when the head of the school's Queer Chorus added her to the choir's Facebook group—prompting her father, who was notified because he was a "friend," to write, "Hell awaits you pervert—good luck singing there."

Sharing for Billionaires

And yet surveillance isn't even the worst of it. The bigger problem with social media is the way they sow uncertainty and amplify hate. Looking back, we might have sensed something amiss at Zuckerberg's introduction of Facebook Ads. The message was cloaked in "Kumbaya"-style verbiage, but in retrospect it wasn't all that subtle:

> Once every hundred years, media changes. The last hundred years have been defined by the mass media. . . . In the next hundred years, information won't be just pushed out to people, it will be shared among the millions of connections people have.

Information will be shared. It sounds so friendly, so generous, almost loving. It doesn't at all suggest the kind of information that has been shared by Red Ice TV, the white-supremacist mouthpiece from Sweden. Or by the Committee for Open Debate on the Holocaust, which promotes "intellectual freedom" to discuss whether Hitler's final solution was a hoax. Or by the Council of Conservative Citizens, the white-supremacist group whose site "educated" the 21-year-old high school dropout who went on to shoot nine people dead in a historic African-American church in Charleston, South Carolina. Or by the neo-Confederate League of the South, one of several far-right groups that helped organize the 2017 Unite the Right rally in Charlottesville, Virginia, which culminated in murder when a young Hitler admirer rammed his car into a crowd of people protesting the rally. Some such Internet pages were taken down in the wake of Charlottesville. Some were not.

Not that deciding what should go is easy, or easy on the people who do it. When a reporter from the online publication *The Verge* spoke with current and former content reviewers for Facebook in Phoenix—contract workers in their twenties and early thirties—he found some deeply traumatized people. A trainee collapsing in uncontrollable sobs after watching a video of a man being stabbed again and again as he screams and begs for his life. A worker losing it over another stabbing video—a guy his own age, bleeding out and crying for his mother. This worker watched so many conspiracy videos claiming 9/11 was an inside job that he started to believe them. Other employees were found having "trauma sex" in the stairwells, in bathroom stalls, in the parking garage. Sometimes they'd joke about going out to hang on the roof—the joke being they might throw themselves off it. They had psychological counselors on call, but nondisclosure agreements prevented them from talking with friends or family about what was happening. A poster on the wall read, "EMPATHY AT SCALE." Almost nobody lasted more than a year.

It was even worse for a group of Facebook content moderators in Europe, the *Guardian* reported, after a data breach exposed the personal profiles of 1,000 moderators to the very organizations they were monitoring. Among them were 40 people working at a counterterrorism center at Facebook's European headquarters in Dublin. One of these—a native of Iraq, early twenties, getting €13 (about $14) an hour—quit his job, left his family, and went into hiding in eastern Europe until his money ran out. His father had been kidnapped and beaten before they left Iraq, his uncle killed. The same could happen to him now. "The punishment from ISIS for working in counter-terrorism is beheading," he said. "All they'd need to do is tell someone who is radical here."

Two years later, in Sri Lanka, a Facebook user posted a wrathful bulletin in the language of the country's Buddhist majority: "Kill all the Muslim babies without sparing even an infant. Fucking dogs!" According to *Businessweek*, the post got 30 likes before anyone flagged it as hate speech. Facebook concluded that it "doesn't go against one of our specific Community Standards," so the post stayed up—one of many spewing hatred for Sri Lanka's Muslims, and for other minorities elsewhere in the world. Finally, after two people were killed in a riot, the government took Facebook offline for three days. "The shutdown got the company's attention," *Businessweek* reported.

For years, Zuckerberg had painted Facebook as a sort of quasi-utopian experiment. There was even a map by a Facebook intern, a midnight blue map with tiny strands of light representing Facebook connections, so layered and bright they sketch out the continents, reaching across the seas, each infinitesimal strand representing a single connection, a friend, a link. Too bad so many of those pale blue lines are actually acid green.

With after-tax income in 2020 of $29 billion and a profit margin of 34 percent, Facebook could well afford to stanch the hate that gushes from its servers, difficult as the task may be. But that's evidently not a priority, even though Facebook exists in the same world Javaad Alipoor conjures up in *The Believers Are But Brothers*. The world in which Atif and Marwan take up the sword to avenge the humiliation of Islam while Ethan/4thelulz rages against the cucks and libtards in California. While I, like most of us, am just trying to hang on in the Grayzone, because I think gray is a beautiful color—capable of endless nuance and subtlety, not harsh and blinding like black or white—and because frankly the alternatives don't look all that great. Lose your mind to some wacko conspiracy theory? Wouldn't *you* rather stock shelves at Tesco?

Okay, maybe not.

Race to the Bottom of the Brainstem

Ultimately it's a question of corporate citizenship. Facebook and other social media sites, YouTube in particular, can dominate the ad market while spewing misinformation and hate because the US has no legal requirement for them to do otherwise. Section 230 of the Communications Decency Act, the 1996 legislation that overhauled US telecom policy for the first time since 1934, absolves Internet service providers, online media platforms (including Facebook, Instagram, YouTube, and Twitter, none of which existed in the nineties), and individual bloggers of responsibility for almost anything that is posted by their users. (Child pornography and intellectual property theft are still beyond the pale.) And in an attention economy, counterfactual information can spread wildly if packaged right.

"This is a problem that Internet platforms did not invent," Roger McNamee, an early Zuckerberg mentor and Facebook investor, points out in his tell-all book *Zucked.* "Existing fissures in society created a business opportunity that platforms exploited. They created a feedback loop that reinforces and amplifies ideas with a speed and at a scale that are unprecedented." A feedback loop that combines the persuasiveness of stories—stories from friends, stories from the media, from ISIS, from Red Ice TV, from who knows where—with the addictiveness of digital attention traps.

Social media becomes an attention trap when it's algorithmically engineered to give us a dopamine rush, usually by nudging us toward some other post that will generate an even bigger reaction. Video game developers routinely build "compulsion loops" into their titles—prompts that promise a reward and deliver it randomly, so you never know if you'll get the reward or not. Compulsion loops prey on the brain's reward system, which releases a dopamine hit in anticipation—not on delivery—of a pleasurable experience. If the experience doesn't come, you're left wanting it all the more. Such loops are hard to escape, particularly for anyone predisposed to addiction, and they are hardly restricted to video games. Like slot machines, smartphones and social media are designed to keep us constantly on edge, constantly seeking more.

"In the absence of a commitment to civic responsibility, the recommendation engine will be programmed to do the things that generate the most profit," McNamee writes. There's a joke in the tech world, he notes, about YouTube's "three degrees of Alex Jones"—its alleged tendency, no matter where you start, to steer you to a video from the notorious *InfoWars* conspiracy monger (The Sandy Hook elementary school massacre was a hoax! 9/11 was a government job! The moon landing never happened! Buy my toothpaste and kill the coronavirus!) within three recommendations. But it turns out that not only is the three-degrees-of-Alex-Jones joke not a joke; you don't even have to go the whole three degrees.

In a 2018 exposé, the *Wall Street Journal* reported that YouTube "often fed far-right or far-left videos to users who watched relatively mainstream news sources, such as Fox News and MSNBC." A YouTube search that year for "FBI memo" turned up Alex Jones among the top results, along with major news and broadcasting networks and a site that described itself as "Dedicated to Watching the End Time Events that Lead to the Return of Our Lord Jesus Christ." By putting fringe conspiracy views on equal footing with legitimate news reports, YouTube's algorithms effectively declared Alex Jones and his ilk as authoritative as any legitimate news organization. Not for the first time, its executives pledged to do better. "We recognize that this is our responsibility," one said, "and we have more to do."

Ah, yes: We Know We Have More Work to Do. "Let's call it W.K.W.H.M.W.T.D. for short," wrote Charlie Warzel in the *New York Times*—"the definitive utterance of the social media era, trotted out by executives whenever their companies come in for a public shaming." WKWHMWTD is kind of a mouthful, so following the example of WYSIWYG (pronounced WIZ-ee-WIG), the "what you see is what you get" design goal of personal computer pioneers in the eighties, let's say WEK-a-WHUM-wa-TEE-dee. WKWHMWTD is everywhere these days, quoted in the news, trotted out at Congressional hearings, and yet progress remains slow. Sometimes the wacko recommendations go down—the flat-Earthers became less ubiquitous after YouTube targeted them, according to an academic paper on the subject—and sometimes they go back up. But they never disappear entirely.

"It's not because anyone is evil or has bad intentions," Tristan Harris, a former "design ethicist" at Google who now heads a San Francisco nonprofit called the Center for Humane Technology, told Anderson Cooper on *60 Minutes*. "It's because the game is getting attention at all costs. And the problem is it becomes this race to the bottom of the brainstem, where if I go lower on the brainstem to get you, you know, using my product, I win. But it doesn't end up in the world we want to live in."

Which brings us to October 2019, and Mark Zuckerberg's speech at Georgetown University. No longer the fresh-faced Harvard dropout, he spoke as the 35-year-old billionaire who controls what is arguably the world's most powerful media company, except it can't be a media company because it assumes no responsibility for what is said or done on its platform—and thanks to section 230, it doesn't have to. The month before, Facebook had announced it would make no attempt to censor politicians' claims or fact-check their ads because anything they say is newsworthy, regardless of whether it's true. Now he doubled down, wrapping himself in the First Amendment, casting his policy in patriotic terms, even suggesting it's more righteous than what news organizations do. "I don't think it's right for a private company to censor politicians or the news in a democracy," he asserted, in what was billed as a major policy declaration. "People having the power to express themselves at scale is a new kind of force in the world—a Fifth Estate alongside the other power structures of society."

It was a thoroughly bogus argument. Private companies "censor" things all the time. The First Amendment prohibits the government from interfering with free expression; it doesn't tell private companies they have to publish anything and everything anybody says. And as an open letter from Facebook employees slyly noted, "Free speech and paid speech are not the same thing." Yet if Zuckerberg has his way, the Fourth Estate—an independent, ad-supported press that takes legal responsibility for what it publishes—will continue to wither and die. Meanwhile, his new "Fifth Estate"—or rather the companies that facilitate it, Facebook chief among them—grows fat off the souls of its users and the money its advertisers pay to access their futures. Certainty for the advertisers; claims and counterclaims, lies and disinformation, truth or consequences for the rest of us.

Targeting the Edge of Your Belief System

We know now where this led: to a rally on the Ellipse in Washington, DC, on January 6, 2021, at which the president of the United States whipped a crowd into a frenzy with lies about the election results. "We will never give up. We will never concede," Trump cried. "We won this election, and we won it by a landslide." The crowd moved on to the Capitol, where some of its members broke into the building, taking over the Senate chamber and almost breaching the House, while communicating with one another via Facebook about the whereabouts of the lawmakers who had fled—people they considered traitors. At one point, according to an affidavit from the FBI, one of them wrote, "All members are in the tunnels under capital seal them in. Turn on gas." The next day, Facebook banned Trump indefinitely.

Thirteen months earlier, as the US election campaign was beginning to heat up, John Borthwick called a meeting. Borthwick is the founder and CEO of betaworks, a venture capital fund that invests in tech start-ups at the seed stage and earlier—among them Tumblr, Kickstarter, and Medium, the social blogging platform that's pioneering a new model of publishing. He'd just had breakfast with Chris Hughes, a cofounder of Facebook when he was Zuckerberg's Harvard roommate, who had recently declared in a *New York Times* opinion piece that Facebook should be broken up. Borthwick and Hughes agreed that something had to be done—not just about Facebook, but about the digital media ecosystem in general.

A week or two later, Borthwick brought together 25 people at the betaworks offices in the Meatpacking District of Manhattan. The result, announced on Medium and signed by Borthwick, Hughes, and 11 others—among them Tristan Harris, Roger McNamee, *Filter Bubble* author Eli Pariser, and former Federal Election Commission chair Trevor Potter—was a list of 10 things the technology platforms could do to safeguard the 2020 elections. The recommendations ranged from the obvious—identifying and deleting fake accounts—to the strangely controversial, like clarifying where the social media giants should draw the line on lying. But the larger problem, beyond the election, is the structure of online discourse.

"The way our media system works, so much is just point-counterpoint," Borthwick told me later. "It not only divides but tends to drive people to extremes. It becomes binary—'I'm against it!' 'I'm for it!'—when the reality is that many things in life get sorted out in the muddy middle." In the Grayzone.

"Our ability to understand what is real is getting very tenuous," Borthwick continued. He cited *Behind the Curve*, a 2018 documentary about the flat-Earth movement: "What you see in it are reasonably intelligent, normal people who are kind of loners, who live in constrained information spheres, and you just see how the algorithm starts to pull you in. They're microtargeting, but that term misses the point. It's that, we know the edge of your belief system. We can't tell you 'flat Earth,' but there's a little crack in your logical belief system, and we target you with an ad or a promo video from somebody you respect. You click on that, and you slowly go down the rabbit hole. And three months later, you're a full-on flat-Earther."

It's the quantitative theory of interestingness at work. Just enough novelty and then, before long, flat Earth, Satan-worshiping pedophiles, a landslide election win viciously stolen from Donald J. Trump. Whatever rabbit hole sucks you in.

"I Wish the Internet Were a Little Bit Kinder"

Thanks to deepfakes—video or audio files that have been digitally altered to show something that never happened—our ability to determine what stories are real is about to get more tenuous still. The technology that enables deepfakes has become simpler to use and increasingly available, with predictable results. In April 2020, for example, the environmental activist group Extinction Rebellion posted a deepfake video in which Sophie Wilmès, the prime minister of Belgium, appeared to say, "Coronavirus is an alarm bell we cannot ignore. Pandemics"—Covid-19, SARS, Ebola, Swine Flu—"are one of the consequences of a deeper ecological crisis." Except that she didn't actually say that. They were words put into her mouth.

Two months later, *Vox* reported that Kristen Bell, star of the NBC series *The Good Place*, had apparently turned up in porn videos—except it wasn't her, it was her face, digitally mapped onto the face of a porn actress. "I wish that the Internet were a little bit more responsible and a little bit kinder," Bell said in response. Wishful thinking indeed: according to a report from Sensity, a betaworks-supported cybersecurity firm in Amsterdam that specializes in detecting "synthetic media," nearly 15,000 deepfake videos had been posted online as early as September 2019, almost all of them involving pornography. Yet even the possibility that political videos might be deepfakes was causing trouble—an attempted coup in Gabon, a hotly debated sex scandal in Malaysia.

In addition to private companies like Sensity (formerly known as Deeptrace), the Pentagon has mounted an effort to identify deepfakes algorithmically by identifying "semantic errors" that suggest a file has been manipulated through AI—mismatched earrings, for example, a fashion faux pas no human would commit. And yet, in quiet moments, the people whose job it is to identify and expose deepfakes online may admit that what they are doing amounts to a high-stakes game of Whac-a-Mole. Anyone can order up a deepfake video from vendors that are easy to find online, at prices that range from a few hundred dollars to $10,000, depending how convincing you want it to be. And the technology is racing ahead, so as with malware and virus protection, constant updating is required to counter new means of forgery—and even then, the chances of catching a particular video before millions of people have seen it are slim.

Those who work in the field don't kid themselves. "It feels like an accident of history," I was told by one who asked to go unnamed in order to speak freely, "that for two centuries from the invention of photography to today, we as humanity started to believe that since there is a recording, therefore it must be factual." And a far shorter time than that if you want to talk about smartphone video, for example, documenting police murders of black people. "It was kind of an accident," this person continued, "a period in time when we were able to produce recordings of events but not to manipulate them. That is where a break with potentially catastrophic consequences is happening now. The next generation is going to be born seeing so much synthetic content that they'll think we were stupid to believe it."

The Apopheniac's Dilemma

At Columbia's Digital Storytelling Lab, Lance Weiler has been developing a different approach to the issue of deepfakes. Early in 2020 he and a DSL colleague, Nick Fortugno, started prototyping a virtual, interactive theater piece called *Project Immerse*. In some ways it's like an extremely participatory version of the anthology television series *Black Mirror*, but instead of merely presenting dystopian visions of the future, it aims to demystify the technologies that give rise to them. At heart, it's a digital literacy initiative—teaching disguised as entertainment.

Project Immerse is an exercise in collective sense-making. It takes place on the web, using Zoom and an online environment called Miro that acts as an infinite digital whiteboard where people can post information and collaborate in real time. The experience is prefaced by a warning that as a participant, you will be misled and lied to. The initial episode involves a teenager who has purchased a bodycam on eBay to use in a high school project. When the teacher announces that his team hasn't done its project properly, everything that went into that project is thrown online for all to see—the first of many data dumps you will encounter. The situation turns from strange to surreal when the teacher steps out, the classroom gets hacked, and you find yourself staring at a hopelessly chaotic computer desktop—is that browser tab open to a bodycam auction on eBay? Then your screen goes black, and when it comes back on, someone new has taken over the class.

Now people are thrown into groups and inundated with more data, along with instructions to write down anything that looks important before it's deleted. You see that the high school student's stepfather is a cop—that's important, right? But then some new person pops up claiming to be you. And more and more of them, until it becomes impossible for anyone to distinguish you from all the other entities claiming to be you. But it's hard to focus anyway because you're being bombarded with random bits of information that lead only to more questions. Where is the student? What did he do? What does the charred skateboard you just saw have to do with it? Has he been radicalized? Is he a victim? Or part of some conspiracy?

By this time, it's impossible to tell what aspects of the story are real and what aspects are fake. You've been desperately looking for patterns, but you're no longer able to distinguish those that mean something from those that don't. You were warned that this would happen, but nonetheless you've fallen victim to apophenia—the tendency to find patterns where none exists, whether in the condensation on a living-room window or in the cryptic utterings of some person, or thing, who goes by Q. The "narrative fallacy," as Nassim Nicholas Taleb calls it in *The Black Swan*. Now, with the game over, you're told that 90 percent of what you've encountered has been generated by a machine—by an AI whose knowledge of the world is based on seventies conspiracy theories, Wikileaks, and other such scenarios. You learn that many of the videos you just saw that looked so damning were deepfakes. That the shared reality you just constructed with the other people in your group was totally bogus. And that everything you've just seen was created with off-the-shelf technology—no computer coding required.

But there's a flip side to this as well. With the help of AI, *Harry Potter* fans can edit themselves into the movies. Kids can become someone else on TikTok. "I can drop into a Buster Keaton film and make it something new," Weiler says. All sorts of possibilities become real. The same technologies that are shredding the fabric of reality, as Doctor Who would have it, are also enabling the tech-savvy among us to tell stories in astonishing new ways.

Inceptionism

One such person is Refik Anadol, an Istanbul-born artist whose medium is data. Anadol, who lives now in Los Angeles, is a bubbly, almost cherubic-looking man who dresses entirely in black. In 2018, commissioned to tell the story of the Los Angeles Philharmonic at the start of its centennial season, he responded by imagining its Frank Gehry–designed concert hall as an enormous artificial intelligence—one that celebrates the orchestra's past and dreams about its future.

Working with Anadol to make it happen were a team from Google AI, the independent AI researcher Parag Mital, and a half-dozen designers in their twenties who worked in Anadol's studio, their faces half-hidden behind enormous computer screens. Every available artifact from the Philharmonic's archives was gathered: millions of photographs, printed programs, and audio and video recordings, each one digitized and algorithmically activated to form a spectacle that played across the Walt Disney Concert Hall's billowing steel superstructure for 10 consecutive nights. In the process, billions of data points came together in a vast web of connections: every performance of every symphony, every trumpet, every oboe, every note the orchestra has ever played. As "WDCH Dreams" reached its climax, all this data—nearly 45 terabytes of it—was fused together in a sort of fantasia that caused the building to, as Anadol put it, "hallucinate."*

"I thought it was time to take these beautiful memories and organize them into a story," Anadol said as we sat in his studio, a former auto repair shop on Hyperion Avenue, just down the street from the site where Walt Disney created Mickey Mouse in 1928. "It's kind of a science fiction story," he went on. "We have concerns about the future because that's where we all live." Key to this story, he added, is "the idea of the machine as collaborator."

AI came into the picture because for the building to "dream," or for that matter to collaborate, the computer code would need some knowledge of what it was doing. Anadol had recently been granted a residency at Google's Artists + Machine Intelligence program, set up to bring artists and engineers together to address such questions as the nature of intelligence and the relationship between humans and machines. Later, when he started on the LA Phil project, Google supplied cloud-computing resources, machine-learning experts, and a procedure called "inceptionism" that had been incubated at the company's lab in Zurich.

Inception, the Christopher Nolan movie, is about "dreams inside dreams inside dreams," says the leader of Artists + Machine Intelligence, Kenric McDowell, a slender young man with shoulder-length hair. Inceptionism is similarly recursive. It's what happens when an artificial neural network stops being trained to recognize images and is instructed instead to show us what it sees—a good

* "WDCH Dreams" received the Columbia Digital Storytelling Lab's 2019 Breakthrough Award. For more information, visit digitaldozen.io/projects/ wdch-dreams/ and refikanadol.com/works/wdch-dreams/.

idea if you want to learn how the machine learns. The results are startling: if the network has been trained to recognize dog faces, it will see dog faces everywhere. Or as McDowell says, "It starts to breathe its own fumes."

Sort of like tech in general. And yet, though it relies on some of the same algorithms that underlie facial recognition, an AI technology that seems increasingly ominous as its potential for abuse becomes clearer, "WDCH Dreams" is a benign work, an unalloyed vision of artificial intelligence as partner rather than threat. "I am very, very optimistic," Anadol says. "I think these are incredible tools to have for creativity." As for the rest—"Technology is a mirror of humankind. A very honest mirror of who we are."

Atonement

How do the rest of us tell stories in a world like this? Carefully, I hope. Thoughtfully. And maybe on a place like Medium, the online writing platform that was set up in 2012 by Evan Williams, the San Francisco–based entrepreneur. Williams was a cofounder of Twitter and before that of Blogger, the early online blogging platform that Google bought in 2003. When he started Blogger in 1999, few people knew what blogging was. Later, with the launch of the "microblogging" platform Twitter, he inadvertently helped send blogging into decline. That was in 2006—the same year Facebook opened itself to anyone with an email address, the same year Google bought the fledgling video site YouTube for $1.65 billion. The year that, though we didn't know it at the time, saw the beginning of industrial-scale social media. You get the feeling that Medium is an act of atonement.

When blogging emerged in the early aughts, it brought a sense of liberation. You didn't have to be a professional writer; you didn't have to be edited; you didn't need to be an Internet savant. If you could type, you could blog. But soon there got to be so many blogs it became harder and harder to be noticed. To build an audience you needed to blog and blog and blog some more and then keep blogging still. And of course there was no money in it. It was so much easier, and often more rewarding, to post on Facebook or Twitter or Tumblr or Instagram, where likes were cheap and followers abounded. Who cared if many of those followers were bots? Who cared, or even realized, that what you were actually doing was setting yourself and your followers up for a data harvest by the social media combines and whoever they'd sold you to?

Medium was meant to be an antidote to all that. Williams introduced it as "a new place on the Internet where people share ideas and stories that are longer than 140 characters and not just for friends." In other words, not Twitter, not Facebook. It's intended, as Williams put it, to be relational rather than transactional. To foster communities rather than herd you algorithmically into attention traps. But with the ad market dominated by Google and Facebook it's not obvious how to make this pay, even to a man who calls his investment vehicle Obvious Ventures. Not without reason did Harvard's Nieman Journalism Lab describe Medium as "an endless thought experiment into what publishing on the internet could look like."

Medium is hardly the only such experiment. Another San Francisco–based startup, Substack, provides the tools you need to start an email newsletter and charge a subscription fee for it. Substack (the name refers to the technology "stack" required to maintain a subscription service) was started in 2017 by a couple of guys who were inspired by the success of *Stratechery*, a newsletter from Taiwan that has become a must-read in tech circles. Ben Thompson, the former Microsoft employee who started *Stratech-*

ery as a blog in 2013 and converted it to a newsletter a year later, is the rare individual who not only has something insightful to say but can master the necessary business and technical details. If Substack could fix it so "you just have to be a great writer and we can take care of the rest—well, that would be transformative," its cofounder and CEO Christopher Best told *NiemanLab*. Note that you would still have to be a great writer—and if you really want to make it pay, you'd better be a great writer in a niche no one else has discovered yet.

This ability to make it pay is a critical distinction between newsletters and blogs. As journalism has withered under the Google-Facebook advertising duopoly and other onslaughts— the *New York Times* reported in September 2020 that more than 30,000 US journalists had been laid off, furloughed, or had a pay cut during the coronavirus pandemic—paid subscription newsletters have been looking better and better to individual reporters and even budding periodicals. "It's a lifeboat for people off the wreck of Old Media—or New Media, for that matter," the Hollywood columnist Richard Rushfield told the *Times*. In early 2019, Substack began hosting podcasts as well, offering podcasters a way to make money and newsletter writers an opportunity to expand into another fast-growing medium. Spotify too has had a big push on podcasts and sells ads against them—but like musicians, podcasters on Spotify need to be superstars if they expect to see any money.

None of this means the Internet's attention traps are going away. "There's a huge buffet," Evan Williams told the *New York Times* columnist Kevin Roose. "If you eat whatever's put in front of you, you're not necessarily going to be making the best choices."

His mention of choices reminded me of a talk I'd come across by David Foster Wallace. The year was 2005, and Wallace was giving a commencement address at Kenyon College in rural Ohio.

At the moment when we stood collectively, unknowingly on the brink of smartphones and industrial-scale social media, Wallace delved into the meaning of "learning how to think," an old-fashioned idea that liberal arts colleges like Kenyon are supposed to teach you:

> It means being conscious and aware enough to *choose* what you pay attention to and to *choose* how you construct meaning from experience. Because if you cannot or will not exercise this kind of choice in adult life, you will be totally hosed.

Choose where your attention goes; choose, as Jerome Bruner might have put it, how you construct reality; choose not to be totally hosed—these are the mark of awareness in an attention economy. If there were only one thing to be learned about stories, or devices, or stories *on* devices, it would be this. That you need to be conscious and aware enough to respond to the signal and not the noise. That you need to break out of the compulsion loops that surveillance capitalism has programmed for you. That you need to construct your own reality rather than buy into someone else's. And that to manage these things successfully, you need to be fully, deeply aware of the sea we are swimming in.

Acknowledgments

As I mentioned at the start of this book, I could not have written it without the experience I've had over the past seven years at Columbia. That I owe to many people, starting with David K. Park, the former dean of strategic initiatives for the Faculty of the Arts and Sciences; Ira Deutchman, the indie film producer and distributor and longtime professor of professional practice at Columbia University School of the Arts; and Lance Weiler, experimental filmmaker and storyteller, who had recently founded the Digital Storytelling Lab at the School of the Arts. David and Ira encouraged me to develop the Strategic Storytelling seminar, and David engineered a first-ever partnership between the School of the Arts and Columbia Business School to present it as an executive education program.

Developing the seminar would have been a great deal harder without Paul Woolmington, a legendary ad man who taught it with me before going back into advertising as CEO of the startup agency Canvas Worldwide. The program has also benefited from the support of Anthony Madonna, Alberto Cruz, Scott Gardner, Amy Schnitzer, and Sarah Czuratis at Columbia Business School; of Mike Malefakis, former head of executive education at the Business School; of Hilary Brougher, Maureen Ryan, Rich

Dikeman, Christina Rumpf, and Alicia Stevens at the School of the Arts; and of Rachel Ginsburg at the Digital Storytelling Lab. I'm especially grateful for the support of Carol Becker and Jana Hart Wright, dean of faculty and of administration respectively at the School of the Arts.

Throughout the book you will have come across ideas from people who have been guest speakers at the seminar—chief among them AIGA medalist Ellen Lupton, author of *Design Is Storytelling* and senior curator at Cooper Hewitt, Smithsonian Design Museum; Christian Madsbjerg, cofounder of the consulting firm ReD Associates and author of *Sensemaking*, a book that celebrates what tends to be known derogatorily as "the human factor"; Matt Locke, formerly in charge of innovation at the BBC and Channel 4, founder more recently of the UK media consultancy Storythings; Karin Timpone, former global marketing officer for Marriott Worldwide; and Columbia Business School professor Rita Gunther McGrath, the strategy and innovation expert whose most recent book is *Seeing Around Corners*. Their generosity has been key to the development of the book and the seminar alike.

The book had its genesis in a toolkit I developed for people enrolled in the seminar, because I wanted them to have a quick summary of what I was trying to convey. My first thought, after reimagining it at book length, was to take it to Brendan Curry at Norton, the editor and the publishing house that brought out *The Art of Immersion* a decade ago. "We're getting the old band together!" Brendan replied, and indeed we were: marketing director Steve Colca, executive art director Ingsu Liu, associate production director Anna Oler, and Jason Booher to design the cover; plus Elizabeth Riley, Dorothy Cook, Bee Holekamp, Rebecca Homiski, Laurie Lieb, and Steven Pace in New York and John Donovan, Victoria Keown-Boyd, Pamela O'Reilly, Judith Pamplin, and Oliver Wearing in London. I'd also like to thank Vittorio Bo and Stefano Milano at my Italian publisher, Codice Edizioni—I'm thrilled to be working with them again as well. And of course I owe a great deal to my agent, Andrew Wylie, and to James Pullen in his London office: thank you.

Beyond that, I'm extremely appreciative of those beyond Columbia who welcomed me to the academic world—among them Henry Jenkins of the Annenberg School for Communications and Journalism at USC; Larry Gross of USC Annenberg Press, founder of the *International Journal of Communication*; Jonathan Taplin, founder of USC's Annenberg Innovation Lab; Erin Reilly of the Moody College of Communication at the University of Texas in Austin; and Martha Russell, executive director of Stanford MediaX. Short passages in the book appeared in different form in the *New York Times, strategy + business,* and the *Milken Institute Review*; I'm grateful to my editors there for encouraging me to explore new ideas. I am grateful to Brian Clark for inspiration, and to many others who offered encouragement and help, among them Susan Bonds, Maia Danziger, Barbara Graustark, Justin Hendrix, Billee Howard, Vaino Leskinen, Mike Monello, Peter Passell, Michael Pressman, Leila Rafla-Demetrious, Robert Schaltenbrand, Benj Steinman, Andrew Taylor, and Barbara Tversky. And above all I owe gratitude to the incomparable Susan Kamil and to my wife, Beth Rashbaum.

Notes

Preface

xvi **"Appetites we share with animals"**: Louis Menand, "What Identity Demands," *New Yorker*, Sept. 3, 2018.

xvi **"Man . . . is the story-telling animal"**: Graham Swift, *Waterland* (New York: Vintage, 1992), 62–63.

Part 1. The Narrative Turn

3 **"There are two modes"**: Jerome Bruner, *Actual Minds, Possible Worlds* (Cambridge, Mass.: Harvard University Press, 1986), 11.

3 **William James had said**: William James, "Brute and Human Intellect," *Journal of Speculative Philosophy* 12, no. 3 (July 1878): 237.

3 **"truly radical claim"**: Rebecca Goldstein, "Hey, Let's Construct Reality!", *New York Times Book Review*, Mar. 23, 1986.

3 **"in a sea of stories"**: Jerome Bruner, *The Culture of Education* (Cambridge, Mass.: Harvard University Press, 1996), 147.

4 *Toward Slavery and Humiliation*: Shoshana Zuboff, *The Age of Surveillance Capitalism: The Fight for a Human Future at the New Frontiers of Power* (New York: PublicAffairs, 2019), 323.

4 **"Nothing that is out there"**: Kirsten Weir, "The Centenarian Psychologist," *Monitor on Psychology* 46, no. 5 (May 2015): 48.

5 **"Why are we so"**: John Crace, "Jerome Bruner: The Lesson of the Story," *Guardian*, Mar. 27, 2007.

5 **"each of us constructs"**: Oliver Sacks, *The Man Who Mistook His Wife for a Hat, and Other Clinical Tales* (New York: Perennial Library, 1987), 110.

6 "'Let's try to formulate'": Robert Coles, *The Call of Stories: Teaching and the Moral Imagination* (Boston: Houghton Mifflin, 1989), 5, 10.

6 **"new narrative orthodoxy"**: Galen Strawson, "Tales of the Unexpected," *Guardian*, Jan. 9, 2004.

7 **"After I read Allen's book"**: Robert J. Shiller, *Narrative Economics: How Stories Go Viral & Drive Major Economic Events* (Princeton, N.J.: Princeton University Press, 2019), ix–x.

7 **"a 'psychology' of literature"**: Bruner, *Actual Minds*, 4.

7 **she asked fellow students**: Melanie C. Green and Timothy C. Brock, "The Role of Transportation in the Persuasiveness of Public Narratives," *Journal of Personality and Social Psychology* 79, no. 5 (Nov. 2000): 701–721.

8 **"the enchanted state"**: J. R. R. Tolkien, *Tolkien on Fairy-Stories*, ed. Verlyn Flieger and Douglas A. Anderson (London: HarperCollins, 2008), 52.

9 **"In each case"**: Richard Gerrig, *Experiencing Narrative Worlds: On the Psychological Activities of Reading* (New Haven, Conn.: Yale University Press, 1993), 2–3.

10 **unless the person challenging them**: Paul J. Silvia, "Deflecting Reactance: The Role of Similarity in Increasing Compliance and Reducing Resistance," *Basic and Applied Social Psychology* 27, no. 3 (Aug. 2005): 277–284.

10 **It's fairly widely accepted**: Nancy Easterlin, "Cognitive Literary Studies and the Well-Lived Life," *Poetics Today* 40, no. 3 (Sept. 1, 2019): 377–394.

10 **This was demonstrated by Geoff Kaufman**: Geoff F. Kaufman and Lisa K. Libby, "Changing Beliefs and Behavior Through Experience-Taking," *Journal of Personality and Social Psychology* 103, no. 1 (July 2012): 1–19.

12 **"nothing is less innocent"**: Tom van Laer, Ko de Ruyter, Luke M. Visconti, and Martin Wetzels, "The Extended Transportation-Imagery Model: A Meta-Analysis of the Antecedents and Consequences of Consumers' Narrative Transportation," *Journal of Consumer Research* 40, no. 5 (Feb. 1, 2014): 797–817.

13 **the spaghetti Western study**: Uri Hasson, Yuval Nir, Ifat Levy, Galit Fuhrmann, and Rafael Malach, "Intersubject Synchronization of Cortical Activity During Natural Vision," *Science* 303 (Mar. 12, 2004): 163–1640.

13 **later study at Princeton**: Uri Hasson, Ohad Landesman, Barbara

Knappmeyer, Ignacio Vallines, Nava Rubin, and David J. Heeger, "Neurocinematics: The Neuroscience of Film," *Projections* 2, no. 1 (Summer 2008): 1–26.

15 **analysis by the Design Management Institute:** "The Power & Value of Design Continues to Grow across the S&P 500," *DMI* 27, no. 4 (Dec. 2016): 5.

15 **"Design is now too important":** Tim Brown, *Change by Design: How Design Thinking Transforms Organizations and Inspires Innovation* (New York: HarperCollins, 2009), 37.

15 **"is an instrument":** Jerome Bruner, *Making Stories: Law, Literature, Life* (Cambridge, Mass.: Harvard University Press, 2002), 15, 17.

16 **"We are finally beginning":** Dan Ariely, "The End of Rational Economics," *Harvard Business Review,* July–Aug. 2009.

17 **"A view of human nature":** Daniel Goleman, *Emotional Intelligence: Why It Can Matter More Than IQ* (New York: Bantam, 1995), 4.

18 *The Black Swan:* Nassim Nicholas Taleb, *The Black Swan: The Impact of the Highly Improbable* (New York: Random House, 2007), 62–63.

18 **An international team of researchers:** Md Saiful Islam et al., "COVID-19–Related Infodemic and Its Impact on Public Health: A Global Social Media Analysis," *American Journal of Tropical Medicine and Hygiene,* Aug. 10, 2020.

19 **"annihilating in effect property":** Dunbar Rowland (ed.), *Jefferson Davis, Constitutionalist: His Letters, Papers and Speeches* (Mississippi Dept. Archives and History, 1923), vol. 5, p. 72, quoted in James M. McPherson, "Southern Comfort," *New York Review of Books,* Apr. 12, 2001.

20 **"the sternest, the strongest":** "He Defends Lynch Law: John Temple Graves of Georgia Says the Mob Is Necessary," *New York Times,* Aug. 12, 1903.

Part II. The Elements of Story

1. Author

28 **"My family and I":** Farhad Mirza, "Recreating Death for a Living: Inside Bosnia's War Hostel," *Al Jazeera,* Apr. 28, 2018.

28 **"Millennials come and say":** Andrew Higgins, "No Bed, No Breakfast. But the Gunfire Is Divine," *New York Times,* Nov. 28, 2018.

30 **"The Netflix of Eyewear":** "Get Framed! A GQ Guide to Glasses," *GQ,* Feb. 28, 2010.

30 **A markup of 1,000 percent:** David Lazarus, "Why Are Glasses So Expensive? The Eyewear Industry Prefers to Keep That Blurry," *Los Angeles Times*, Jan. 22, 2019.

31 **In a TED talk:** Simon Sinek, "Start with Why: How Great Leaders Inspire Action," TEDx Puget Sound, Sept. 28, 2009.

32 **a survey on attitudes about digital vs. physical:** "Embracing Analog: Why Physical Is Hot," JWT Intelligence/Frank Rose, Mar. 2013.

33 **When the marketing agency Merkle:** "Why Millennial Women Buy: The Behavior and Motivations of the Most Powerful Purchasing Segment," Merkle + Levo, Mar. 8, 2018.

35 **"It's sophisticated":** Rob Brunner, "Dynamic Duos: 5 Brilliant Business Lessons from Warby Parker's CEOs," *Fast Company*, Aug. 23, 2013.

36 **"we're lower-case":** Laura Jacobs, "Deuce of Spade," *Vanity Fair*, May 2002.

36 **"It was about this world":** Tom Foster, "How to Create a Cool Brand," *Inc.*, Apr. 2014.

37 **"What does it say":** Ibid.

37 **"can be covered up with a smile":** Daphne Merkin, "Kate Spade and the Illness Hidden With a Smile," *New York Times*, June 7, 2018.

37 **"It seems straightforward now":** Foster, "How to Create a Cool Brand."

38 **"I wasn't in some high-end jewelry store":** Jeff Harder, "The Razor Wars Have Begun and Somebody's Going to Get Hurt," *Boston Globe Magazine*, June 21, 2017.

38 **"I was like, 'How did I' ":** Bernhard Warner, "Why This Shaving Startup Made a $100 Million Gamble on a 100-Year-Old Factory," *Inc.*, May 2016.

40 **"an important air of credibility":** Hayden Copolen, "Inside the Small-Town, Century-Old German Factory Making Your Razors," *Gear Patrol*, Oct. 18, 2016.

40 **it was a mini-documentary:** "Harry's—Meet the Shaving Company That's Fixing Shaving [Full Length]," www.supermarche .nyc/harrys.

40 **between 2010 and 2016:** Sharon Terlep, "Gillette, Bleeding Market Share, Cuts Prices of Razors," *Wall Street Journal*, Apr. 4, 2017.

41 **Nelson Peltz, the billionaire:** Berkeley Lovelace Jr., "Billionaire Activist Blasts P&G for Letting Online Shave Clubs Obliterate Gillette," CNBC, July 17, 2017.

42 **"In the apex":** Dan Bigman, "Big Risk, Big Reward: Felix Baumgartner and Red Bull Deserve All the Marketing Buzz They Get," *Forbes*, Oct. 14, 2012.

42 **In a 2017 survey:** "Is There an #adlergic Epidemic? Ad Blocking across Media," Deloitte, 2017.

44 **One recent survey:** "Younger Generations Expect Brands to Take a Stance on Social Issues," eMarketer, Dec. 15, 2020.

44 **"We're five years old":** Jack Neff, "Harry's Explores Manhood in Rare Tear-Jerker Razor Ad," *Adweek*, Feb. 26, 2018.

2. Audience

45 **"I still don't know":** Matt Locke, "From Clapping to Likes, and Back Again," *A Brief History of Attention*, Medium, Sept. 19, 2017.

46 **"By the time I started":** Matt Locke, "Empires of Attention" (audio), *Four Thought*, BBC Radio 4, Oct. 23, 2013; "Empires of Attention" (text), *A Brief History of Attention*, Medium, Oct. 23, 2013.

46 **"the call and response":** Ibid.

47 **"It felt like eternity":** William Grimes, "Lights, Mirrors, Instagram! #ArtSensation," *New York Times*, Dec. 1, 2013.

50 **medieval drama depended:** Stephen Greenblatt, "Witness to a Mystery," *New York Review of Books*, June 11, 2020.

52 **"the sensation of being surrounded":** Janet Murray, *Hamlet on the Holodeck: The Future of Narrative in Cyberspace* (Cambridge, Mass.: MIT Press, 1998), 98.

52 **2013 survey:** "10 Trends for 2014 and Beyond," JWT Intelligence, Dec. 2013.

52 **2016 report:** "Unreality: Next-Gen Fantasy, Utopias, and Unquantified Landscapes in a World of Hyper-Digital Realism," JWT Intelligence, May 2016.

52 **Van Gogh's bedroom:** B. David Zarley, "How Van Gogh's Bedroom Was Rebuilt as a Living Masterpiece," *Vice*, Mar. 5, 2016.

53 **Not for nothing:** Seth Porges, "Theater for the Video Game Generation," *Forbes*, Oct. 29, 2012.

54 **"We're never going to be totally immersive":** David S. Cohen, "George Lucas & Steven Spielberg: Studios Will Implode; VOD Is the Future," *Variety*, June 12, 2013.

56 **"frighteningly immersive":** Rosemary Macaulay, "Secret Cinema Presents 'The Shawshank Redemption,'" *Telegraph*, Dec. 3, 2012.

58 **"People want to be":** Frank Rose, "Can Disney Tame 42nd Street?," *Fortune*, July 24, 1996.

58 **"Experiences have always been around":** B. Joseph Pine II and

James H. Gilmore, *The Experience Economy*, rev. ed. (Boston: Harvard Business School Press, 2011), 3.

58 **"Two guys tossing pizza dough"**: Ibid., 163.

58 **"audience = customers"**: Ibid., 210.

59 **"The Creative Class is experience driven"**: Richard Florida, *The Rise of the Creative Class, Revisited* (New York: Basic Books, 2012), 134–135.

59 **"seems more like the experimental theater"**: C. K. Prahalad and Venkat Ramaswamy, "Co-opting Customer Competence," *Harvard Business Review*, Jan.–Feb. 2000.

59 **the concept of "co-creation"**: C. K. Prahalad and Venkat Ramaswamy, "The Co-Creation Connection," *strategy+business*, Q2 2002.

60 **"Advertising does not work"**: Anca Cristina Micu and Joseph T. Plummer, "On the Road to a New Effectiveness Model: Measuring Emotional Responses to Television Advertising," American Association of Advetising Agencies/Advertising Research Foundation Task Force Study Findings, Mar. 2007.

61 **"Focus group folly"**: Gerald Zaltman, *How Customers Think: Essential Insights into the Mind of the Market* (Boston: Harvard Business School Press, 2003), 121–122.

61 **"take people out of the context"**: Christian Madsbjerg, *Sensemaking: The Power of the Humanities in the Age of the Algorithm* (New York: Hachette, 2017), 12.

63 **"Human memory is story-based"**: Roger C. Schank, *Tell Me a Story: A New Look at Real and Artificial Memory* (New York: Scribner, 1990), 11–12.

64 **"Description begins"**: Stephen King, *On Writing: A Memoir of the Craft* (New York: Scribner, 2010), 174.

64 **"The creative act is not performed"**: Marcel Duchamp, "The Creative Act," Convention of the American Federation of Arts, Houston, Texas, April 1957.

66 **"If only Daddy would have known"**: E. J. Schultz, "After Kendall Jenner Ad Debacle, What's Next for Pepsi?," *Ad Age*, Apr. 6, 2017.

65 *Slate* **published a list**: "30 Questions for Pepsi About Its Protest Imagery–Inspired Soda Commercial," *Slate*, Apr. 5, 2017.

66 **"There really isn't anything they can say"**: Schultz, "After Kendall Jenner Ad Debacle."

67 **"I looked at the ad again and again"**: Beth Kowitt, "PepsiCo's CEO Opens Up About Trump, Amazon, and That Kendall Jenner Ad," *Fortune*, Sept. 21, 2017.

67 **told a story about bunny rabbits:** Herbert A. Simon, "Designing Organizations for an Information-Rich World," in Martin Greenberger (ed.), *Computers, Communications and the Public Interest* (Baltimore: Johns Hopkins University Press, 1971), 40–41.

69 **when attention becomes the scarce resource:** Richard A. Lanham, *The Economics of Attention: Style and Substance in the Age of Information* (Chicago: University of Chicago Press, 2006), xi–xii.

69 **"'Design' is our name":** Ibid., 18.

70 **"The surface, he said":** Ibid., 49.

70 **"the currencies of the experience economy":** B. Joseph Pine II and James H. Gilmore, "The Experience Economy: Past, Present and Future," in Jon Sundbo and Flemming Sørensen (eds.), *Handbook on the Experience Economy* (Cheltenham, Eng.: Edward Elgar, 2013), 30.

71 **A 2018 Expedia survey:** "Generations on the Move," Expedia and The Center for Generational Kinetics, Jan. 2018, 5.

71 **A 2019 Deloitte survey:** "The Deloitte Global Millennial Survey 2019," Deloitte, May 2019, 5.

71 **"Tourism seems an oddly self-destructive":** Lanham, *Economics of Attention*, 2.

72 **"one of the defining media companies":** Felix Gillette, "Scott DeLong's Success Formula for Viral Nova," *Bloomberg Businessweek*, Apr. 24, 2014.

73 **"attention units":** Simon, "Designing Organizations for an Information-Rich World," 41.

73 **"Time is the only unit":** Michael Sebastian, "Is Digital Advertising Ready to Ditch the Click?," *Ad Age*, Sept. 29, 2014.

74 **"Very few entities":** Anita Elberse, *Blockbusters: Hit-Making, Risk-Taking, and the Big Business of Entertainment* (New York: Henry Holt, 2013), 47.

74 **Disney had seven of the top 10:** Rebecca Rubin, "Global Box Office Hits New Record in 2019 With $42.5 Billion," *Variety*, Jan. 10, 2020.

74 **"The impulse to make a film":** "So Many Indie Films, So Many Reasons," *New York Times*, Jan. 9, 2014.

74 **"There's just too much stuff":** Nick Clark, "Too Many Films Are Released Each Year, Says British Film Institute," *Independent*, July 24, 2014.

76 **"What will the Big Data approach":** Andrew Leonard, "How Netflix Is Turning Viewers into Puppets," *Salon*, Feb. 1, 2013.

80 **"Then the Audience Insight team":** Matt Locke, "Readers, Families, Users and Mobs," *How to Measure Ghosts*, Substack, July 8, 2019.

3. Journey

82 **"That river of words"**: Frank Rose, "The Beats' Ferment, Still Bubbling," *New York Times*, Aug. 28, 2016.

82 **"Time is the context"**: Iain McGilchrist, *The Master and His Emissary: The Divided Brain and the Making of the Western World* (New Haven: Yale University Press, 2010), 75–76.

83 **"sets the story in motion"**: Syd Field, *Screenplay: The Foundations of Screenwriting*, rev. ed. (New York: Delta, 2005), 129.

85 **"But at its core"**: David Kudler, "MythBlast | Separation, Initiation, and Return," Joseph Campbell Foundation, April 19, 2020.

86 **many experiences begin**: Ellen Lupton, *Design Is Storytelling* (New York: Cooper Hewitt, 2017), 24–25.

86 **"low tolerance"**: J. R. Georgiadis and M. L. Kringelbach, "The Human Sexual Response Cycle: Brain Imaging Evidence Linking Sex to Other Pleasures," *Progress in Neurobiology* 98 (2012): 49–81.

86 **In a Dutch study**: Gert Holstege, Janniko R. Georgiadis, Anne M. J. Paans, Linda C. Meiners, Ferdinand H. C. E. van der Graaf, and A. A. T. Simone Reinders, "Brain Activation during Human Male Ejaculation," *Journal of Neuroscience* 23, no. 27 (Oct. 8, 2003): 9185–9193.

88 **researchers at Oxford**: Georgiadis and Kringelbach, "Human Sexual Response Cycle."

89 **"Each section is like a short story"**: Field, *Screenplay*, 139.

90 **experiment in nonlinear storytelling**: Anna-Lisa Cohen, Elliot Shavalian, and Moshe Rube, "The Power of the Picture: How Narrative Film Captures Attention and Disrupts Goal Pursuit," *PLoS One* 10, no. 12 (Dec. 10, 2015).

90 **"innate preference for linear narrative"**: Max Green, "How the Brain Reacts to Scrambled Stories," *Atlantic*, Jan. 27, 2016.

91 **"really is a question"**: Anthony Kaufman, "Mindgames: Christopher Nolan Remembers 'Memento,'" *IndieWire*, Mar. 16, 2001.

92 **"a movie about worlds and levels"**: Patrick Goldstein, "Why Is It That the Older You Are the More You Can't Stand 'Inception'?," *Los Angeles Times*, Aug. 2, 2010.

92 **"he shook his head"**: Lynda Obst, "Selling 'Inception': How Hollywood Marketing Works," *Atlantic*, Sept. 1, 2010.

93 **worth more than $30 billion**: 2019 Theatrical and Home Entertainment Market Environment (THEME) Report, Motion Picture Association, Mar. 2020.

94 **In a fascinating essay:** Charlie Collier, "The Waltons to Walter White: The Rise of Immersive Content," *ReDef,* Jan. 26, 2016.

97 **HBO even posted:** "Reality of A.I." (video), HBO, Oct. 10, 2016.

97 **"When I heard, 'Western robot theme park' ":** Tom Bissell, "On the Ranch with the Creators of 'Westworld,' " *New Yorker,* Dec. 15, 2016.

97 **"culturally very Chinese":** Amanda Fortini, "With 'Westworld,' Lisa Joy Is Rewriting Women's Power Story Line in Hollywood and Beyond," *Elle,* Apr. 2018.

97 **"But, in a way, traditional Westerns":** Bissell, "On the Ranch."

98 **The idea that animated the show:** Fortini, "With 'Westworld.' "

98 **And their "why" means something:** Adam Grant, "The *Westworld* Creators Think Real Androids Might Be a Bad Idea," *Esquire,* Apr. 23, 2018.

99 **"Point of view is worth":** Andy Hertzfeld, "Creative Think," *Folklore,* July 1982.

4. Character

105 **"These doctors and these nurses":** "Jack's Story," MSK Kids, Memorial Sloan Kettering Cancer Center.

105 **"the campaign portrays cancer":** David Gianatasio, "Ad of the Day: Memorial Sloan Kettering Tells Three Powerful, Inspiring Cancer Stories," *Adweek,* June 30, 2015.

105 **the second best-liked Super Bowl ad:** Alan Siegel, " 'Puppy Love' Is Champion of Ad Meter Super Bowl Bracket," *USA Today,* Jan. 31, 2018.

106 **"If you watch @Budweiser's #BestBuds ad":** Maura Judkis, "Budweiser 'Puppy Love' Commercial for Super Bowl Wins America's Heart," *Washington Post,* Jan. 31, 2014.

107 **"Our marketing has featured":** E. J. Schultz, "Budweiser Pulls Puppies from Super Bowl Ad Plans," *Ad Age,* Nov. 16, 2015.

108 **"Focus on making":** "The 8095 Exchange: Millennials, Their Actions Surrounding Brands, and the Dynamics of Reverberation," Edelman/StrategyOne, Oct. 14, 2010, quoted in Bryan Roth, "AB InBev Is (kind of) Losing and It's All the Millennials' Fault (Again)," *This Is Why I'm Drunk,* Nov. 22, 2013.

109 **"the emotional forces working on your character":** Field, *Screenplay,* 49–50.

111 **"These are blink and you miss moments!":** "All the background 'words' in episode 3," r/sharpobjects, Reddit.

111 **What might be called "mystery box" storytelling:** Kathryn Van-Arendonk, "Sharp Objects Broke the Mystery Box," *Vulture*, Aug. 26, 2018.

5. World

114 **"This process of world-building":** Henry Jenkins, "Transmedia Storytelling 101," *Confessions of an Aca-Fan* (henryjenkins.org), Mar. 21, 2007.

114 **"a natural human activity":** Tolkien, *Tolkien on Fairy-Stories*, 52.

115 **"*Star Wars* is a completely made-up universe":** Kevin Kelly and Paula Parisi, "Beyond *Star Wars*," *Wired 5.02*, February 1997.

116 **"the most perfect reasoning and observing machine":** Arthur Conan Doyle, "A Scandal in Bohemia," in *The Complete Sherlock Holmes* (New York: Doubleday, 1930), 161.

116 **"was as cozily self-contained as a snow globe":** Michael Saler, *As If: Modern Enchantment and the Literary Prehistory of Virtual Reality* (New York: Oxford University Press, 2012), 33.

117 **"It was the dawn of fandom":** Scott Brown, "Scott Brown on Sherlock Holmes, Obsessed Nerds, and Fan Fiction," *Wired*, May 2009.

120 **somewhere beyond Uppsala:** Stieg Larsson, *The Girl with the Dragon Tattoo* (New York: Vintage, 2009), 76.

121 **"Isn't it strange":** Werner Heisenberg, *Physics and Beyond: Encounters and Conversation* (New York: Harper & Row, 1971), 51, quoted in Gordon Mills, *Hamlet's Castle: The Study of Literature as a Social Experience* (Austin: University of Texas Press, 1976).

123 **"Six seasons of polar bears":** Mary McNamara, "Of Love 'Lost'," *Los Angeles Times*, May 24, 2010.

124 **"Do we all agree":** "Game of Thrones: Worst Finale Ever?" *New Republic*, May 20, 2019.

124 **"I wasted eight years":** @Outkick, Twitter, May 20, 2019.

124 **"can the M.C.U. really keep expanding?":** Maya Phillips, "The Narrative Experiment That Is the Marvel Cinematic Universe," *New Yorker*, Apr. 26, 2019.

6. Detail

125 **One study tried to fathom:** Deborah A. Small, George Loewenstein, and Paul Slovic, "Sympathy and Callousness: The Impact of Deliberative Thought on Donations to Identifiable and Statistical Victims,"

Organizational Behavior and Human Decision Processes 102 (Mar. 2007): 143–153.

126 **A subsequent study in Sweden:** Daniel Västfjäll, Paul Slovic, Marcus Mayorga, and Ellen Peters, "Compassion Fade: Affect and Charity Are Greatest for a Single Child in Need," *PLOS One* 9, no. 6 (June 2014): 1–10.

128 **"sensory glimmers":** Jane Alison, *Meander, Spiral, Explode: Design and Pattern in Narrative* (New York: Catapult, 2019), 47.

130 **"But it was above all at mealtimes":** Gustave Flaubert, *Madame Bovary: A Norton Critical Edition*, trans. and ed. Paul de Man (New York: Norton, 1965), 47.

131 **"Emma's world as it now appears":** Erich Auerbach, "The Realism of Flaubert," in Flaubert, *Madame Bovary: A Norton Critical Edition*, 384.

131 **"She glorified adultery":** Gustave Flaubert, *Madame Bovary: A Tale of Provincial Life* (London: M. Walter Dunne, 1904), vol. 2, appendix, 17.

132 **"the finest style of writing":** James Wood, "How Flaubert Changed Literature Forever," *New Republic*, Jan. 18, 1999.

132 **"the reality effect":** Roland Barthes, "The Reality Effect," in *The Rustle of Language* (New York: Hill & Wang, 1986), 141.

133 **"Kurosawa created historical realism":** John Powers, "star wars: a new heap," *Triple Canopy 4: War Money Magic*, Nov. 11, 2008.

135 **Hillary Clinton's campaign organization:** Jesse Singal, "How Internet Trolls Won the 2016 Presidential Election," *New York*, Sept. 16, 2016.

135 **Furie himself seemed indifferent:** Adam Serwer, "It's Not Easy Being Meme," *Atlantic*, Sept. 13, 2016.

135 **"a nightmare":** Matt Furie, "Pepe the Frog's Creator: I'm Reclaiming Him. He Was Never About Hate," *Time*, Oct. 13, 2016.

135 **"catnip for the trolls":** Singal, "How Internet Trolls Won."

136 **"Another vice of this style":** *Collected Works of Paul Valéry* (Princeton, N.J.: Princeton University Press, 1968, 2017), vol. 9, 335, quoted in Wood, "How Flaubert Changed Literature Forever."

136 **"his passion for the *mot juste*":** John Barth, "A Few Words About Minimalism," *New York Times Book Review*, Dec. 28, 1986.

136 **"the revelatory power":** Tom Bissell, "Everything about Everything: *Infinite Jest*, Twenty Years Later," Foreword to David Foster Wallace, *Infinite Jest* (New York: Little, Brown, 1996, 2016), xv.

136 **"hysterical realism":** James Wood, "Human, All Too Inhuman," *New Republic*, July 24, 2000.

137 **Your honor, eminent counsel:** Moe Levine, "Double Amputation Case," in *Moe Levine on Advocacy* (Portland, Ore.: Trial Guides, 2009), 477.

139 ***"The adverb is not your friend":*** King, *On Writing*, 124.

139 **"a mortal sin":** Elmore Leonard, "Easy on the Adverbs, Exclamation Points and Especially Hooptedoodle," *New York Times*, July 16, 2001.

7. Voice

140 **"Why did Virgin Brides fail?":** John Lockett, "A History of Richard Branson's Harebrained Hobbies," *Vanity Fair*, March 19, 2015.

142 **The Virgin folks summed it up:** "The Virgin Way: Our Brand Purpose," Virgin Group, Sept. 2012.

142 **"our purpose is to change business for good":** "What Makes Us Virgin?," www.virgin.com/about-virgin.

142 **"a global, growth investor":** "Virgin Group Overview," www.virgin .com/about-virgin/virgin-group/overview.

142 **"most resembles a huge 'family office'":** Sarah Gordon, "Virgin Group: Brand It like Branson," *Financial Times*, Nov. 5, 2014.

144 **US consumer intelligence firm Motista:** Scott Magids, Alan Zorfas, and Daniel Leemon, "The New Science of Customer Emotions," *Harvard Business Review*, Nov. 2015.

145 **"We're trying to bring Richard":** Laura Slattery, "Richard Branson Centre Stage in Virgin Media Ireland Campaign," *Irish Times*, Mar. 4, 2016.

145 **Virgin Media employee Q&A:** Kat Hall, "'Faceless' Liberty Global Has 'Sucked the Very Soul' out of Virgin Media," *The Register*, Sept. 23, 2016.

146 **"I love Virgin":** Matt Krupnick, "Virgin America Fans Ask if Alaska Airlines Takeover Will Mean Loss of Cool," *New York Times*, Apr. 11, 2016.

146 **"I'm told some people":** Richard Branson, "Dear Virgin America," Richard's Blog, Virgin.com, Mar. 22, 2017.

146 **"You've got a choice":** Michael Manning, "Virgin America Doing Things Differently," *Airways Magazine*, June 2014.

147 **"The Face on the Tail":** Brad Abrahams (dir.), "Alaska Airlines: The Face on the Tail," bradabrahams.net.

148 **Alaska's CEO:** Michael Addady, "Why Alaska Airlines' CEO Is Losing Sleep over the Virgin America Merger," *Fortune*, June 16, 2016.

148 **"In a world increasingly filled":** James H. Gilmore and B. Joseph

Pine II, *Authenticity: What Consumers* Really *Want* (Boston: Harvard Business School Press, 2007), 1.

149 **"People no longer accept":** Ibid., 5.

149 **Ira C.** Herbert: "Top 20 Slogans | 13: Coca-Cola (1940s)—It's the Real Thing," *Creative Review*, Feb. 2012.

149 **Pine and Gilmore's test:** Gilmore and Pine, *Authenticity*, 96.

150 **advertising, as Pine and Gilmore note:** Pine and Gilmore, "Experience Economy."

151 **an eye-opening account in *BuzzFeed*:** Dan Nosowitz, "Something Borrowed, Something Blue," *BuzzFeed*, Sept. 28, 2014.

152 **It reached the point:** Claire Bothwell, "Burberry versus the Chavs," *The Money Programme*, BBC Two, Oct. 28, 2005.

152 **"clad top to toe":** Laura Barton and Nils Pratley, "The Two Faces of Burberry," *Guardian*, Apr. 14, 2004.

152 **"I felt very uncomfortable":** Jess Cartner-Morley, " 'I'm Just Not Snobby': How Christopher Bailey Restyled Burberry," *Guardian*, Mar. 24, 2018.

152 **"You didn't aspire to do anything":** Sarah Mower, "Christopher Bailey on Going Back to His Roots," *British Vogue*, Dec. 2017.

153 **"There's nothing wrong":** Angela Ahrendts, "Burberry's CEO on Turning an Aging British Icon into a Global Luxury Brand," *Harvard Business Review*, Jan.–Feb. 2013.

153 **She and Bailey decided:** Ibid.

155 **"Honestly, it makes no difference":** Paul Sonne, "Mink or Fox? The Trench Gets Complicated," *Wall Street Journal*, Nov. 3, 2011.

156 **Bailey's Burberry "projected":** Cartner-Morley, " 'I'm Just Not Snobby.' "

157 **An analyst in Paris:** Rupert Neate, "Christopher Bailey Takes Over from Angela Ahrendts as Burberry Chief," *Guardian*, Oct. 16, 2013.

158 **"shockwaves reverberated":** Olivia Singer, "Riccardo Tisci Outlines His Revolutionary Vision For Burberry," *British Vogue*, February 2019.

159 **"the final chapter":** Jess Cartner-Morley, "Christopher Bailey Bows Out from Burberry Under a Bold Rainbow," *Observer*, Feb. 17, 2018.

159 **"Suicide is not fashion":** liz.kennedy, Instagram, Feb. 17, 2019.

159 **"so deeply sorry":** Reis Thebault, "Burberry Sweatshirt Featuring Noose for Drawstrings Condemned for Evoking Suicide, Lynching," *Washington Post*, Feb. 19, 2019.

160 **Gucci apologized "deeply":** Avery Anapol, "Gucci Apologizes, Pulls Sweater Resembling Blackface," *The Hill*, Feb. 7, 2019.

160 **Prada claimed to "abhor":** Robin Givhan, "Seriously, Prada, What

Were You Thinking? Why the Fashion Industry Keeps Bumbling into Racist Imagery," *Washington Post*, Dec. 15, 2018.

160　**"This shit is for attention"**: "Prada, Gucci and Now Burberry: Are Brands Under Fire for Offensive Designs Doing It on Purpose?," *Salon*, Feb. 20, 2019.

160　**That pool was getting shallower**: "16–17-Year-old Population: All Persons," Office for National Statistics, Sept. 10, 2019. Source dataset: Labour Market Statistics Time Series.

161　**"Their world is digital"**: Matthew Waksman and Rob Fullerton-Batten, "Helping a New Generation Find Where They Belong in the British Army," WARC, 2018.

161　**"The benefit was *each other*"**: Ibid.

162　**"The need to belong"**: Roy F. Baumeister and Mark R. Leary, "The Need to Belong: Desire for Interpersonal Attachments as a Fundamental Human Motivation," *Psychological Bulletin* 117, no. 3 (May 1995): 497–528.

162　**The result:** Waksman and Fullerton-Batten, "Helping a New Generation."

163　**"It's Fine To Cry"**: Deborah Haynes, "It's Fine to Cry, Army Tells New Recruits," *Sunday Times*, Jan. 10, 2018.

163　**"It's no good just having an army"**: Nicholas Cecil, "Ex-Army Chief: Force Must Be Tough, Not 'Jolly Nice' to Everyone," *Evening Standard*, Jan. 10, 2018.

163　**"assault on modern masculinity"**: Rebecca Stewart, "Those British Army 'Snowflake' Ads Have Encouraged the Most New Recruits in Years," *The Drum*, Mar. 20, 2019.

164　**"dangerous political correctness"**: Richard Kemp, "The British Army Has Always Been the Best in the World so We Should Target Call of Duty Fans . . . Not Bawl of Duty," *Sun*, Jan. 11, 2018.

164　**"Images of combat"**: Matthew Weaver, "Army Accused of Political Correctness in Recruitment Campaign," *Guardian*, Jan. 10, 2018.

164　**But despite the flak:** Dominic Nicholls and Ellie McKinnell, " 'Snowflake Generation' Recruitment Adverts See Applications to Join the Army Almost Double, MoD Reveals," *Telegraph*, Feb. 8, 2019.

166　**five key dimensions of brand personality:** Jennifer L. Aaker, "Dimensions of Brand Personality," *Journal of Marketing Research* 34, no. 3 (Aug. 1997): 347–356.

167　**Mailchimp, for example, the email marketing platform:** "Voice and Tone," Mailchimp Content Style Guide, 2019, styleguide.mailchimp.com.

8. Platform

169 *The Walking Dead*: Collier, "Waltons to Walter White."

170 **"Vagueness abounds":** David L. Rogers, *The Digital Transformation Playbook: Rethink Your Business for the Digital Age* (New York: Columbia University Press, 2016), 55.

171 **Airbnb had some seven million listings:** Jane Lanhee Lee, "Airbnb Says Second-Quarter Revenue Topped $1 Billion," Reuters, Sept. 19, 2019.

171 **Marriott had 174,000 employees:** Marriott International Inc., Form 10-K, Annual Report for the Fiscal Year Ended Dec. 31, 2019, 7, 9.

172 **Another intriguing fact:** Andrew McAfee and Erik Brynjolfsson, *Machine | Platform | Crowd: Harnessing Our Digital Future* (New York: Norton, 2017), 140–141.

173 **Building on their work:** David S. Evans and Richard Schmalensee, "The Industrial Organization of Markets with Two-Sided Platforms," in *Platform Economics: Essays on Multi-Sided Businesses*, ed. David S. Evans (Chicago: Competition Policy International, 2011), 5.

174 **more than half of all digital advertising in the US:** "Digital Ad Revenues, by Company, US," eMarketer Forecasts Oct. 1, 2020.

174 **nearly 70 percent of that:** Nina Goetzen, "The Duopoly's Share of the UK Ad Market Will Dip Below 66%," eMarketer, Aug. 19, 2020.

175 **As Rogers points out:** Rogers, *Digital Transformation Playbook*, 66.

175 **Steve Ballmer:** David Lieberman, "CEO Forum: Microsoft's Ballmer Having a 'Great Time,'" *USA Today*, Apr. 29, 2007.

176 **when a lot of free apps:** McAfee and Brynjolfsson, *Machine | Platform | Crowd*, 161.

176 **"Can any product or service":** Geoffrey Parker, Marshall Van Alstyne, and Sangeet Paul Choudary, *Platform Revolution: How Networked Markets Are Transforming the Economy and How to Make Them Work for You* (New York: Norton, 2016), 76.

177 **"what business are you in?":** Peter High, "How Best Buy, The New York Times, and John Deere Have Become Digital Leaders," *Forbes*, Aug 27, 2018.

178 **"they assumed themselves to be in the railroad business":** Theodore Levitt, "Marketing Myopia," *Harvard Business Review*, July–Aug. 1960.

178 **the World Wide Web:** McAfee and Brynjolfsson, *Machine | Platform | Crowd*, 138.

180 **As defined more than a century ago:** Irving Fisher, "What Is Capital?," *Economic Journal* 6, no. 24 (Dec. 1896), 509–534.

180 **a somewhat more recent blog post:** Robin Sloan, "Stock and Flow," *Snarkmarket*, Jan. 10, 2010.

183 **"I get email after email":** Michael Mechanic, "Brains, Blood, and BBQ: Welcome to Greg Nicotero's Zombie School," *Mother Jones*, Mar.–Apr. 2014.

184 **During season 7:** "TV Season in Review: The Top Social Moments of the 2016–17 Season," Nielsen, June 7, 2017.

185 **"Even during Walt Disney's lifetime":** Neal Gabler, "When You Wish upon Pixar," *New York Times*, Feb. 2, 2006.

186 **"Sony is not one company":** Frank Rose, "The Civil War Inside Sony," *Wired* 11.02, Feb. 2003.

186 **"bigger is not always better":** Frank Rose, "There's No Business Like Show Business," *Fortune*, June 22, 1998.

187 **Books that "allow families":** "Disney Celebrates Family Bonds and Epic Storytelling in New *Frozen* Product Collection Available at Retail Now," Business Wire, Nov. 6, 2013.

187 **article by Todd Zenger:** Todd Zenger, "What Is the Theory of Your Firm?," *Harvard Business Review*, June 2013.

187 **tweeted the chart:** @jack, "The actual strategy drawing . . . ," Twitter, June 24, 2013, twitter.com/jack/status/6139172167 15710464.

188 **David Evans and Richard Schmalensee:** Evans and Schmalensee, "Industrial Organization of Markets," 3.

9. Immersion

193 **"So there you have it":** "Fake Products, Real Products," Consumer Eyes blog, Feb. 23, 2017.

195 **"original content that celebrates":** Mailchimp Presents, mailchimp.com/presents.

195 **"A herd of cows":** Beth Timmins, "Vegetarian Farmer Saves Cow Herd from Abattoir by Donating It to Animal Sanctuary," *Independent*, June 14, 2017.

199 **"young men with uncertain futures":** Lyn Gardner, "Javaad Alipoor: 'The Response to Radicalism Is to Shut Down Debate for Young People,'" *Guardian*, Aug. 15, 2017.

202 **Robert Shiller noted:** Shiller, *Narrative Economics*, 100–101.

202 **A less helpful constellation:** Julian Kozlowski, Laura Veldkamp, and Venky Venkateswaran, "Scarring Body and Mind: The Long-Term Belief-Scarring Effects of Covid-19," Working Paper 27439, National Bureau of Economic Research, June 2020.

203 **"the self too is an imaginary story":** Yuval Noah Harari, *Homo Deus: A Brief History of Tomorrow* (New York: HarperCollins, 2017), 306.

Part III. The Shape of the Future

208 **SuperData was expecting VR sales:** "2019 Year in Review: Digital Games and Interactive Media," SuperData, Jan. 2020.

208 **when the coronavirus struck:** "Dealing with Covid-19," Otherworld, other.world/covid-19-safety.

210 **"Hiro's not actually here at all":** Neal Stephenson, *Snow Crash* (New York: Bantam, 1992), 22.

210 **Dick was saying:** Philip K. Dick, "How to Build a Universe That Doesn't Fall Apart Two Days Later," in *The Shifting Realities of Philip K. Dick: Selected Literary and Philosophical Writings*, ed. Lawrence Sutin (New York: Vintage, 1995), 262.

210 **"when the universe":** Frank Rose, *The Art of Immersion: How the Digital Generation Is Remaking Hollywood, Madison Avenue, and the Way We Tell Stories* (New York: Norton, 2011), 319.

211 **the *Wall Street Journal* ran:** Eleanore Park, "What Is QAnon? What We Know About the Conspiracy Theory," *Wall Street Journal*, Aug. 17, 2020.

212 **historian Richard Hofstadter:** Richard Hofstadter, "The Paranoid Style in American Politics," *Harper's Magazine*, Nov. 1964.

213 **average membership:** Deepa Seetharaman, "QAnon Booms on Facebook as Conspiracy Group Gains Mainstream Traction," *Wall Street Journal*, Aug. 13, 2020.

213 **One of them was Adrian Hon:** Adrian Hon, "What ARGs Can Teach Us About QAnon," *MSSV*, Aug. 2, 2020.

215 **A decade and a half ago:** Gary Baum, "The Secret Past of a Hollywood Futurist," *Hollywood Reporter*, Nov. 13, 2019.

216 **an insight from Jürgen Schmidhuber:** Jürgen Schmidhuber, "Simple Algorithmic Theory of Subjective Beauty, Novelty, Surprise, Interestingness, Attention, Curiosity, Creativity, Art, Science, Music, Jokes," *Journal of SICE* 48, no. 1 (2009): 21–32.

217 **surprising uptick in flat-Earth sentiment:** Ian Sample, "Study Blames YouTube for Rise in Number of Flat Earthers," *Guardian*, Feb. 17, 2019.

219 **The latter, *Wired* explained:** Steve G. Steinberg, "Netheads vs Bell-heads," *Wired* 4.10, Oct. 1996.

219 **which lost so much money:** Deirdre Carmody, "In a Changing Marketplace, Publishers Turn Elsewhere to Improve Their Bottom Line," *New York Times*, Nov. 13, 1995.

220 **Apple cleared more than $57 billion:** Apple Inc., SEC Form 10-K, Annual Report for the Fiscal Year Ended Sept. 26, 2020, 34.

220 **Microsoft made $39 billion:** *Fortune* 2020 Global 500, ranked by profits.

220 **"surveillance capitalism was invented":** Zuboff, *Age of Surveillance Capitalism*, 85.

221 **Google lost nearly $15 million:** Google Inc., Amendment No. 9 to Form S-1 Registration Statement, Aug. 18, 2004, 48.

221 **Google made $100 million:** Google Inc., Amendment No. 9, 48.

221 **Zuboff dubbed this "the watershed year":** Zuboff, *Age of Surveillance Capitalism*, 75.

223 **the North Carolina college student:** Louise Story and Brad Stone, "Facebook Retreats on Online Tracking," *New York Times*, Nov. 30, 2007.

223 **The woman in Michigan:** Ellen Nakashima, "Feeling Betrayed, Facebook Users Force Site to Honor Their Privacy," *Washington Post*, Nov. 30, 2007.

223 **such complaints were met:** Story and Stone, "Facebook Retreats."

223 **"People have really gotten comfortable":** Bobbie Johnson, "Privacy No Longer a Social Norm, Says Facebook Founder," *Guardian*, Jan. 11, 2010.

223 **"If you have something":** Richard Esguerra, "Google CEO Eric Schmidt Dismisses the Importance of Privacy," Electronic Frontier Foundation, Dec. 10, 2009.

223 **"As a person who is being stalked":** Marshall Kirkpatrick, "Why Facebook Is Wrong: Privacy Is Still Important," *ReadWriteWeb*, Jan. 11, 2010.

223 **University of Texas student:** Julia Angwin, *Dragnet Nation: A Quest for Privacy, Security, and Freedom in a World of Relentless Surveillance* (New York: Times Books, 2014), 10–11.

224 **"Once every hundred years":** David Kirkpatrick, *The Facebook Effect* (New York: Simon & Schuster, 2010), 247.

224 **by the Council of Conservative Citizens:** Associated Press, "Don't Blame Us for Church Shootings, Council of Conservative Citizens Says," NBC News, June 23, 2015.

225 **When a reporter from:** Casey Newton, "The Trauma Floor," *The Verge*, Feb. 25, 2019.

225 **It was even worse:** Olivia Solon, "Revealed: Facebook Exposed Identities of Moderators to Suspected Terrorists," *Guardian*, June 16, 2017.

226 **Two years later, in Sri Lanka:** Sarah Frier, "Facebook's Crisis Management Algorithm Runs on Outrage," *Businessweek*, Mar. 19, 2019.

226 **a midnight blue map:** Paul Butler, "Visualizing Friendships," Facebook Engineering, Dec. 13, 2010.

226 **With after-tax income:** Facebook Inc., SEC Form 10-K, Annual report for the Fiscal Year Ended Dec. 31, 2020, 65.

227 **"This is a problem":** Roger McNamee, *Zucked: Waking Up to the Facebook Catastrophe* (New York: Penguin, 2019), 94.

228 **"In the absence of a commitment":** McNamee, *Zucked*, 92–93.

228 **Buy my toothpaste:** Luis Ferré-Sadurní and Jesse McKinley, "Alex Jones Is Told to Stop Selling Sham Anti-Coronavirus Toothpaste," *New York Times*, Mar. 13, 2020.

228 **"We recognize that this is our responsibility":** Jack Nicas, "How YouTube Drives People to the Internet's Darkest Corners," *Wall Street Journal*, Feb. 7, 2018.

229 **"Let's call it W.K.W.H.M.W.T.D.":** Charlie Warzel, "Facebook Can't Be Reformed," *New York Times*, July 1, 2020.

229 **the flat-Earthers became less ubiquitous:** Marc Faddoula, Guillaume Chaslot, and Hany Farid, "A Longitudinal Analysis of YouTube's Promotion of Conspiracy Videos," arXiv:2003.03318 [cs.CY], Mar. 2, 2020.

229 **"It's not because anyone is evil":** "Brain Hacking," *60 Minutes*, CBS News, April 9, 2017.

230 **"I don't think it's right":** Cecilia Kang and Mike Isaac, "Defiant Zuckerberg Says Facebook Won't Police Political Speech," *New York Times*, Oct. 17, 2019; Ryan Tracy, "Facebook's Mark Zuckerberg Rebuffs Calls for Tighter Controls, Saying Free Speech Must Be Preserved," *Wall Street Journal*, Oct. 18, 2019.

230 **"We will never give up.":** Aaron Blake, "What Trump Said Before His Supporters Stormed the Capitol, Annotated," *Washington Post*, Jan. 11, 2021.

231 **communicating with one another via Facebook:** US Dist. Court for the District of Columbia, United States v. Thomas Edward Caldwell, Donovan Ray Crowl, and Jessica Marie Watkins, Polian Aff ¶ 48, Jan. 19, 2021.

231 **who had recently declared:** Chris Hughes, "It's Time to Break Up Facebook," *New York Times*, May 19, 2019.

231 **The result, announced on Medium:** John Borthwick, "Ten Things

Technology Platforms Can Do to Safeguard the 2020 U.S. Election," *Render*, Medium, Jan. 7, 2020.

232 **the environmental activist group:** Gabriela Galindo, "XR Belgium Posts Deepfake of Belgian Premier Linking Covid-19 with Climate Crisis," *Brussels Times*, April 14, 2020.

233 **"I wish that the Internet":** Cleo Abram, "The Most Urgent Threat of Deepfakes Isn't Politics. It's Porn," *Vox*, June 8, 2020.

233 **According to a report from Sensity:** Henry Ajder, Giorgio Patrini, Francesco Cavalli, and Laurence Cullen, "The State of Deepfakes: Landscape, Threats, and Impact," Deeptrace, Sept. 2019.

237 **"I thought it was time":** Frank Rose, "Frank Gehry's Disney Hall Is Technodreaming," *New York Times*, Aug. 14, 2018.

237 **It's what happens:** Alexander Mordvintsev, Christopher Olah, and Mike Tyka, "Inceptionism: Going Deeper into Neural Networks," Google AI Blog, June 17, 2015.

239 **"a new place on the Internet":** Evan Williams, "Welcome to Medium," Medium, Aug. 14, 2012.

239 **"an endless thought experiment":** Laura Hazard Owen, "The Long, Complicated, and Extremely Frustrating History of Medium, 2012–Present," *NiemanLab*, March 25, 2019.

240 **If Substack could fix it:** Ricardo Bilton, " 'Stratechery as a service': Substack Aims to Streamline the Creation of Independent Subscription News Sites," *NiemanLab*, Oct. 5, 2017.

240 **more than 30,000 US journalists:** Marc Tracy, "Journalists Are Leaving the Noisy Internet for Your Email Inbox," *New York Times*, Sept. 23, 2020.

240 **"It's a lifeboat":** Tracy, "Journalists Are Leaving."

240 **"There's a huge buffet":** Kevin Roose, "And for His Next Act, Ev Williams Will Fix the Internet," *New York Times*, May 9, 2018.

241 **"It means being conscious":** David Foster Wallace, *This Is Water: Some Thoughts, Delivered on a Significant Occasion, about Living a Compassionate Life* (New York: Little, Brown, 2009), 54–55.

Index